THE DISRUPTIVE POWER OF
ONLINE EDUCATION

THE DISRUPTIVE POWER OF ONLINE EDUCATION: CHALLENGES, OPPORTUNITIES, RESPONSES

EDITED BY

ANDREAS ALTMANN

MCI Management Center Innsbruck, Austria

BERND EBERSBERGER

University of Hohenheim, Stuttgart, Germany

CLAUDIA MÖSSENLECHNER

MCI Management Center Innsbruck, Austria

DESIREE WIESER

MCI Management Center Innsbruck, Austria

United Kingdom – North America – Japan – India – Malaysia – China

Emerald Publishing Limited
Howard House, Wagon Lane, Bingley BD16 1WA, UK

First edition 2019

Copyright © 2019 Emerald Publishing Limited

Reprints and permissions service
Contact: permissions@emeraldinsight.com

No part of this book may be reproduced, stored in a retrieval system, transmitted in any form or by any means electronic, mechanical, photocopying, recording or otherwise without either the prior written permission of the publisher or a licence permitting restricted copying issued in the UK by The Copyright Licensing Agency and in the USA by The Copyright Clearance Center. Any opinions expressed in the chapters are those of the authors. Whilst Emerald makes every effort to ensure the quality and accuracy of its content, Emerald makes no representation implied or otherwise, as to the chapters' suitability and application and disclaims any warranties, express or implied, to their use.

British Library Cataloguing in Publication Data
A catalogue record for this book is available from the British Library

ISBN: 978-1-78754-326-3 (Print)
ISBN: 978-1-78754-325-6 (Online)
ISBN: 978-1-78754-327-0 (Epub)
ISBN: 978-1-78754-328-7 (Paperback)

INVESTOR IN PEOPLE

Acknowledgements

We would like to express our gratitude for the support through the Tyrolean Science Fund.

We would like to thank our Graphic Designer, Nikoleta Grozdanova, for her inspiring ideas in the design of the book cover.

Contents

List of Figures *ix*

List of Tables *xi*

About the Editors *xiii*

About the Authors *xv*

Introduction: The Disruptive Power of Online Education: Challenges, Opportunities, Responses
Andreas Altmann, Bernd Ebersberger, Claudia Mössenlechner and Desiree Wieser   *1*

PART I: ONLINE PROGRAMMES AND PROGRAMME DESIGN

Chapter 1 Scaling Online Learning: The Case for a Programme-level Approach
Regina Obexer   *7*

Chapter 2 LOGIC LEADS LEARNing: MOOCs in the Middle East
Yusuf M. Sidani   *27*

Chapter 3 The Power of Technology in Customised Executive Education
Lynette J. Ryals, Ruth Bender and Toby Thompson   *43*

Chapter 4 Internationalisation of Online Learning: A Double Degree Model
Charles Krusekopf   *63*

PART II: CHANGING CLASSROOM DYNAMICS IN THE DIGITAL TEACHING SPACE

Chapter 5 Engagement in Online Learning: It's Not All About Faculty!
Kathy Bishop, Catherine Etmanski and M. Beth Page   83

Chapter 6 Social Collaborative Learning Environments: A Means to Reconceptualise Leadership Education for Tomorrow's Leaders and Universities?
Anja P. Schmitz and Jan Foelsing   99

Chapter 7 Online, Not Distance Education: The Merits of Collaborative Learning in Online Education
Desiree Wieser and Jürgen-Matthias Seeler   125

Chapter 8 Disrupting Higher Education in Alaska: Introducing the Native Teacher Certification Pathway
Paul Berg, Kathryn Cruz, Thomas Duening and Susan Schoenberg   147

Chapter 9 Academic Rigour and Video Technology: A Case Study on Digital Storytelling in Graduate-level Assignments
Eva Malisius   167

Chapter 10 Game-based Learning as Education Method in the Digital Age: Experiences at the Highest Military Education Institution in Germany with Online and Offline Game Formats Related to Developing Competencies
Ronald Deckert, Felix Heymann and Maren Metz   185

Index   205

List of Figures

Chapter 2

Figure 2.1 LOGIC LEADS LEARNing. 32

Chapter 3

Figure 3.1 Co-creation at Each Stage of the Process. 51

List of Tables

Chapter 3

Table 3.1	Contextual Differences between Customised Executive Education and MOOCs	47
Table 3.2	How Client and Academic TEL Skills Influence Course Design	49

Chapter 7

Table 7.1	Overview Key Features	135
Table 7.2	Strengths and Weaknesses of the Study Programme	139

Chapter 9

Table 9.1	CAM 'My Digital Conflict Story' Assignment	176
Table 9.2	CAM 'My Digital Conflict Story' Learning Outcomes	177
Table 9.3	MAGL 'Presenting a Community in Conflict' Assignment	179
Table 9.4	MAGL 'Presenting a Community in Conflict' Learning Outcomes	180

Chapter 10

Table 10.1	Description of the Competencies Based on HRK, KMK and BMBF (2005); World Economic Forum (2015, 2016); Tenberg (2014)	188
Table 10.2	Comparing Digital and Non-digital Game Settings with Regard to Competencies	198

About the Editors

Andreas Altmann studied Business Administration and Economics at the Universities of Linz and Innsbruck, and International Relations at the Johns Hopkins University, SAIS Bologna. He received his doctoral degree in Public Finance from the University of Innsbruck in 1993 and entered his academic career as a Postdoctoral Researcher, first at the Department of Finance and later on at the Department of Strategic Management. There he got involved in building up a new school from scratch, now known as MCI Management Center Innsbruck – The Entrepreneurial School®. He became its founding Director and Rector in 1995 and has successfully led MCI to an internationally acknowledged autonomous university institution with currently 3,300 students, 1,000 full-time and adjunct faculty, 250 partner universities and numerous successful alumni from around the world. His research focuses on university regulation, governance and management, including the competitive environment and market behaviour in the higher education and research sector.

Bernd Ebersberger is Professor for Management of Innovation with the University of Hohenheim, Stuttgart, Germany. Previously, from 2007 to 2018 he has been with MCI Management Center Innsbruck. From 2004 to 2006, Ebersberger was with the Innovation Systems and Policy Department of Fraunhofer ISI in Karlsruhe, Germany. From 2002 up until 2004 he was Senior Researcher and Team Leader at VTT Technology Studies, Espoo, Finland, at the same time Visiting Researcher at Statistics Finland, Helsinki, Finland. From 1997 to 2002, he was a Researcher at the University of Augsburg. His current research interests focus on management of innovation, entrepreneurship, and management of higher education. Bernd has authored and co-authored numerous books and more than 30 papers published in international peer-reviewed journals.

Claudia Mössenlechner, in her current function as a Head of MCI Learning Solutions, is responsible for developing e-learning solutions and products. She has conceptualised MCI's first online programme and courses for tertiary education as well as for private and public companies in Austria and Italy. In addition, she has extensive experience as an examiner and accreditor (European Higher Education Space). Claudia has lead and coordinated 'quality in online teaching' approaches at Management Center Innsbruck and serves as Deputy Head of the MCI Academic Council. Her research focus lies on the implications of online teaching and online business models.

Desiree Wieser is a Research and Teaching Assistant at MCI Management Center Innsbruck, and a PhD Student in Management at the University of Innsbruck in Austria. Her main research area focuses on higher education management, in particular on online education and the successful implementation of online education in higher education institutions. At MCI, Desiree works in the Department of Research, Innovation and Entrepreneurship and coordinates different publication and research projects. At the moment she is responsible for the research projects 'Virtual Campus' and 'The Disruptive Power of Online Education'. Together with her team, she is currently also participating in the EU project 'Embedding Entrepreneurship Education', an initiative to foster entrepreneurship education throughout Europe. Next to her engagement in research and the coordination of different projects, Desiree also acts as junior faculty and teaches in different management study programmes at MCI.

About the Authors

Ruth Bender is Professor Emerita of Corporate Financial Strategy at Cranfield University, UK. Ruth started creating and using technology-enhanced learning in 1996 for both MBA courses and executive education. Much of her work is on blended courses. Ruth chairs The Case Centre, a not-for-profit organisation promoting the case study method in education.

Paul Berg has worked in the field of cross-cultural education as a Teacher in public and private schools, an educational specialist in the Alaska Department of Education, a Professor with the University of Alaska and as a Cultural Education Specialist for an Alaska Native Educational Foundation.

Kathy Bishop is Associate Professor and Program Head for Royal Roads University's Master's of Arts in Leadership, one of Canada's largest graduate programmes promoting leadership development. She completed her PhD in Interdisciplinary Studies (Leadership Studies and Theatre) at the University of Victoria (2015). She can be reached at Kathy.Bishop@royalroads.ca.

Kathryn Cruz of ansrsource, USA, serves as an Educational Specialist for a tribal non-profit and has co-taught and designed several culturally responsive university courses in collaboration with local elders, universities and school districts. Kate recently wrote a short story addressing historical actions and trauma affecting today's Alaskan Native communities.

Ronald Deckert is Dean of Faculty and Professor for Business Administration and Engineering. His research focuses on the topics of Digitalisation and Industry 4.0. He has been also involved in projects for federal state ministries and institutions in Germany in the areas of research, strategy, education and logistics.

Thomas Duening is the El Pomar Chair for Business and Entrepreneurship, and Associate Professor of Management in the College of Business at the University of Colorado. Duening is a leader of online education in the College and is an early adopter and tester of many distance education technologies.

Catherine Etmanski is a Professor and Director in the School of Leadership Studies (SoLS) at Royal Roads University. She received her PhD from the University of Victoria in 2007 with a focus on leadership, adult education and participatory engagement. She can be reached at Catherine.Etmanski@royalroads.ca.

Jan Foelsing is a 'Learning and NewWork Designer' who is passionate about modernising our education system and the way we learn and work together in organisations. At the University of Pforzheim, he is responsible for research regarding social collaboration tools and ways to use these tools for modern learning arrangements.

Felix Heymann is a career Soldier and holds a diploma in Education. He is also a Certified Business Coach. He is an expert in serious gaming and its implementation and application in the field of instruction on the Leadership Academy of the German Army.

Charles Krusekopf is a Professor in the School of Business at Royal Roads University. He has published papers and book chapters on topics in international economics and business. He has a PhD in Economics from the University of Washington, and a MA in International Relations from Johns Hopkins University SAIS.

Eva Malisius is an Associate Professor in the School of Humanitarian Studies at Royal Roads University, Canada. She is a conflict engagement specialist, educator and scholar-practitioner. Her research interests focus – among other topics – on constructive conflict engagement and transformative learning and teaching in online and face-to-face classrooms.

Maren Metz is a Graduate Psychologist, Coach and Communication Trainer who has academic interests in learning via online media. Her work centres on e-coaching and the use of serious gaming. She is currently a leader of two distance study programs, psychology and business psychology in a private school in Hamburg.

Regina Obexer is a Senior Lecturer at Management Center Innsbruck, Austria. She has worked in the field of Digital Education and eLearning in Higher Education for nearly two decades and has held various management and leadership positions at universities in Austria and Australia.

M. Beth Page owns Dream Catcher Consulting and serves as Associate Faculty at Royal Roads University, Canada. Beth holds degrees from Pepperdine University, Western Illinois University and Carleton University, and she completed her PhD at the University of Victoria. She can be reached at beth@dreamcatcher-consulting.com

Lynette J. Ryals is Pro-Vice Chancellor and Dean of the School of Management at Cranfield University, UK. Her focus is on how education should evolve to meet the needs of the future workplace. This includes developing 'learning pathways' to support people as they progress through their careers.

Anja P. Schmitz is a Professor of Human Resources Management/HRM and a member of the Human Resources Competence Center of the Pforzheim University of Applied Sciences (HRCC). Her research interests include Personnel and Organizational Development, Employee Experience, Social Collaboration in organisations and education, as well as HR processes.

Susan Schoenberg of ansrsource, USA, is passionate about educational technology. She graduated magna cum laude from Harvard University and began her career as a software engineer creating learning games and interactive media for K-12 math and science learners. She has worked in numerous learning companies writing experiential educational software for all ages.

Jürgen-Matthias Seeler is Professor and Head of Department and Studies at Management Center Innsbruck, Austria. He introduced MCI's first academic Online Programmes 'Business Administration' Online (BA) and 'Corporate Governance and Finance' Online (MA). Previously, he was consultant in Central Africa, where he worked in the field of Governance and Anti-Corruption.

Yusuf M. Sidani is Professor of Leadership and Business Ethics at the Olayan School of Business, American University of Beirut, Lebanon. His research, which appeared in several leading international peer-reviewed academic journals, focuses on business ethics, gender and diversity, and employee behaviour with special attention to the Middle East.

Toby Thompson is the Networked Learning Director at Cranfield University, UK. Toby consults with clients on designing and implementing networked learning interventions appropriate to their context. His PhD is in the philosophy of executive education. His research interest is in how time and temporality are conceived in executive education and development practices.

Introduction: The Disruptive Power of Online Education: Challenges, Opportunities, Responses

Andreas Altmann, Bernd Ebersberger, Claudia Mössenlechner and Desiree Wieser

By the end of this decade, more than half of the world's population will be digitally connected (Kraft & Jung, 2016). The internet and technology are changing social norms and societal structures as well as corporate values (Holladay, 2017) bringing about transformations that are hard to discern in their overall global impact at this point in time (McAfee & Brynjolfsson, 2015).

Worldwide, the higher education sector is seriously being disrupted through the effect technological innovations have on markets and the way they work (Christensen & Eyring, 2011). Traditional, on-site education is enhanced, supplemented or even replaced by teaching and learning in the digital space. As digital technologies are spreading rapidly, higher education institutions must embrace these developments to meet the needs of their learners (Delich, 2005), who are deeply embedded in the digital world, and to adapt their programmes to increase the impact regarding the curriculum taught, in terms of teaching formats and design and in relation to the overall impact of their business model.

Additionally, competition in the educational market is growing in that new third-party competitors like EduTech companies and online educational providers have entered the market. Even twenty years ago, information technology and competition in higher education have been described using the metaphor of dancing with the devil (Katz, 1999). The situation has certainly not improved, as these new competitors operate in more independent and profit-oriented frameworks that are not necessarily primarily addressing the higher education market but are attractive for exactly that market.

In higher education, we observe disruption through, what Christensen and Eyring (2011) call, online universities. These online universities challenge traditional universities that adopt a Harvard model of teaching, research and outreach. Subsequently, we see traditional universities respond on two levels: First, on a programme/product level with programmes including some elements of online education or online formats. And second, we observe a change triggered by shifting the teaching environment to the digital space, which calls for a different balance of teaching interventions and pedagogy.

In an attempt to address these challenges, universities identify and use different windows of opportunities by applying their expertise in research and teaching, by adjusting their systems and organisational structures, by adapting their products and services and by truly putting their learners in the centre of the frameworks they operate in.

This book explores how higher education institutions across the globe respond to and address the necessary changes in regard to both programme design and pedagogy. It offers a view on upcoming challenges as well as giving an insight into ways how institutions deal with online education in practice.

I.1. Online Programmes and Programme Design

Regina Obexer opens the discussion and explores the topic of eLearning and online programme development by describing and discussing the 'whole-of-programme approach' regarding the design and implementation of an online degree programme.

Yusuf M. Sidani then looks at Massive Open Online Courses (MOOCs) by describing a joint project between a traditional university in the Middle East and a MOOC provider as a new form of partnership. When presenting his case study, the author also presents a framework to operate in (LOGIC – LEADS – LEARNing) during such endeavours in order to address the issues and needs of key partners and stakeholders involved and make the project a successful one.

Lynette J. Ryals, Ruth Bender and Toby Thompson focus on online programme design in the context of executive education programmes, a 'competitive landscape' that finds itself on a completely different territory than for-credit university programmes or, for example, providers of MOOCs. First, the authors look at collaborative course design involving the client and then look at the impact technology-enhanced learning has on course design, delivery and evaluation in customised settings. The authors conclude with some observations of what they call 'considerable institutional disruptions' as far as the expectations concerning the business models for higher education are concerned.

Charles Krusekopf, by embracing the internationalisation of online learning, introduces a case study on a blended double-degree Business Master's programme. Thereby he highlights the insufficient attention that has been paid to how online learning and internationalisation can be combined to enfold mutually supportive powers, and provides suggestions on how such powers can be exploited efficiently.

I.2. Changing Classroom Dynamics in the Digital Teaching Space

As key educational services, i.e. teacing, change, not only the nature and the design of higher education programmes are affected, but also classroom dynamics and teaching activities as such. Roles of faculty change through the use of technology. In their chapter, Kathy Bishop, Catherine Etmanski and M. Beth Page claim that student engagement is the vital element for student learning also in an online environment and when teaching adults. Hands-on and drawing on their own teaching experience, the authors creatively present and literally show a diverse range of student-centred activities and scenarios they use to build online communities as a base for student engagement. By way of example; i.e. by using dialogue scripts, they discuss the teaching principles they apply, at the same time giving the reader an insightful impression of teaching moves that intentionally disrupt the role of the teacher and create space for student engagement and community building.

A strong student community and space for student engagement is the ideal ground for social-collaborative learning. Anja P. Schmitz and Jan Foelsing argue that personalised and social-collaborative learning processes enabled through Social Collaboration Platforms, used as primary learning environment, hold the potential for dealing with the challenges faced by traditional universities and their business models. The authors introduce a case study of a total reconceptualisation of a Bachelor's course in leadership that is enhanced by social collaboration elements and supported by a technological learning environment. On the basis of the illustrated case, they show how a redesign of traditional teaching settings that considers the expectations of the new student generation becomes possible, and develop a flexible framework that captures how learners can be prepared for the new demands in the business world, profiting from sustainable communities of practice and how this will open up new business models for universities.

Collaborative learning approaches might also help to overcome social isolation phenomena, an often cited as a hurdle for students in online education. This is an aspect co-editor Desiree Wieser and Jürgen-Matthias Seeler focus on in their chapter. They see the merits of collaborative learning in the fact that student collaboration is a major factor in overcoming what they call a 'key disadvantage' in online education, namely geographical distance. In a practical case analysis, they outline an example of the implementation of a blended online programme that has been designed using a mix of teaching and learning formats.

The question of geographical distance and possible social isolation effects in teacher training and development is addressed by Paul Berg, Kathryn Cruz, Thomas Duening and Susan Schoenberg when they describe an innovative concept based on a competency-based, bilingual online programme for teacher certification in rural Alaska. The proposed project is a perfect example of how teaching in the online space can help overcome geosocial and cultural divides and significantly increase both the educational and societal impact.

In her chapter, Eva Malisius shows that video technology and digital storytelling can be used without compromising academic rigour and as a way to assess students in graduate-level courses. At the same time, her chapter is a valuable contribution to the ongoing discussion on assessment methods for the twenty-first century, and prove for the impact the use of technology in itself can have on students and the generic skills they develop through online programmes.

Ronald Deckert, Felix Heymann and Maren Metz look at the game- and simulation-based learning and the impact especially serious games can have for the development of social and management competencies in students. While the field of digital serious games and simulations for learning is still very young, the authors contribute a valuable discussion to this book by looking at some of the major concepts in the field and matching competency tables for management students with the possibilities game- and simulation-based learning offers.

The ongoing rapid development of information technologies and new media will further and distinctively change higher education programme design as well as the teaching and learning environments of the future. We hope that the chapters of the book will both inform and inspire teaching professionals and leaders, managers and administrators; in other words, all those involved in strategic decision-making and the design and implementation of online educational offers in higher education.

Together, the chapters of this book provide a base for discussion that needs to be led to further develop or establish online learning in an organisation. It is our hope that *The Disruptive Power of Online Education: Challenges, Opportunities, Responses* will help to spark, inspire and inform these discussions in a positive way.

References

Christensen, C., & Eyring, H. J. (2011). *The innovative university: Changing the DNA of higher education from inside out* (1st ed.). San Francisco: Jossey-Bass Wiley.

Delich, P. (2005). *Pedagogical and interface modifications: What instructors change after teaching online*. Malibu, CA: Pepperdine University.

Holladay, P. (2017). Pedagogy for online tourism classes. In P. Benckendorff & A. Zehrer (Eds.), *Handbook of teaching and learning in tourism* (pp. 141–153). Cheltenham: Edward Elgar Publishing.

Katz, R. N. (1999). *Dancing with the devil: Information technology and the new competition in higher education*. Jossey-Bass Higher and Adult Education Series. San Francisco, CA: Jossey-Bass Publisher.

Kraft, P., & Jung, H. H. (Eds.). (2016). *Digital vernetzt. Transformation der Wertschöpfung.: Szenarien, Optionen und Erfolgsmodelle für smarte Geschäftsmodelle, Produkte und Services*. München: Carl Hanser Verlag GmbH Co KG.

McAfee, A., & Brynjolfsson, E. (2015). The digitization of just about everything. *Rotman Management Magazine, Fall*, 39–42.

PART I
ONLINE PROGRAMMES AND PROGRAMME DESIGN

Chapter 1

Scaling Online Learning: The Case for a Programme-level Approach

Regina Obexer

Abstract

Whilst online and blended learning approaches are now widely used by many higher education institutions, the extent and depth of eLearning implementation often depend more on the efforts of enthusiastic individual lecturers rather than effective institution-wide strategies. Innovation is thus frequently restricted to local settings and the enrichment of existing educational approaches rather than radically questioning current paradigms and creating new ways of delivering education. In recent years, there has been more urgency in calling for a deeper re-thinking of how higher education can be made more flexible, scalable and individualised not only at the level of courses but in a systemic and strategic way. This article describes a strategic approach to implementing blended learning at Management Center Innsbruck in Austria. I argue that the whole-of-programme approach taken in this case is an effective way to strategically introduce sustainable and scalable blended learning, and thus not only respond to but actively shape the disruption brought about by online education.

Keywords: Online learning models; programme development; sustainable innovation; scalability; systems approach; eLearning implementation

1.1. Introduction

After nearly three decades of innovation and gradually increasing use, online and blended learning approaches have entered the mainstream, and some argue that the mere concept of eLearning will be obsolete in the near future as there will be no learning without technology (Cavanagh, 2012). However, the extent of eLearning implementation both in terms of breadth and depth varies significantly across the higher education landscape. Countries with a long tradition of distance education (Australia, Canada, USA) and highly developed technological infrastructure have embraced eLearning as the next step in providing educational opportunities to those not able to participate in traditional learning programmes, and to enhance and expand learning for all students (Brooks & Pomerantz, 2017; Gunn & Herrick, 2012). The UK, given its cultural closeness to those nations, has developed equally advanced eLearning strategies (Walker, Voce, & Jenkins, 2016). Nations with significant unmet needs in education, such as India, China, countries in Africa and South America, are looking to eLearning as the means that will provide their people with the education they seek (Murphy, Farley, Dyson, & Jones, 2017; Pulist, 2013; Rivers, Rivers, & Hazell, 2015), and some are already leapfrogging in terms of the development of new and efficient technologies and methods to fill those unmet needs (Biswas & Hazra, 2016; Ng'ambi, Brown, Bozalek, Gachago, & Wood, 2016).

In Germany and Austria, however, things seem to be taking a slower pace, despite significant investment in eLearning initiatives both at national and at European Union level over the past two decades (Bratengeyer et al., 2016; EACEA, 2014. e-teaching.org, 2017; Gaebel, Kupriyanova, Morais, & Colucci, 2014). The reasons for this lag are multi-layered, and it would go beyond the scope of this paper to discuss them. Instead, what is presented here are two forward-looking propositions: the first is that the current status and pace of digitisation does not suffice anymore in the face of economic, technological and social developments, and the second is that eLearning development and implementation at the programme level is an effective approach for Higher Education institutions to fast-track eLearning adoption, make it more sustainable, and create a better experience for stakeholders. A case study of Management Center Innsbruck, where such an approach was implemented, illustrates the programme-level approach as a practical example.

1.2. Setting the Scene: Where Are We?

During an initial period in the late 1990s, eLearning projects and initiatives were supported by significant government funding across the developed world. Projects mainly involved the implementation of various eLearning technologies (with a strong focus on Learning Management Systems) as well as specific, often course based eLearning content and tool developments (Euler & Seufert, 2011). After the various project funding sources had dried up in the early years of the new millennium, it proved to be challenging for many institutions to continue the innovations and achievements of these early projects, and to embed the changed practices into everyday teaching and learning in a systemic way. Most universities in Austria, for example, have now implemented an institution-wide Learning Management System and sometimes a handful of other centrally supported tools and systems that enable various eLearning activities (Bratengeyer et al., 2016). Generally, there is some degree of support for teaching staff, mostly in the form of technical support (including basic training) and to a varying degree and in various forms, didactic support to assist in the development of learning resources and in approaches to designing online teaching and learning as well as assessment strategies. eLearning at an institutional level means for many universities that they make resources available online, that there is some degree of communication with students via electronic means, and that eAssessment is carried out, particularly through online quizzes in large classes.

However, despite significant investment and efforts at institutional, national and European levels, the progress made in implementing online education approaches across the Higher Education sectors in Austria can at best be described as incremental and evolving rather than strategic and systemic. Whilst there is some evidence of efforts to embed strategic approaches to eLearning at an institutional level, and there are indications that the shift towards more student-centred learning approaches is gaining wider traction, the existing educational paradigms are mainly unchallenged by and at best augmented with technologies. Many enthusiastic and engaged teachers are trialing various innovative eLearning and eTeaching approaches and are often successful at the level of their particular course or group of students. However, many of these individual successes have little or no effect beyond the local level, and evidence of systemic approaches to implementing eLearning or blended learning at a wholeof-programme level is sparse (Germ & Mandl, 2009; High Level Group on the Modernisation of Higher Education, 2014). A more systemic approach as described in the following is starting to emerge as an important aspect. For example, a recent strategy paper developed by the German initiative *Hochschulforum Digitalisierung* notes:

> In the current phase of digitalising academic programmes, the use of digital teaching and learning formats should only be promoted as an integral part of complex study programmes. This suggestion involves abandoning the exclusive promotion of special digitalisation projects in favour of supporting complete study programmes relating to specialist areas or faculties. (Hochschulforum Digitalisierung, 2017, p. 19)

So far, however, the discussion about strategic measures necessary to achieve institution-wide adoption of eLearning use seems to have failed to translate into practice at a wider scale.

1.3. Strategic Imperative: Why We Need to Go Beyond Gradual Adaptation

While the lack of strategic and systemic adoption may not have been seen as problematic so far, even as eLearning was considered by many to reach maturity during the turn of the decade, the tone in the discourse about technology innovation in education has changed radically in recent years. Especially the hype around Massive Open Online Courses (MOOCs) has put into question the very nature of Higher Education, and other developments (Open Educational Resources or OER, Learning Analytics, adaptive learning, etc.) are widely debated as game changers (Christensen & Eyring, 2011; Oblinger, 2012). Commercial providers are aggressively pushing into an exploding online higher education market. Industry demands for graduates with a range of evolving skills are putting pressure on education and training systems worldwide, whilst in developing countries such as India and China, the new middle class is clamouring for education at a scale that is impossible to realise with traditional educational models. At the same time, it is recognised that the need for lifelong learning has to move beyond political rhetoric in the face of an ageing demographic, rapidly changing technology developments and the ever-increasing amount of information we have to deal with in this century's knowledge society and economy. These aspects require people to be engaged in continuing education while they are working, be it in formal degree programmes or in more modular and tailored professional development opportunities, including social and informal learning.

We are currently experiencing a confluence of factors that seems indeed to become a catalyst for the long-awaited transformation of Higher Education through technology. Barber, Donnelly, and Rizyi (2013) describe the main drivers for this increased urgency, arguing that higher education must change due to a number of economic pressures. These include a changing global economy, the global financial crisis and its consequences, the rising costs of education, but at the same time the falling value of a degree, and the fact that global competition in the higher education sector is rising significantly. According to Barber et al. (2013), the changes ahead are significant and will overhaul the existing sector in such a way that institutions that are not prepared risk becoming obsolete in the face of a diversified higher education sector, in which each institution will need to find its particular niche, be clear about their target student population, and articulate clearly their value proposition. In a similar vein, Christensen and Eyring (2011) argue that higher education is facing what other industries have already been going through – disruptive innovation through digitisation. They list a number of examples which illustrate how existing business models were completely transformed through the availability of new technologies or digitally enabled processes. In this scenario, it is mostly new competitors in the market who succeed by employing radically different and new business models rather than existing (and often well established) businesses who may find it difficult to completely change their approach to a new mindset. Christensen and Eyring (2011) maintain that Higher Education is now at a point where the services it offers (or, in the authors' words, 'the job to be done') can be delivered in a much cheaper and more accessible way through online education. The quality may not be as good, but it is good enough and certainly better than the alternative for many, which is no education or training at all.

Oblinger (2012) argues that educational technology can play a significant role in changing education and that in this changed and significantly accelerated environment, more radical strategies are necessary to cater for the needs of higher and further education of today and tomorrow:

> Information technology can be a game changer in higher education, as it has been in other sectors. [...] Information technology enables new models. It can disaggregate and decouple products and processes, allowing the creation of new value propositions, value chains, and enterprises. These new models can help higher education serve new groups of students, in greater numbers, and with better learning outcomes. (Oblinger, 2012, p. 11)

Many other voices agree. The mere 'enrichment' character of eLearning in higher education, i.e. the use of technologies to augment existing teaching and learning, will need to morph into the 'new normal' (Cavanagh, 2012). New forms of learning and teaching (not those mirroring the current paradigm) are emerging and will partly need to be invented to truly cater to the needs of this millennium. Indeed, a changed frame of reference is necessary that does not simply attempt to improve current models of delivering education but re-invent them based on the affordances of the digitalisation taking place in the 21st century. This requires a shift from integration to digitisation and serious re-consideration and exploration of how new models of education enabled by technology can work, and what they mean in terms of our existing systems, including institutional and sectorial culture, process and practice, legal and regulatory frameworks, (changing) roles of the various stakeholders (in particular the academic workforce) and others (Boud & Brew, 2013; McFarlane, 2011).

1.4. Strategic Scope: Online Learning Is Not a One-(wo)man Show

Given this degree of disruption and transformation, it is important that higher education institutions have a strategic approach to dealing with the challenges described above, and proactively participate and shape the transformation processes and strategic development required to create the higher education model of tomorrow (Bischof & Stuckrad, 2013; Seufert & Meier, 2013).

In order to be able to achieve this transformational shift, it will be necessary to start with bolder experiments beyond those occurring in individual classrooms, taking into account that the transition from traditional models of teaching to new paradigms is complex and requires significant institutional vision, support and investment.

Many higher education institutions understand that there are changing demands on them which result in requirements to fundamentally rethink their offering, however, there are few institutions that are able to approach this challenge strategically and with confidence. For example, a recent study of eLearning at Austrian Universities shows that whilst the technical eLearning infrastructure is implemented across most if not all institutions, only very few organisations have a specific online learning strategy (Bratengeyer et al., 2016). The study shows that there is an investment in online learning and an understanding that it is important to move towards more digital offerings. Beyond the technical infrastructure, many institutions have implemented various support measures and structures such as eLearning support centres, staff development programmes for online learning, technical support, and various incentives. However, these initiatives are generally geared to support early adopters – those enthusiastic individual teachers who want to experiment with various technologies to enhance their teaching. When driven by this group of early adopters, innovation is usually based on the objectives, interests and abilities of the teacher, very much tailored to their teaching approach and subject area, and it rarely goes beyond their individual courses. Many of the projects funded during the early years of eLearning introduction in Europe were of this character. While some of the projects resulted in innovations and improvements to practice and processes, there were also many that had to be abandoned when project money dried up, or when key individuals left the project or organisation (Haug & Wedekind, 2009; Singh & Hardaker, 2014). A report to the European Commission on new modes of learning and teaching in higher education states:

> There remains a culture of conservatism within European higher education which needs to change. [...] While a broad range of good practice is already emerging across Europe, this is happening to a large degree in an uncoordinated bottom-up approach. (High Level Group on the Modernisation of Higher Education, 2014, p. 11)

This has been one of the issues with eLearning implementation in Higher Education and is one of the reasons why – despite significant investment – sustained and deeply embedded digitisation is still the exception rather than the norm. This model of the individual teacher implementing isolated digital innovations in their courses termed the 'Lone Ranger' approach by Bates and Sangrá (2011, p. 138), is problematic in several respects.

Viewed from a student's point of view, at best they conceive the new approach as interesting, innovative, and as an opportunity to enhance their digital skills. At worst, students are confused about what to do and how to do it, why they are using the technology or study online, and where to get technical support when needed. Online learning also requires a change in learning the culture and the different skills, which students often do not have, and in an individual course, approach will find more difficult to gain without support.

From the teacher's point of view, whilst this approach provides freedom in terms of how, in what depth, and with what tools online learning is implemented, it also means that individual teachers often work in isolation, as lone rangers, without much opportunity to exchange ideas, challenge existing policies that might be obstructing their plans, or view their course – and their students' needs – in a wider context, both in terms of the curriculum and of the overall student experience. Additional workload is often not seen by the institution and can lead to frustration and overwork in the long term.

From the point of view of the institution, this approach is generally quite resource-intensive in that it either requires the teacher to do it all by themselves (which is often the case, and it should be mentioned that this also often happens in the enthusiastic teacher's own time), or support services such as instructional design, staff development, and technical support for students is provided to the individual on a singular needs basis rather than as part of an overall framework of larger scale implementation and development. In addition, innovation resulting from these inputs seldom spreads to other contexts and is frequently lost when the individual leaves the organisation, or loses interest or energy for their novel approach (Bates & Sangrá, 2011).

1.5. Beyond a Lone Ranger Approach: Programme-level Development and Implementation

1.5.1. What Is a Programme-level Approach to Online Learning Development and Implementation?

So what can universities do to accelerate innovation in this space, and to create more sustainable models of online learning implementation? Based on the shortfalls of an individual course development approach discussed above and the urgency caused by swiftly changing demands on higher education, it is proposed here that in order to be successful, consistent and sustainable, the introduction of online strategies is best planned and implemented at programme level; i.e. at the level of the curriculum and as an integral part of the planning and review process of a new or existing programme. Programme-level eLearning developments and implementations have the following characteristics:

- They are developed by a team, including the programme head, teaching staff, if appropriate administrative support staff from the academic area or department, and staff from support services such as eLearning support centres, the library, and IT services.
- They plan for consistent technology use across the programme.
- They plan for consistent and appropriate online teaching approaches across the programme (with appropriate variation to suit learning requirements and specific competency development in various subjects).
- They plan for quality assurance across the programme.
- They consider staff development requirements for both teaching and support staff, and plan for (team) development of the competencies and skills required.
- They consider student (online) learning development needs, and ideally include these as part of the curriculum.
- They plan for student and staff just-in-time support.
- They plan for consistent strategies to develop or acquire online learning content and resources, and integrate these with the teaching approaches.
- They take into consideration and plan for necessary changes to institutional policies and processes.

- They take a project management approach to the development of the programme and employ project management tools and methods.

1.5.2. Advantages of a Programme-level Approach: An Overview

Considering the drawbacks of individual developments as described above, the advantages of a successful programme-based implementation include the following:

1.5.2.1. For Students

Students in holistically designed and developed study programmes generally appreciate the predictability and consistency in experience at several levels. If implemented well, there is easy-to-use and functional technology, well-organised student support, consistent communication and clear expectations, streamlined processes, and digital skills development to enable them to fully participate in the programme. This is often included in an online orientation phase or offered through support materials provided at various and appropriate stages during their studies. If all these prerequisites are in place, students know what they sign up for, they have the technology to participate fully, and they receive the necessary support and training to do well in their online studies.

1.5.2.2. For Teaching Staff

Although teaching staff involved in developing and teaching an online programme in a team rather than an individual approach may lose some autonomy in terms of their own course or subject, they gain many advantages. On the one hand, working in a team which is ideally supported by other professionals such as instructional designers, multimedia developers, graphic designers, or library professionals, they enjoy ongoing support and commitment from the institution. Engaging in joint discussion and development of the curriculum and programme, they will develop a better understanding of their own contribution to the whole (which in turn often improves the quality and consistency of the programme). Participating in skills development together with their colleagues in the context of their own programme development will enable them to build competencies together, trial new technologies and approaches in a safe space, and immediately apply what they have learned together with their peers. Programme development approaches often also have the effect that departments or programme teams become more cohesive and get to know each other better, thus often leading to deeper and ongoing collaboration and exchange. What is more, additional workload – often seen as a hidden barrier to eLearning implementation – becomes more transparent and one of the issues to be considered, rather than something that just has to be accepted as is often the case when individuals embark on online learning activities on their own.

1.5.2.3. For the Institution

From the point of view of the organisation, the advantages in taking a programme development approach are significant in many ways. The shift to online or blended learning is a considerable investment for higher education institutions, and there should be a focus on their sustainability and ideally their scalability. Scalability is often referred to in relation to growing student numbers in this context. Another aspect of scalability relates to the possibility to transfer the models, approaches and processes developed for one programme to others, thus making the implementation of programme transformation more scalable by reducing effort and risk and increasing efficiencies.

Programme-level development is efficient in that it provides central services such as staff development, instructional design, resource development or selection, and student supports for groups of people rather than individuals. A team approach to skill development not only reduces the demand on support providers, but also enables a different outcome as skills are developed in a context of real needs, with immediate applicability, and in exchange with peers who work in the same context. Instructional design support can be provided more efficiently when considering the whole programme and will result in better outcomes if designing high-level learning outcomes, assessment and knowledge and competency development across the programme rather than the individual course.

Programme-level approaches are not always easy to implement, and their success depends on several dimensions and conditions. The remainder of this article describes the different facets of a programme-level approach, including the key aspects to be considered by institutions choosing this approach as well as the necessary conditions and challenges associated with this method. In order to provide concrete examples of how this approach can work, the case of online learning implementation at MCI Management Centre Innsbruck (Austria) will be used to illustrate a successful programme-level implementation.

1.6. A Short Profile of Management Centre Innsbruck (MCI)

The MCI Management Centre Innsbruck was founded in 1995/96 and has grown over the years to accommodate over 3,400 students at the time of writing. Focusing on disciplines relating to business and society as well as science and technology, the MCI offers a range of undergraduate and postgraduate degrees both in German and in English, including offerings in the area of executive education and customised programmes.

Until a few years ago, the MCI was fairly typical in its national and regional context when it comes to the use of technologies in learning and teaching to provide added value within existing paradigms. Whilst innovation was occurring, particularly with regards to new resource formats and in terms of encouraging a more active role of the student in the learning process, these did not disrupt the existing model of higher education as such but were rather incremental improvements of the existing model.

In 2014, the MCI decided to extend its existing, face-to-face model of delivery and − after a period of intensive market research and planning − started its first undergraduate business degree in blended learning mode, a bachelor in business administration offered in German. In 2016, the second track in English was introduced to extend the market reach and to provide an additional trajectory for students who are more internationally oriented. At postgraduate level, an online MBA in international business was first offered in 2015 as part of the executive education portfolio, and a Master in Corporate Governance and Finance started in fall 2017.

Traditionally, the MCI has a strong philosophy of excellent student services, highly personalised student support, innovative, highly applied, current and practical teaching approaches and low student to staff ratios. The new online programmes need to be designed to live up to these expectations associated with the strong MCI brand. Considering this context and the culture of the institution, the MCI decided to opt for a blended learning mode rather than fully online programmes. It should be noted that this does not change in principle the design and development parameters, as both blended and online programmes require similar considerations.

1.7. eLearning Implementation at Programme Level: Key Aspects to Consider

The following section explains in more detail the key aspects that require consideration when planning for a programme-level approach to eLearning implementation. It should be noted that the aspects described here are not exhaustive and that a range of institutional characteristics and contexts (e.g. organisational culture, the rationale for eLearning implementation, available resources and existing infrastructure) will have an impact on how these play out. However, the aspects discussed in this section can be seen as the backbone of a systemic, programme-level implementation of online and blended learning programmes.

1.7.1. Strong Leadership and Institutional Commitment

The arguably most important aspects in implementing eLearning at a higher education institution are strong leadership and institutional commitment. This presupposes that the organisation has thought strategically about the value of introducing eLearning, and can articulate a clear reason why this investment is necessary, which goes beyond the mere mantra that 'digitisation is upon us'. Ideally, there is a clearly articulated strategy that lays out the motives and drivers for implementing eLearning and explains how the institution will enact this strategic intent. This strategy should be visibly aligned with the vision and the mission of the institution and reflect its culture and spirit. How this strategy is developed will depend very much on the culture of the organisation, on the leadership style of university management, the nature of faculty engagement and involvement, and also on the circumstances and drivers that determine why eLearning is being implemented (Valente, 2018).

At the MCI, there was clear strategic reasoning for introducing the blended learning programme: firstly, to provide more flexible and accessible programmes for prospective students with work and family commitments; secondly, to increase the MCI market reach to students who live too far away to travel to Innsbruck regularly; and thirdly to create an incubator that introduces eLearning at the institution and accelerates innovation.

The institutional commitment was initially clearly visible through significant resource investment in the new programme, including hiring several academic staff experienced in online delivery to lead the programme and an explicitly articulated view by university leadership that the change was important for the MCI's future development. The establishment of a central support service, the Learning Solutions Team, was a cornerstone of the strategy, designed to both support the new programme, and to drive, increase and sustain the development of blended learning approaches in other programmes across the institution. In addition, a broad information campaign was rolled out across the institution to create a shared language and understanding about the new approach – a key initial strategy to carry innovation beyond the borders of the programme and expand cultural change across the organisation.

1.7.2. *Supporting and Developing Teaching Staff in the Transition*

Developing online programmes is different from preparing for teaching face-to-face. Many teachers coming from a traditional, face-to-face environment do not have the skills to teach online. The question of how to best support staff in the transition to blended or online learning depends to a certain extent on the culture of the institution. At the MCI, where there is only a small body of tenured teaching staff, and a large number of sessional staff, it was decided to hire several new teaching staff with extensive online experience who spearheaded the first offering of the blended learning programme. Together with the internal, existing planning team (who had developed the curriculum), an instructional designer and the multimedia team, they developed the first iteration of the offering, and in the process brought other teaching staff along with them.

One of the most important success factors in online programme implementation is the capability development of staff teaching in the programmes. Staff development needs for online teaching range from an expanding set of technical skills in using the available technology to didactical skills in reframing teaching and student learning for an online learning environment. Capability development in this space has been discussed extensively and can take on a range of formats and approaches (Herman, 2012; McQuiggan, 2012).

At the MCI, a staff development programme was implemented that covers core skills and competencies both in terms of technology use and in terms of didactic strategies in alignment with and geared towards the programme-level teaching approach. It was decided to offer both group workshops and individual coaching sessions. The core staff participated in an introductory workshop on blended learning, where different teaching formats, learning designs as well as approaches to resource development were discussed. In addition, workshops were offered on the use of the Learning Management System and the web-conferencing platform Adobe Connect used in the programme. Learning resources such as handbooks and user guidelines were also developed and made available to the teaching team, including an introduction to blended learning, guidelines on planning and delivering webinars and moderating online discussions, and various user handbooks for the tools available. For staff joining the core team after the initial phase, the Learning Solutions team offered individual coaching sessions where the programme approach and didactical options were discussed in addition to an in-depth introduction to the technology used. The coaching sessions were offered both face-to-face where teachers were onsite and online for those not able to come to the campus. Over time, more informal support mechanisms have emerged in addition to the institutional offering, with peer support between more experienced staff and their colleagues new to teaching online becoming increasingly common.

In addition to internal faculty development programmes, it is also important to look beyond institutional boundaries and engage with and learn from professional discourse and development opportunities in higher education at national and international level. This should occur for all stakeholders involved in blended learning programme implementation, including the leadership team, faculty, support services and administration teams. There are many networks, conference, special interest groups, and professional associations which can provide a wealth of knowledge and information, and can be accessed through a variety of channels, be it online or face-to-face. The same is true for online learning opportunities such as MOOCs, Webinars, discussion groups, email lists, Twitter chats, etc., which are abundantly available in the area of digital learning. Encouraging staff to participate and contribute to these networks, e.g. through conference attendance and presentations, engagement in networking events and knowledge exchange, social network use and contributions to various initiatives not only allows for deepening and extending stakeholder awareness, knowledge and know-how but also increases the visibility of the own institution in the academic community.

1.7.3. Supporting Students in Adapting to a New Way of Learning

Support for students must be a focus when introducing online and blended learning programmes, especially in part-time programmes where the student population is more diverse and has different needs. At the MCI, it was found that this support impacts directly on students' success in the programme. As online programmes are often designed for students who work and have family or other commitments, the target group has typically not engaged in formal education for some time. The average age of MCI students in blended learning programmes is around 28 years, and students self-report that they have concerns both about their ability to 'get into studying again' and about using learning technologies (Mössenlechner, Obexer, Sixl-Daniell, & Seeler, 2015). Despite all the talk about 'digital natives', many students clearly need support in using learning technology, particularly when it comes to participating actively in webinars.

The support provided at the MCI includes an intensive orientation course as an integral and compulsory first part of the curriculum in blended learning programmes. This covers technology use as well as learning support, time management and general study skills. The course includes both face-to-face and online components and is delivered over a two- to three-week period. Students are also encouraged to form self-organised support groups amongst themselves, for example through WhatsApp groups, but also by organising social events during residencies. A buddy system between second-year students and first-year students complements the support provided.

1.7.4. Technology Use at the Programme Level

Whilst Learning Management Systems (LMS) are often criticised for not being user-friendly, for stifling innovation and putting the straight-jacket on teacher creativity (Brown, Dehoney, & Millichap, 2015; Dahlstrom, Brooks, & Bichsel, 2014), they are nevertheless still an important component of systemic online programme development. An LMS makes available both a set of tools and a structure for programme teams to design online courses and does so consistently across a programme. In most cases, it will not be up for discussion on what system to use at programme level as many organisations have implemented a particular LMS at the institutional level. What can and should be discussed, however, is:

- how individual course sites are designed and used;
- what tools within the LMS are useful for the particular programme and should, therefore, be available as a standard in each individual course;
- what tools are useful only for particular courses and should be added on an individual basis; and
- if there are any requirements the LMS cannot fulfil that need to be met. If this is the case, there are a range of external tools that can be made use of.

At Management Center Innsbruck, the open community LMS Sakai is being used, and in addition the web-conferencing software Adobe Connect. From the start, a common design and look and feel were developed for the Sakai course websites in each blended learning programme. Individual lecturers are able to use additional tools for a range of purposes, however, there is a clear standard for communication between lecturer and student, for assignment submission via the LMS assignment tool, and in parts also for content provision. Whilst some may perceive this standardisation as limiting and against the spirit of freedom of teaching, it is essential for online programmes to provide and implement a certain degree of structure and to also expect each lecturer to follow the given standards. Where this is not the case, students are likely to be confused, to complain about having to re-orient themselves in terms of navigation, the location of resources, communication procedures, etc. each time they start a new course. They are also likely to waste much time in simply finding things (out) rather than actually studying. This can result in increased support requests, frustrated students, and in the worst case, higher attrition over time.

Where individualisation and variation are of course possible, and in some cases necessary, is in the way each lecturer uses the tools available (and possibly builds in additional ones) to meet the needs of their individual teaching styles and their students' learning requirements. For example, in several online classes at MCI additional, freely accessible collaboration and communication tools are used to augment learning. However, the cornerstones of the virtual learning environment remain stable in each course.

1.7.5. Learning Resources

Learning resource development and selection (e.g. developing new resources, using textbooks or open educational resources, etc.) is another area that requires joint deliberation and a common direction to ensure consistency for students and in many cases cost-effectiveness. Here, organisational culture, support resources and availability of existing materials play a role and require careful planning. Important aspects to consider when making these decisions include investigating what Open Educational Resources could be used, the availability, quality and affordability of commercial materials, and the availability of online library resources. If existing materials are not a feasible option and materials need to be developed, factors such as required formats (print, online, video, audio, etc.) as well as the capacity and capability of staff (both content experts and development specialists if required) need to be considered. What is also important in this context is that lecturers are aware of and understand what they can and cannot do with regards to copyright and fair use (another important topic for capability development).

At MCI, it was decided that lecturers in the programme would develop consistently formatted course readers which were made available online in each course. The variation between programmes here depends on the availability and accessibility of teaching materials for each programme area. Where materials were developed in-house, a clear policy determining intellectual property rights, compensation for development efforts and re-use of materials was implemented.

1.7.6. Institutional Change, Administrative Processes and Policy Development

eLearning implementation always involves institutional change, and that comes with challenges and opportunities. The first challenge is to create a common understanding and shared language to enable the community to understand and discuss what is happening and what this concept of online education is actually all about. Ideally, this occurs throughout the institution, or at least at the programme level. At MCI, this first stage was supported by engagement of the senior leadership team as a first step, followed by a series of information sessions for all staff that explained different concepts, terminology and models related to online learning as well as the MCI's plans in this space. Thirdly, a coherent staff development programme was launched to allow everyone, also staff in programmes that were not online or blended, to gain new skills in teaching online. After one semester of running the first programme, lecturers and other staff in that programme were able to start sharing their experiences and learnings with colleagues in other programmes.

eLearning implementation at scale also requires significant change with regards to administrative processes and policy. Some of the questions that tend to come up very quickly include:

- How do we deal with student attendance requirements (if any), especially in blended learning programmes?
- Is teaching online different from face-to-face teaching with regards to assigning load or (for external staff) remuneration?
- How is additional staff investment in resource development and other activities compensated?
- What are the regulations with regards to intellectual property rights of materials developed for online programmes?
- Will I (the lecturer) make myself redundant over time?

These and related questions need to be tackled transparently, and even if set policies are not evident from the start, staff need to have a sense of their concerns being heard and considered.

At MCI, the first set of policies and practices around these and similar questions have been established, and new blended and online programmes being developed can be based on these. However, as programmes become more sophisticated and are scaled to accommodate higher numbers of students, new and different questions emerge, which need further development of the institution as a whole.

1.7.7. Quality and Quality Assurance

Ensuring and maintaining quality in online programmes should be a strong focus from the start. Quality aspects include amongst others quality of teaching, quality of student support, quality of learning outcomes and quality of institutional support and development.

There are various processes and practices that can assist in measuring, maintaining and continually improving quality, and it would go beyond the scope of this paper to discuss these in detail. At MCI, it was decided not to treat blended and online programmes as a different category when it comes to quality assurance. These programmes undergo the same procedures and are measured according to the same standards in terms of teaching evaluation. They also undergo the same quality assurance processes when it comes to various accreditations (e.g. AACSB, FIBAA). Certain special aspects of online and blended learning programmes are quality assured through internal processes (e.g. course templates are provided at course level, course materials developed undergo a rigorous quality assurance process through the programme's department and the learning solutions team) and through regular exchange between those responsible for quality in the departments (especially programme directors and/or heads of department) and the learning solutions team. Benchmarking with national and international partners is another instrument employed (currently informally) to measure and continually improve the quality of the MCI blended learning programmes.

1.7.8. Systemic Innovation and Sustainability

As argued throughout this article, programme level implementation of online and blended programs has many advantages, and is a significant lever in scaling online learning implementation up and out. A team approach to programme development, shared planning and implementation of the curriculum, and institution-wide commitment to new formats are the basis for making innovation more sustainable and systemic. Rather than taking a 'slow and emergent conversion' approach to eLearning implementation; i.e. leaving it up to motivated individual teachers to introduce eLearning components to their courses, a programme level approach may seem radical and 'top down' to some. However, it is an effective approach to making innovation happen at the speed that today's rapidly changing environment requires. By approaching online learning implementation at programme rather than course level, new practices, processes and skills are developed collaboratively, are shared across the programme team if not further, and are thus made more sustainable, even when key individuals leave the organisation or focus on other areas. Addressing and planning for the key aspects discussed above in a coherent, systemic manner will ensure that there is a shared understanding of the processes, practices, resources, skills and requirements across the programme team and that these are also appropriately documented and made transferable to other contexts.

New online or blended learning programmes implemented in this manner can be catalysts for change across the institution as they function as incubators for new ways of teaching, and they also highlight emerging issues at administrative, HR, policy, technology and resource level as discussed above.

Finally, a holistically designed and developed online or blended learning programme will benefit students most in the end in that they can enjoy a coherent, well-designed and professionally facilitated the learning experience.

1.8. Conclusion

In summary, programme-level design and development approaches view online learning deployment as a systems issue, where changes are required in many if not all parts of the organisation.

As such, their implementation requires institutional commitment, the preparedness to question and change existing processes and practices, and investment in change management, skills development and adequate support for students and staff. It requires commitment from the members of the programme team, including teaching staff, but also administrative staff and support services, as well as the necessary physical, technical and human resources.

In contrast to more individual, uncoordinated and bottom-up approaches, which are valuable at some level but arguably less effective, it is argued here that programme-level approaches are more efficient and sustainable. They are organised at team level including all relevant stakeholders, take a project approach and take into consideration aspects such as faculty development, technology and resource deployment, and deep embedding of the new approach in the overall system of the institution. They allow for a more consistent student experience across courses, for continuity beyond individual teacher engagement, and for strategic development of an institution's educational offering towards more flexible approaches to teaching.

The disruptive effect of digitisation on higher education may be seen as a threat to some. Employing the approach described here will enable higher education institutions to become active shapers of their own future rather than victims of disruption.

References

Barber, M., Donnelly, K., & Rizyi, S. (2013). *An avalanche is coming: Higher education and the revolution ahead.* Institute for Public Policy Research. Retrieved from http://www.ippr.org/assets/media/images/media/files/publication/2013/03/avalanche-is-coming_Mar2013_10432.pdf

Bates, A. W., & Sangrà, A. (2011). *Managing technology: strategies for transforming higher education.* San Francisco, CA: Jossey Bass.

Bischof, L., & Stuckrad, T. V. (2013). *Die digitale (R)evolution? Chancen und Risiken der Digitalisierung akademischer Lehre.* Gütersloh: CHE. Retrieved from http://www.che.de/downloads/CHE_AP_174_Digitalisierung_der_Lehre.pdf

Biswas, S., & Hazra, S. (2016). Digital India: A unique step towards E-learning in India. International Research. *Journal of Interdisciplinary & Multidisciplinary Studies, 1*(7), 64–70. ISSN: 2394-7950.

Boud, D., & Brew, A. (2013). Reconceptualising academic work as professional practice: Implications for academic development. *International Journal for Academic Development, 18*(3), 208–221.

Bratengeyer, E., Steinbacher, H., Friesenbichler, M., Neuböck, K., Kopp, M., Gröblinger, O., & Ebner, M. (2016). *Die österreichische Hochschul-E-Learning-Landschaft. Studie zur Erfassung des Status quo der E-Learning-Landschaft im tertiären Bildungsbereich hinsichtlich Strategie, Ressourcen, Organisation und Erfahrungen.* Verein Forum neue Medien in der Lehre Austria. Norderstedt: Books on Demand.

Brooks, C., & Pomerantz, J. (2017). *2017 Student and faculty technology research studies.* Educause Center for Analysis and Research. Retrieved from https://library.educause.edu/resources/2017/10/ecar-study-of-undergraduate-students-and-information-technology-2017

Brown, M., Dehoney, J., & Millichap, N. (2015). *The next generation digital learning environment: a report on research.* Educause Learning Initiative White Paper. Retrieved from https://library.educause.edu/~/media/files/library/2015/4/eli3035-pdf.pdf

Cavanagh, T. (2012). The postmodality era: How online learning is becoming learning. In Oblinger, D. (Ed.), *Game changers: Education and information technologies* (pp. 215–228). Washington, DC: EDUCAUSE.

Christensen, C., & Eyring, H. J. (2011). *The innovative university: changing the DNA of higher education from the inside out*. San Francisco, CA: Jossey-Bass. ISBN-10: 1118063481.

Dahlstrom, E., Brooks, C., & Bichsel, J. (2014). *The current ecosystem of learning management systems in higher education: student, faculty, and IT perspectives*. Research report. Louisville, CO: ECAR. Retrieved from https://library.educause.edu/~/media/files/library/2014/9/ers1414-pdf.pdf

EACEA. (2014). *Lifelong learning program. statistics*. Retrieved from http://eacea.ec.europa.eu/llp/results_projects/statistics_en.php

e-teaching.org. (2017). *E-learning-förderung in Deutschland*. Retrieved from https://www.e-teaching.org/projekt/politik/foerderphasen

Euler, D., & Seufert, S. (2011). Change management in der Hochschullehre: Die nachhaltige Implementierung von e-Learning-Innovationen. *Zeitschrift für Hochschulentwicklung*, *5*(4), 3–15. ISSN 2219-6994. Retrieved from https://www.zfhe.at/index.php/zfhe/article/view/187

Gaebel, M., Kupriyanova, V., Morais, R., & Colucci, W. (2014). *E-learning in European higher education institutions*. Brussels: European University Association (EUA). Retrieved from http://www.eua.be/Libraries/publication/e-learning_survey

Germ, M., & Mandl, H. (2009). Warum scheitert die nachhaltige Implementation von eLearning in der Hochschule? In U. Dittler, J. Krameritsch, N. Nistor, C. Schwarz, & A. Thillosen (Eds.), *E-Learning: Eine Zwischenbilanz. Kritischer Rückblick als Basis eines Aufbruchs* (pp. 275–290). Münster: Waxmann.

Gunn, C., & Herrick, R. (2012). *Sustaining eLearning innovations. A research study report*. Australian Council of Open, Distance and eLearning. Retrieved from http://www.acode.edu.au/pluginfile.php/160/mod_resource/content/1/Sustaining_eLearning_Innovations_Report.pdf

Haug, S., & Wedekind, J. (2009). Adresse nicht gefunden – auf den digitalen Spuren der e-teaching-Förderprojekte. In U. Dittler, J. Krameritsch, N. Nistor, C. Schwarz, & A. Thillosen (Eds.), *E-Learning: Eine Zwischenbilanz. Kritischer Rückblick als Basis eines Aufbruchs* (S. 19-37). Münster: Waxmann.

Herman, J. (2012). Faculty development programs: The frequency and variety of professional development programs available to online instructors. *Journal of Asynchronous Learning Networks*, *16*(5), 87–106.

High Level Group on the Modernisation of Higher Education. (2014). *Report to the European Commission on new modes of learning and teaching in higher education*. Retrieved from http://ec.europa.eu/dgs/education_culture/repository/education/library/reports/modernisation-universities_en.pdf

Hochschulforum Digitalisierung. (2017). *The digital turn – pathways for higher education in the digital age*. Arbeitspapier Nr. 30. Berlin: Hochschulforum Digitalisierung.

McFarlane, D. (2011). Are there differences in the organizational structure and pedagogical approach of virtual and brick-and-mortar schools? *Journal of Multidisciplinary Research*, *3*(2), 83–98.

McQuiggan, C. A. (2012). Faculty development for online teaching as a catalyst for change. *Journal of Asynchronous Learning Networks*, *16*(2), 27–61.

Mössenlechner, C., Obexer, R. Sixl-Daniell, K., & Seeler, J. M. (2015). E-learning degree programs – a better way to balance work and education? *International Journal of Advanced Corporate Learning, 8*(3), 11–16. doi:10.3991/ijac.v8i3.4844

Murphy, A., Farley, H., Dyson, E., & Jones, H. (Eds.), (2017). *Mobile learning in higher education in the Asia-Pacific Region. Harnessing trends and challenging Orthodoxies.* Education in the Asia-Pacific Region: Issues, Concerns and Prospects 40. Singapore: Springer. doi:10.1007/978-981-10-4944-6_18

Ng'ambi, D., Brown, C., Bozalek, V., Gachago, D., & Wood, D. (2016). Technology enhanced teaching and learning in South African higher education – a rearview of a 20-year journey. *British Journal of Educational Technology, 47*(5), 843–858.

Oblinger, D. (2012). IT as a game changer. In D. Oblinger (Ed.), *Game changers: Education and information technologies* (pp. 37–51). Washington, DC: EDUCAUSE.

Pulist, S. K. (2013). *eLearning in Commonwealth Asia 2013.* New Delhi: CEMCA.

Rivers, P., Rivers, J., & Hazell, V. (2015). Africa and technology in higher education: trends, challenges, and promise. *International Journal for Innovation Education and Research, 3*(5), 14–31. Retrieved from http://www.ijier.net/ijier/article/view/354

Seufert, S., & Meier, C. (2013). E-learning in organisationen. Nachhaltige Einführung von Bildungsinnovationen. In M. Ebner & S. Schön (Eds.), *Lehrbuch für Lernen und Lehren mit Technologien (L3T).* Retrieved from http://l3t.eu/homepage/das-buch/ebook-2013/kapitel/o/id/124/name/e-learning-in-organisationen

Singh, G., & Hardaker, G. (2014). Barriers and enablers to adoption and diffusion of eLearning: A systematic review of the literature—a need for an integrative approach. *Education and Training, 56*(2), 105–121. doi:10.1108/ET-11-2012-0123

Valente, A. (2018). Leading the implementation of a successful community college e-learning program. In A. A. Pina, V. L. Lowell, & B. R. Harris (Eds.), *Leading and managing e-learning. What the e-learning leader needs to know.* Educational Communications and Technology: Issues and Innovations (pp. 351–367). Cham, Switzerland: Springer. https://doi.org/10.1007/978-3-319-61780-0_3

Walker, R., Voce, J., & Jenkins, M. (2016). Charting the development of technology-enhanced learning developments across the UK higher education sector: a longitudinal perspective (2001–2012). *24*(3), 438–455. Retrieved from https://doi.org/10.1080/10494820.2013.867888

Chapter 2

LOGIC LEADS LEARNing: MOOCs in the Middle East

Yusuf M. Sidani

Abstract

This chapter presents a case study of a 'Massive Open Online Courses' (MOOCs) structure that is offered through an agreement between a traditional university and a MOOC provider. This arrangement has been helping in reaching very large numbers of learners in the Middle East. In implementing this agreement, I categorise the concerns of three key stakeholders (administrators, faculty and students) regarding this mode of instruction. A framework (abbreviated as LOGIC – LEADS – LEARNing) is proposed that could be of use to higher education institutions when they embark on non-traditional education. A common concern among the primary stakeholders was the issue of legitimacy of such an education. I argue the MOOCs so far do not represent a substitute or a threat to traditional face-to-face education. In addition, there are no foreseen reputational risks for universities if MOOCs are included as a mode of education. The value from MOOCs needs to be seen from the perspectives of students and other stakeholders. MOOCs have the potential to lead to positive consequences for the university – as a whole – and other relevant stakeholders as well. However, MOOCs in the Middle East are not likely to operate under a workable business model, at least not in the short run. As MOOCs rise to make more sense to students, their disruptive power would become more tangible. This, however, will take some time and will only be threatening if educational institutions become complacent in response to the novel ways by which the new generation is approaching learning.

Keywords: MOOC; Lebanon; Arab world; Edraak; American University of Beirut; legitimacy of online education

2.1. Introduction

The last couple of decades have witnessed an explosion in unconventional teaching opportunities. This has been facilitated by technological advancements, most notably the internet revolution. One of the unconventional teaching technologies has been the growing interest in Massive Open Online Courses (MOOCs), (Liyanagunawardena, Adams, & Williams, 2013). This chapter represents a case study about a MOOC experience emanating from an agreement between a traditional university and a MOOC provider. This experience has allowed educational access to large numbers of students from across the Arab world. Beyond the particulars of this case study, a framework is proposed (abbreviated as LOGIC – LEADS – LEARNing) that is argued to be of use to higher education institutions as they embark on non-traditional education.

The current trend in MOOCs emerged in 2011 when three computer science courses were offered by Stanford University (Vardi, 2012). Since then, there has been a phenomenal growth in MOOC initiatives provided both by universities and independent providers. Although many definitions of MOOCs are continuing to emerge (e.g. Daniel, 2012; Kolowich, 2013), one common understanding of a MOOC is that it represents a course which offers wide participation to members of the public who have an online access:

> A MOOC integrates the connectivity of social networking, the facilitation of an acknowledged expert in a field of study, and a collection of freely accessible online resources. Perhaps most importantly, however, a MOOC builds on the active engagement of several hundred to several thousand 'students' who self-organise their participation according to learning goals, prior knowledge and skills, and common interests.
> (McAuley, Stewart, Siemens, & Cormier, 2010, p. 5)

MOOCs, by definition, can accommodate large numbers of individuals. While some MOOCs that target very specialized audiences (such as a class in medieval history within a specific narrow context) may attract relatively lower numbers, the general rule is that MOOCs draw very large numbers of students often numbering in the thousands and more. In addition, MOOCs are not necessarily tied to a specified formal academic degree. Accordingly, they mostly attract those who want to know more about a specific subject without committing to a long academic journey.

MOOCs utilise the internet to reach students, so they do not require the usual face-to-face meetings. Thus they offer the opportunity to transcend geographic borders so learners can be enroled in a course irrespective of where they are located. In most cases, all that is needed is a willing student who has an online connection. With such an approach, a lot of flexibility is built into the teaching experience. Students can log from home, work, a public library or any place that has an online connection.

Many approaches have been suggested to build a workable sustainable model for MOOCs at universities (Burd, Smith, & Reisman, 2015; Daniel, Cano, & Cervera, 2015; Dellarocas & Van Alstyne, 2013; Kalman, 2014). The prevalent 'business model' for the MOOC is generally based on a no-fee structure or a low-fee one. In some cases, such as for Coursera (Coursera, 2018), many courses are offered for free, but students have to pay if they want a certificate. For some other MOOC providers, such as Edraak (Edraak, 2018), all courses are offered for free with a certificate upon completion. For universities, some suggested that one option is to move from a 'freemium' to a 'premium' mindset (Daniel et al., 2015). Others suggested that workable business models could be implemented through tuition, governmental subsidies, employers, or sponsors (Dellarocas & Van Alstyne, 2013). Yet, some MOOC providers seem to have decided that the only available route is the non-profit one relying mainly on grants and similar avenues of funding (Korn & Levitz, 2013). In the US, there are many examples of what appears to be business models for MOOCs that have started to appear; this is not the case in Europe (Epelboin, 2017). The issue becomes even harder in many developing countries where there is a lack of funding and the potential tuition fees could be prohibitive. The case for a sustainable business model thus becomes harder. For many universities in many parts of the world, there appears to be no workable 'business model' for MOOCs.

Some MOOC providers offer students the chance to get an online certificate when they take a series of courses. MOOCs have also been used towards a fully recognised academic degree. The Gies College of Business at the University of Illinois at Urbana-Champaign, for example, offers a completely online MBA degree (iMBA) which is comprised of two components. The first is based on self-paced MOOC classes through Coursera. The second is done through the Illinois online platform (iMBA Program Overview, 2018). The case remains, however, that in most cases, MOOCs are not part of a standard degree programme. They generally have no or low admission requirements, especially when compared to traditional university education. Many universities are still exploring and experimenting with including a form of MOOC offering in their standard educational system.

The question of whether MOOCs will present a case of a disruptive power is an interesting field of enquiry. Within the disruptive technology discourse, a successful new technology is the one that replaces the existing technology after a point-in-time; usually, it doesn't happen immediately (Bower & Christensen, 1995; Christensen, 1997; Tellis, 2006). It may take some time for the disruptive technology to be able to be perfected and made cost-efficient before it becomes attractive to the mainstream market (Christensen & Overdorf, 2000). To address whether MOOCs can have a disruptive power, some questions need to be addressed. One key question is: Is the MOOC methodology just another way of transmitting education (that is, another delivery mechanism), or does it present an alternative mode of learning that threatens traditional education?

Based on earlier research on disruption, one may conclude that a methodology becomes disruptive to a traditional university when an incumbent fails to allocate the necessary resources needed to tackle the new technology. Another threat is that when incumbents become too focused on a certain class of customers thus failing to be sensitive to changing customer demographics.

> In higher education, online courses now typically offer lower-end and more convenient access to courses that can improve students' credentials or help them switch careers, which is often precisely what the student customers want to accomplish by enrolling. (Christensen & Eyring, 2011, p. 47)

In this chapter, I am presenting the case of MOOCs as a disruptive technology within the context of an agreement between the American University of Beirut (AUB)-Edraak[1], a MOOC provider. Some questions that I hope my analysis will uncover pertain to whether and how AUB, as a prestigious traditional university, is allocating resources to alternative modes of education, specifically MOOC arrangements. I am also interested in assessing the extent to which AUB is aware of the changes that are happening in its potential 'customers'. Finally, I am curious as to the perspectives of the various stakeholders on the issue.

AUB is located in Beirut the capital of Lebanon in the Middle East. Lebanon is an Arab country that has vibrant commercial and educational sectors with strong ties to the Western world (Sidani, 2002). AUB is a prestigious institution of higher learning in Lebanon which celebrated its 150th anniversary in 2016. It has more than 8,500 students distributed across more than 130 programs in the undergraduate and graduate levels. Its mission is 'to provide excellence in education, to participate in the advancement of knowledge through research and to serve the peoples of the Middle East and beyond [...]' (American University of Beirut, 2018).

In 2014, AUB launched its first MOOC in collaboration with Edraak. Edraak, an Initiative of the Queen Rania Foundation for Education and Development, is a MOOC platform headquartered in Amman Jordan with a partnership with edX. It offers original courses in Arabic, in collaboration with carefully selected Arab-speaking professors from all over the world. Edraak has offered MOOCs in collaboration with a number of Arab institutions of higher education and other educational organisations across a number of disciplines including entrepreneurship, business communication, nutrition and health, computer science and programming, graphic design and filmmaking. The AUB-Edraak agreement emerged after negotiations between the two parties which had to be reviewed and updated in 2016. The range of courses that have been offered under this agreement is still very limited and till now none can be used to pursue a degree programme.

---

[1]Despite the fact that data was collected through facilitation from both parties, all opinions and analysis found in this chapter – unless otherwise indicated – are the author's and do not necessarily represent either those of AUB or Edraak.

This case study provides a window into this initiative and how it is unfolding. In seeking feedback from the most relevant stakeholders, this case study explores AUB's embryonic journey thus far into this type of non-traditional education. In doing this, I uncover some of the best practices that institutions of higher education can implement as they explore non-traditional routes for the delivery of quality education. In addition, common pitfalls in such initiatives are explored with hopes that future initiatives would evade unnecessary effort and time.

2.2. Methodology

This case study first emerged out of a personal experience in designing and delivering a MOOC through the AUB-Edraak agreement. I was involved in a course titled 'Success skills' which was produced in 2015 and offered twice. The course proved to be very successful, drawing thousands of students; it is now part of the permanent self-paced courses at the Edraak platform. This means that the course can now be taken anytime and anywhere by anybody who has access to an internet connection. This experience provided the opportunity to have access to student feedback from hundreds of students. With the help of Edraak executives, I also had the opportunity to get access to feedback to other courses at Edraak. The author also participated in sessions targeting faculty members from across the university in various disciplines, where he addressed questions and concerns about MOOCs. A 2017 regional conference hosted by Edraak in Amman (Jordan) about 'Reimagining Education in the Arab World' was instrumental in completing the picture. The author's notes during meetings with faculty members of the Olayan School of Business at AUB also provided significant insights into this topic. Moreover, the Edraak team, including the Chief Executive officer Mr Nafez Dakkak, were specifically interviewed for the purpose of this study. Those multiple opportunities provided insights into the potential that MOOCs offer, in addition to expectations and concerns. The information was corroborated and complemented through a thorough review of other non-traditional modes of education currently underway at the university. AUB has been allocating resources to blended-learning approaches which also provided some key information about the direction that AUB is heading into in regards to integrating more technology in its programs. All of those variant sources provided ample data regarding the potential of MOOCs and online education in advancing or constraining the accomplishment of learning objectives in the context under study.

2.3. MOOC – Key Issues

Based on all the data collected so far, I present the key issues, expectations and concerns raised by the various stakeholders in regards to MOOCs. I am going to concentrate on three key parties; administrators, faculty members and students. Understanding the positions of those primary stakeholders vis-à-vis MOOCs also illuminates on the issues that could be raised by other secondary stakeholders such as parents, technology providers, donors and alumni.

In categorising the concerns of those three key stakeholders I have used a mnemonic/acronym (LOGIC – LEADS – LEARNing) to reflect a framework for issues that are of importance to higher education institutions when they embark on such education (Figure 2.1). A common concern among the primary stakeholders was the issue of legitimacy or credibility of such an education. That's why all the three mnemonic words start with the letter 'L' to denote the legitimacy concerns raised by all parties.

2.3.1. Key Issues Raised by Administrators

The framework uses the acronym LOGIC to summarise the administrative concerns about MOOCs as they were discussed: 'L' stands for legitimacy, 'O' stands for 'our' name and reputation; 'G' stands for the guiding principles behind such education, 'I' stands for influence and 'C' stands for competition.

2.3.1.1. 'L': Do MOOCs Represent a Legitimate Way of Delivering Education?

While some administrators were quite knowledgeable about MOOCs, there is still some ambiguity about what does a MOOC really mean, and whether it is a legitimate way of educating students. Among the team that negotiated the deal with Edraak, there were administrators who very well understood how it generally worked and the model on which such a mode of education is based. Yet when the discussion reached a more extensive network of administrators, it was clear that some had some concerns about its credibility as a mode of education for the university. A good response for this concern came from the Edraak team who indicated that *'online education will improve education both online and offline, while increasing access to education to learners of all ages.'* In other words, MOOCs are not there to replace but to improve a university's educational offerings. This question about legitimacy often led to the next question.

ADMINISTRATORS	INSTRUCTORS	STUDENTS
Legitimacy	Legitimacy	Legitimacy
Our name	Effort	Effort
Guiding Principles	Appreciation	Attention
Influence	Discipline	Recognition
Competition	Sense	Net outcome

Figure 2.1. LOGIC LEADS LEARNing. *Source*: The author's representation.

2.3.1.2. 'O': Why Should We Do It? What Are the Implications on Our Brand Name?

AUB has always been a centre of excellence for many generations in the region. It is often ranked among the very elite universities. In 2018 it ranked 235 at a global level and thus positioning itself among the top 250 universities in the world (AUB Office of Admissions, 2018). In 2017, AUB was ranked the number 1 university in the Arab region as per QS university rankings (AUB Press Release, 2017). Part of the attractiveness of AUB relates to its legacy of quality education that has mostly been traditional quality education. Its beautiful campus provides students with the opportunity to get involved into a captivating student experience. This campus has been ranked among the most attractive campuses in the world, ranked the 18th most beautiful in the world (Rami, 2016). There is a lot of tradition and a lot of legacies, some of it tied to its location, its historic buildings and its heritage. So the natural question that is raised relates to whether the university would be compromising part of its brand name by engaging in a type of education that requires less physical presence? What would make this institution – given its history, culture and prestige – enter into an arena with all that comes in terms of suspicious standards and ambiguity? This question is usually handled by referring to recent experiences among top North American and European universities, with lots of heritage, which have nevertheless entered into that field. Concerns relating to legitimacy and reputation are usually satisfactorily tackled when the names of Harvard, MIT and Oxford are put forward as universities that have been involved in this type of non-traditional education.

2.3.1.3. 'G': What Are the Guiding Principles?

This dimension reflects on the impact of a MOOC on the university resources. Once the 'why' and 'should we' questions are settled, questions arise regarding the guiding principles by which MOOCs are run. From an administrator perspective, one needs to know what an involvement in MOOC means for university resources. What type of investment would this require both in terms of financial budgeting and faculty/staff allocation? 'What sort of financial resources would that require?' is a common question. 'Should we invest in such new technology and at what level of priority?' is another key question. Those questions are usually handled by noting that under agreements such as the AUB-Edraak agreements, universities provide the course content and subject-matter expertise and the MOOC partner provides the platform and all the technological underpinnings required, including any sophisticated media-related resources. This means that a university does not have to substantially invest, at least in the short run, in the technical aspect of this endeavour. Once this new technology is tested and feedback is assessed, the university would be in a better position to judge how to go forward with such technologies.

A related question pertains to faculty workload. Sometimes universities reduce the teaching loads of instructors who are involved in course design. In addition, extra support could be given to faculty; this is not generally perceived as too costly for the university. AUB leadership has publicly announced that online education is something that is seriously studied and continuously assessed given the competitive context in the higher education landscape (Khuri, 2017). This is a clear indicator that the university is willing to allocate the necessary resources into various modes and forms of education after careful analysis and study.

2.3.1.4. 'I': How Can We Measure Our Instructional Effectiveness?

Like any other credible institution of higher learning, AUB always assesses instructional effectiveness through various means of assessment. In traditional education, those include student assessments of performance through the typical evaluation forms, peer and chairperson evaluations and accreditation mechanisms related to the assessment of learning outcomes. A question raised pertained to 'how can the institution reasonably be able to assess the effectiveness of its instructors?' There was a concern that some of the traditional ways of assessing teacher performance are not available in an online environment.

What is usually noted in response to this concern is that actually technology provides universities with a vast – even wider – means of assessing teacher and instructional effectiveness. For example, in the course that I delivered, the course management team was able to collect specific, relevant and often detailed quantitative and qualitative feedback from more than 800 students. Understandably, this number only represented a portion of those who took the course as filling the evaluation forms was voluntary. Yet the number is quite large compared to classes that I usually deliver in traditional face-to-face education. Such a number actually provides a broader opportunity to give instructors the sort of comprehensive feedback that would be less available in smaller classes.

2.3.1.5. 'C': Would We Be Able To Compete? How Can We Scale This Up?

One of the concerns that were raised pertained to the ability of the institution to compete given the fact that big names, on a global scale, are already in this market. Some key universities – many of which are involved in MOOCs – already have presence in the Arab Middle East region, through affiliations, satellite campuses and other strategic educational ventures. From an administrator perspective, the game is global. So, looking at other players in the educational field, there could be hesitancy to enter into an arena when the likes of Harvard and MIT are already there. Another related concern pertains again to the costs involved, from a competitive perspective. Producing MOOCS and other forms of online educational presence requires a set of skills and resources that could be expensive to acquire or build in-house. 'If we as an institution are not able to enter 'big' into a certain market, then isn't staying outside the arena – at least in the foreseeable future – a better alternative?'

The AUB-Edraak arrangement actually helps satisfy this concern. Edraak has developed a set of resources that could be used in a win-win arrangement with AUB. The courses developed so far have proven to be very well done where AUB and its professors were able to concentrate on what they know best, the art of teaching, not only in English but also in Arabic. The technical development and hosting of the MOOCs have been delegated to Edraak which has performed an equally impressive job. Another issue is that AUB is perfectly situated to compete with big names in some disciplines, given its legacy and positioning in the region. For example, AUB is in an excellent position to deliver courses in the humanities and social sciences that have regional implications. Courses such as 'Middle Eastern politics' and anything related to Arabs or Muslims is something that AUB has a competitive advantage in. This also includes courses in the sciences of regional relevance such as 'Public Health in the Middle East' or gender studies.

2.3.2. Key Issues Raised by Faculty

The framework uses the acronym LEADS to summarise faculty/instructor concerns about MOOCs as they were discussed: 'L' stands for legitimacy, 'E' stands for 'effort', 'A' stands for appreciation expected, 'D' stands for discipline and 'S' stands for sense.

2.3.2.1. 'L': Do MOOCs Represent a Legitimate Way of Delivering Education?

Faculty members often raised the issue of the legitimacy of this form of education. There were some qualms as to the value of this mode of education. Some raised the issue that MOOCs would dilute 'real education'. One faculty member noted that 'parents are paying a lot of money for their kids to be educated by experienced and knowledgeable scholars. They are not paying money for teachers to delegate teaching to an intelligent machine.' Some instructors worried whether it would be legitimate to offer courses with lower expectations from students? They noted, for example, that they require three major work-load items for a traditional face-to-face 3-credit course. A student work-load item is any major aspect of assessment including a major test, a major project, or a bunch of other work assignments. This is usually not expected in some online courses and thus the opportunity for better assessing learning outcomes becomes more limited. This brings to question the credibility of this approach.

An obvious response to this concern – that was specifically corroborated by Edraak executives – is that MOOCs or other forms of online education are not there to replace traditional education. This form of education caters to the varying needs of learners. Learners learn differently and such type of teaching caters to the various abilities and preferences of many learners, especially among the younger generations who are more used to technology, often better than their instructors. 'The abundance of data generated by online education allows us to better understand the needs of learners and tailor content to them' (*Edraak team*).

Another response to this concern is the fact that MOOCs under the agreement are delivered in Arabic and most learners may not qualify to be admitted to AUB given the language barrier (the teaching language at AUB is English). So the objective is to reach a large number of students across a wide geographic area in the Arabic language. This could be seen as part of increasing the 'brand equity' and the reputation of the university. Yet, it could also be seen as part of the social responsibility of the institution to non-traditional learners who cannot join AUB due to economic (they cannot afford), geographic (they are outside Lebanon), or admissibility (they cannot properly converse in English and thus cannot join AUB) reasons. This helps make institutions more inclusive and welcoming to a broad section of potential learners.

2.3.2.2. 'E': How Much Effort Does It Require?

Another main concern among faculty members was the intensity of effort required to participate in such a teaching endeavour. This is a serious and valid concern. MOOCs and other forms of online education require significant amounts of work and time investment from faculty members. Once faculty members realise this, a related question is raised pertaining to the support that they will get in return for such investment. Teachers who are developing MOOC teaching materials usually get a certain level of support in terms of reduction in other teaching assignments and assistance. They still have to balance between the support that they are getting and the final outcomes of such endeavours.

In my own experience, the amount of reduction in teaching given to me to prepare for the MOOC was perhaps less than the amount of effort expended. Yet, looking back at the final outcome and the student reach that my course had, I would not hesitate to do it all over again. In my meetings with faculty members, I usually explain to them that the intangible reward received is often more important than the tangible support given. This links back to the earlier question as to why faculty members do that. As corroborated with the Edraak team '*Most of the academic instructors that have worked with Edraak have done so to increase their impact/reach to more students and to experiment with the future of education*'.

2.3.2.3. 'A': What Sort of Appreciation and Acknowledgement Would I Get?

Teachers ask about how their employer would recognise their efforts in developing the online course. This question is the other side of the earlier one. Teachers wonder whether the efforts they put towards developing a course are justified given the support that they get and the potential pay that they receive. Naturally, universities recognise the efforts put into such endeavours in annual assessments and promotion decisions as 'teaching excellence and innovation' are part of the criteria by which all faculty members are evaluated against.

2.3.2.4. 'D': Do MOOCs Work in My Discipline?

This was raised by two groups of faculty members. The first group belonged to disciplines that are quantitatively oriented such as those in the sciences or engineering. A typical question is: 'It is well-understood that an online delivery could work in the humanities and the arts, but would it work in engineering and the sciences?' The answer is in the affirmative. Edraak, and of course other MOOC providers, have a wide array of courses that are given, including courses in the sciences and in engineering. Many of Edraak's successful MOOCs are in such quantitative fields of study.

The second group that questioned whether there were any disciplinary constraints came mostly from faculty members in such fields as sociology and political science. The question particularly related to whether there were limits on academic freedom. In a traditional classroom, instructors are not hesitant to raise sensitive, yet relevant issues. In good higher institutions of learning, the freedom of instructors and students to engage in healthy and relevant conversations and debates is, not only respected but actually encouraged. The objective of institutions like AUB is to graduate thinkers with critical minds who do not object to challenge – or be challenged by – others on controversial issues as long as this is done in a civilised manner relevant to the topics under discussion. But what about an online course about sensitive issues such as 'women's rights in the Middle East' in a sociology class, or 'political rights and situation of minorities' in a political science class? Would there be censorship on the type of ideas that instructors can raise?

This is again a very important and relevant question. What I can say so far that I am neither aware of any idea presented by an instructor that has been censored nor has there been any case of an instructor being encouraged not to raise an issue or delve into a specific topic. It is also not expected that this would be an issue for institutions which do not compromise on the value of academic freedom. For the wider Middle Eastern educational landscape, this is a challenge that has to be addressed within each specific context.

2.3.2.5. 'S': Does This Make Sense for Me Personally?

The final concern, which was shared among many faculty members, pertained to whether MOOCs make sense for them personally. Given what they know in terms of effort, support, credibility of such programs, they wondered whether an involvement in MOOCs is something that they want to do given each person's specific situation and in line with their unique career positioning at a certain period of time. The answer would obviously differ from one person to another and is best addressed by the person involved.

2.3.3. *Key Issues Raised by Students*

The framework uses the acronym LEARNing to summarise student concerns about MOOCs as they were discussed: 'L' stands for legitimacy, 'E' also stands for 'effort', 'A' stands for the expected attention that they would get from their instructors, 'R' stands for the type of recognition they would receive (certificate or diploma) and 'N' stands for the net outcome they would get from such an education.

2.3.3.1. 'L': Do MOOCs Represent a Legitimate Way of Delivering Education?

Various discussions with students and looking into their feedback about their involvement in a MOOC, the issue of legitimacy is also a recurring question. Compared to traditional face-to-face education, they would ask, to what extent do MOOCs represent a legitimate way of getting an education? Reading through the hundreds of students' feedback statements, this seems to be a recurring one. Yet, it seems that student legitimacy concerns are lesser than those raised by faculty members. Many students seem to be satisfied by the opportunity to learn new things from professors who are considered to be among the best in the Arab world. Definitely, AUB's name and reputation play a role in disseminating the view that what is being offered is real, sound and credible knowledge delivered by people affiliated with reputable credible institutions.

2.3.3.2. 'E': How Much Effort Does It Require? How Much Time Should I Invest?

In most cases, MOOC learners are not full-time students at the institution offering the MOOCs. Most are either students at other institutions in their home countries, or are employed with fulltime or part-time jobs. Yet some are not employed. MOOCs present an opportunity for all of them to be exposed to a new body of knowledge or learn a new set of skills. They cannot usually allocate a full-time schedule for a MOOC.

Course instructors are aware of this fact and usually have varying time requirements for each MOOC that are sometimes modest and can be as low as two hours per week but could be much longer. This allows learners to assess which MOOC to take given their specific time commitments.

2.3.3.3. 'A': Will I Get Individual Attention from My Instructor?

Students require attention from their instructors in terms of addressing their specific questions and needs. The discussion available within the MOOC platform allows them to post various questions to their professors. Due to a large number of students enroled, it is often the case that course instructors cannot individually attend to each student's request or question. This is one of the disadvantages of a MOOC compared to traditional education which usually has a substantially lower number of students. Nevertheless, as course instructors and administrators become more familiar with various students' requests, it becomes apparent that many such questions are in fact similar, and thus they would be able to generally address many such common questions or concerns. I had about 3,000 active students in my course out of which hundreds contributed each week. While my assistants and I tried our best to address every concern and question, the number of questions was overwhelming the first time the course was offered. The second time the course was offered, we were able to anticipate for common issues and pre-empt many questions. The number remained, however, extremely high for us to categorically conclude that we were able to address individual learning points to maximum effectiveness.

2.3.3.4. 'R': What Sort of 'Recognition' Will I Receive?

Students often ask whether they would be able to get a diploma or a certificate after they complete a specific MOOC. They also ask whether the MOOC course can be made equivalent to university credits if they decide to join the university.

As it stands now, AUB students get a certificate from Edraak with the professor's name on it. Yet this is not an AUB diploma nor can it be used for credit at the institution. Still, many employers may look positively at a certificate, even if it is not within a for-credit programme if they realise that this is linked in some way to a subject-matter expert from a credible institution. As the brand recognition of Edraak increases, such certificates would have even a higher value in the marketplace. Thus, beyond extending their knowledge about specific topics of interest, this certificate will increase the skillset of students making them more relevant in the workplace.

2.3.3.5. 'N': What Is the Net Outcome for My Enrolment in A MOOC?

At a global level, some MOOCs are free. Others require learners to pay a registration fee. Edraak, by definition and in line with its motto *'knowledge for those who seek it'*, offers free education to anyone seeking to be educated. Accordingly, enrolment under the AUB-Edraak agreement is free. This makes it much easier for potential students to decide which courses to be enroled in as the monetary investment is zero.

In terms of whether a MOOC is worth the time invested, this is not very different than traditional face-to-face education. Some MOOCs are very successful, and students sense the value that they are receiving. The feedback provided by many students for successful MOOCs leads to the conclusion that they saw their time investment worthwhile. In other less successful MOOCs, more students would question the futility of registering in such a course as the net outcome was negative in that case. More research would be needed to assess whether there has been an increase in the employability of students because of the various MOOCs provided.

2.4. Conclusion

The above themes reflect the major issues, fears, challenges and hopes associated with this educational approach. In my opinion, this agreement adds tremendously to the visibility of the institution across the whole Middle East region. This extends the reach of the university to audiences that it never reached before. Those places include places in North Africa – from Morocco to Egypt – and as far as Yemen and Oman in Western Asia. Yet if any university jumps too soon on the opportunity without adequate preparation, it risks tarnishing its institutional image in an enormous manner. Institutions like AUB are aware that there are big players in the online education business. Some realise that the market now is globally accessible with a cost structure that is not easily met by smaller local players. What is of concern is that smaller players would not be able to compete. In this case, the disruptive power of MOOCs may be more felt by those smaller institutions.

MOOCs have the potential to impact students in many ways. The AUB-EDRAAK agreement has the potential to support them with their current academic coursework by leveraging the MOOC as supplementary/remedial material. In addition, according to Edraak's experience so far, MOOCs would help in improving their job prospects. Finally, beyond employability, MOOCs – especially those designed in this context – help students in gaining life skills that are not otherwise available in traditional education. As MOOCs rise to make more sense to students, their disruptive power would become more tangible. This, however, will take some time and will only be threatening if educational institutions become complacent in response to the novel ways by which the new generation is approaching learning.

MOOCs and similar approaches to education could contribute in an instrumental way to the struggling educational system in Lebanon and the Arab world (Sidani & Thornberry, 2010). The key learning points for AUB and, in effect, every institution of higher education in a similar context, includes realizing the following:

(1) MOOCs represent a mode of teaching not a substitute for the traditional face-to-face programs. So the disruptive power of MOOCs does not mean that traditional instruction would cease to exist at any time in the foreseeable future. As such MOOCs do not yet meet the test of a disruptive technology that is going to replace an old technology (face-to-face education). Currently, MOOCs do not represent good substitutes for traditional education nor are they expected to be in the near future, at least not in the context under study.

(2) If done right, there are no reputational risks associated with MOOCs being offered as a mode of education. There is actually a risk if a university chooses to ignore this trend. This is where online education, as a disruptive technology, would become threatening to a university's reputation and image. A university needs to have a clear vision and buy-in from relevant stakeholders in the university, otherwise MOOCs – or any other form of online education – will not work. A university needs to adopt a daring and innovative entrepreneurial spirit, not afraid to take reasonable risks and capitalise on the technologies available.

(3) MOOCs in the Middle East are not likely to operate under a workable business model, at least not in the short run. This type of education requires investments, and there could be significant financial and human resources that need to be put in place without expecting direct financial returns. From a disruptive technology point of view, the lack of a workable 'business model' is actually good news to private universities. It is unlikely, in the context under study, that a business model for MOOC delivery will create an institution (a non-university) that would drive traditional educational institutions 'out of the market' or significantly threaten their presence. From a strategy perspective, this acts as a barrier to entry into the educational market.

(4) The value from MOOCs needs to be seen, not only from a student perspective but also how it works for other stakeholders. Teachers specifically are particularly positioned to benefit a lot from the MOOC experience both in

terms of tangible and intangible outcomes. They would add a lot to their skill sets in terms of getting acquainted with new modes of teaching. They will also be able to reach students much beyond what they ever imagined, thanks to advanced technology and online presence. This would almost invariably lead to positive consequences for the university -as a whole- and other relevant stakeholders as well.

The AUB-EDRAAK agreement has helped in reaching vast numbers of learners all across the Arab world. AUB's brand recognition across the Arab region has certainly improved as the MOOC experience allowed AUB instructors to reach various corners of the Arab world, audiences it would rarely reach under traditional modes of education. Taking this route, higher education institutions are expected to use the disruptive power of the online technology to their benefit rather than suffering its negative consequences.

References

American University of Beirut. (2018). Facts and figures. Retrieved from http://www.aub.edu.lb/aboutus/Pages/facts.aspx. Accessed on February 28, 2018.

AUB Office of Admissions. (2018). QS World University Rankings. Retrieved from http://website.aub.edu.lb/admissions/applications/Pages/ApplytoAUB.aspx

AUB Press Release. (2017, October 17). For the first time: AUB no. 1 university in the Arab region as per QS university rankings. Retrieved from http://website.aub.edu.lb/communications/media/Documents/Oct-17/AUB-Ranking-First-in-QS-Ranking-EN.pdf#search=ranking

Bower, J. L., & Christensen, C. M. (1995). Disruptive technologies: Catching the wave. *Harvard Business Review, 73*(1), 43–53.

Burd, E. L., Smith, S. P., & Reisman, S. (2015). Exploring business models for MOOCs in higher education. *Innovative Higher Education, 40*(1), 37–49.

Christensen, C. M. (1997). *The innovator's dilemma: When new technologies cause great firms to fail*. Boston, MA: Harvard Business School Press.

Christensen, C. M., & Eyring, H. J. (2011). *The innovative university: Changing the DNA of higher education from the inside out*. San Francisco, CA: John Wiley & Sons.

Christensen, C. M., & Overdorf, M. (2000). Meeting the challenge of disruptive change. *Harvard Business Review, 78*(2), 66–77.

Coursera. (2018). Retrieved from https://www.coursera.org/

Daniel, J. (2012). Making sense of MOOCs: Musings in a maze of myth, paradox and possibility. *Journal of Interactive Media in Education*, (3), Art. 18. doi:10.5334/2012-18

Daniel, J., Cano, E. V., & Cervera, M. G. (2015). The future of MOOCs: Adaptive learning or business model? *International Journal of Educational Technology in Higher Education, 12*(1), 64–73.

Dellarocas, C., & Van Alstyne, M. (2013). Money models for MOOCs. *Communications of the ACM, 56*(8), 25–28.

Edraak. (2018). Retrieved from https://www.edraak.org/en/. Accessed on January 2, 2017.

Epelboin, Y. (2017). MOOCs: A viable business model? In M. Jemni, K. Kinshuk, & M. Koutheair (Eds.), *Open Education: from OERs to MOOCs* (pp. 241−259). Springer: Berlin, Heidelberg.

iMBA Program Overview. (2018). Retrieved from https://onlinemba.illinois.edu/get-info-contact-form/

Kalman, Y. M. (2014). A race to the bottom: MOOCs and higher education business models. *Open Learning: The Journal of Open, Distance and e-Learning, 29*(1), 5−14.

Khuri, F. (2017). AUB in its 150th anniversary. *Harvard Business Review Arabia*. Retrieved from https://hbrarabic.com

Kolowich, S. (2013). The professors who make the MOOCs. *The Chronicle of Higher Education*, 18.

Korn, M., & Levitz, J. (2013, January 2). Online courses look for a business model. *The Wall Street Journal*, B8.

Liyanagunawardena, T. R., Adams, A. A., & Williams, S. A. (2013). MOOCs: A systematic study of the published literature 2008−2012. *The International Review of Research in Open and Distributed Learning, 14*(3), 202−227.

McAuley, A., Stewart, B., Siemens, G., & Cormier, D. (2010). The MOOC model for digital practice. Retrieved from www.elearnspace.org/Articles/MOOC_Final.pdf

Rami. (2016). AUB chosen among the most beautiful universities in the world. *Blog 961*. Retrieved from http://www.plus961.com/2016/01/aub-chosen-among-the-most-beautiful-universities-in-the-world/

Sidani, Y. (2002). Management in Lebanon. In M. Warner (Ed.), *International Encyclopedia of Business and Management* (2nd ed., pp. 3797−3802). London: Thomson Learning.

Sidani, Y. M., & Thornberry, J. (2010). The current Arab work ethic: Antecedents, implications, and potential remedies. *Journal of Business Ethics, 91*(1), 35−49.

Tellis, G. J. (2006). Disruptive technology or visionary leadership? *Journal of Product Innovation Management, 23*(1), 34−38.

Vardi, M. Y. (2012). Will MOOCs destroy academia? *Communications of the ACM, 55*(11), 5−5.

Chapter 3

The Power of Technology in Customised Executive Education

Lynette J. Ryals, Ruth Bender and Toby Thompson

Abstract

Customised executive education, designed for and delivered to individual client companies by Higher Education Institutions (HEIs), differs in important ways from award-bearing courses. One area in which these differences are surprisingly extensive is in the use of technology. We explore the impact of technology-enhanced learning (TEL) on course design, delivery and evaluation of customised executive education. In doing so, we contrast this form of learning with MOOCs, which use TEL in a different way, for a different audience.

We begin with the 'two-client' problem. In customised executive programmes, course design is done collaboratively between the HEI and the corporate client, reflecting the particular learning needs of the selected participants as perceived by the commissioning client. We find that the level of TEL in any programme will reflect the learning needs, and also the level of TEL sophistication, of both client and academics.

We then consider the successful integration of TEL into customised executive education. TEL can enrich a course great, but will also mean a loss of academic control, as a significant amount of the learning will be peer-to-peer, and much of the information-gathering can take place outside the classroom.

We conclude with the outcomes and success measures of customised executive education. The institutional disruption of TEL to the HEI is considerable, as their traditional business model is based on rewarding academics for research and for classroom-hours. This needs to be rethought where the classroom element is reduced, but there is constant online interaction with participants.

Keywords: Executive education; executive development; customised executive education; technology-enhanced learning; andragogy; course design

3.1. Introduction

This chapter examines the disruptive impact of technology on non-award-bearing customised executive education which is designed with, and tailored to, the specific needs of individual companies or organisations. This type of education is typically aimed at developing middle to senior managers and improving their role performance. It consists of closed courses, available only to designated employees of that organisation and occasionally to members of their supply chains. Such courses may contain high levels of proprietary information such as financial and management reports, or case studies or projects based on the particular organisation. We consider how the adoption of technology-enhanced learning (TEL) has fundamentally changed the way in which this type of education is designed and delivered, either as a Small Private Online Course (SPOC) or, more commonly, in a blended learning environment. We contrast this type of course, highly tailored to a client context, with Massive Open Online Courses (MOOCs), which by their nature occupy a position at the other extreme of the spectrum of online courses.

Reflecting the chronological sequence of these educational interventions we consider the teaching and learning process in three stages: course design; course delivery; and evaluation and outcomes. We outline how TEL affects the discussion between university and corporate client on course design prior to delivery; how it impacts on course delivery; and how the impact on client companies and on participants[1] can be assessed. We conclude with some observations on the business model for universities wanting to offer online and blended executive education and some inhibitors that they might face.

Our paper makes several contributions to the field. We discuss how TEL has changed executive education, showing how it differs from MOOCs, and how technology plays an active part in course design as well as delivery. We explore the necessary three-way liaison between learner, university, and corporate client and consider how to reconcile the sometimes conflicting goals of these three very different stakeholders. In addition, we make observations about the specific business model issues and what this might mean for Higher Education Institutions

---

[1]In the context of client-defined executive education courses, learners are generally referred to as 'participants' or 'delegates', distinct from the 'students' who attend formally accredited courses.

(HEIs). Furthermore, we comment specifically on the objectives and success criteria for corporate executive education.

3.2. Customised Executive Education: The Context

The context in which this chapter is set is the provision of what the market calls 'executive education' to the middle and upper echelons of executives within multinational companies. These companies may have a European or North American head office but have multinational operational sites, from whose regions our provision is often commissioned and, in the case of blended courses, delivered. The authors carry out related functions in this context: client management and business development; education delivery; and education technologist. As we will discuss later, there is considerable overlap between these roles. All three also work closely with the Executive Development Directors (EDD) for these programmes. EDDs are responsible for the whole client relationship. They orchestrate the design of programmes, select and brief the appropriate academics and liaise with the learning technologist on the requirements for the learning management system and all online aspects of the programme. Acting as a bridge between client, participant and academic, they lead the webinars, attend most classroom sessions and provide relevant feedback to all parties involved in the intervention.

The purpose of these courses of education (often termed 'development' or 'training' programmes by the commissioning companies) is defined principally by the commissioning client – often an executive or group of executives within the Human Resources (HR) or related functions. This is done in conjunction with those responsible for customising the executive education provision within the HEI. As such, the provision is commissioned *on behalf of* a specified population of executives, rather than by individuals in search of a personalised developmental provision. The end purposes of such courses will vary considerably, but could include knowledge transfer; *in situ* development of a company's top team; exposure to new thinking and new business approaches; the enactment of new behaviours; or full-scale organisational development for entire executive populations in support of a strategic corporate imperative.

The fact that the commissioning client is not the eventual programme participant leads to a 'two-client problem', which is a feature of corporate executive education that has no parallel within the student or MOOC environment. The commissioning client will have a very strong influence on the course content and delivery modes, but this team will be commissioning the course(s) for others, so there are also the interests of the individual participants themselves to consider. A factor influencing the design and delivery of executive education is that the two parties' interests may not coincide. One example is a tension between what the HEI regards as an essential component to the education or development of a participant – given the HEI's andragogic expertise, allied to their specialist fields of research – and what a particular corporate client regards as essential, given the contingencies of the corporate's immediate needs. Resolution of this tension is one of the hallmarks of successful university-based customised executive education.

Another, surprisingly common problem in corporate executive education is that the course content or delivery method originally specified by the commissioning client might not always match that desired by the participants. This problem may arise because the commissioning client has misidentified the executive education need, or at least misattributed its cause. The problem may not manifest itself until delivery starts, at which point the 'participant client' becomes more influential than the 'commissioning client'. Post delivery, focus swings back to the commissioning client as the effectiveness of the education is considered, thereby introducing into the mix the mediational skills required of the HEI educational technologist to ensure the skill (and comfort) gap does not affect the quality of the outcome.

Another contextual difference from student courses and MOOCs is the competitive landscape. Competition in award-bearing courses, whether online or traditional, is largely between universities. In the executive education context, the competitive landscape is much more intense, including traditional universities, independent universities, consultancies and increasingly the client company's own training and development team or corporate university (UNICON, 2014). The competition will be based on multiple criteria including course design and technology, the pricing model, contextual appreciation of the organisation, region, or market and the profile of academic faculty delivering the programme.

Aside from the non-massive and non-open constraints that are a consequence of supplying multiple single-clients with a bespoke education provision, there are further contextual differences between executive education and the MOOC environment.

Firstly, the client expectation is of 100% completion. Participants may have been specifically selected to attend the course. This is often a sign of esteem within the client company, and participants may need corporate sponsors. Dropping out of an executive education course provided by your company is not generally acceptable and may even have career-limiting implications. In this respect, executive education has more in common with a selection of students for award-bearing courses than it has with MOOCs[2].

Secondly, individual executive participants are not generally expected to return for further courses (although the corporate client may); so, executive education is purely about education and training, and, from the point of view of the institution, does not contain a marketing element. This contrasts sharply with MOOCs, often positioned as 'tasters' leading to further study.

Thirdly, executive courses are distinct from MOOCs in that with corporate courses the participants have a common corporate background, and might be working with each other now or in the future. On these courses, whether

---

[2]It has been shown that overall, only 5–6% of those enroling for a MOOC actually complete the course although completions rise to 22–24% for those who enrol intending to complete, rather than just to browse (OCR, 2016; Reich, 2014).

delivered in a traditional manner or with TEL, participants enter into a relationship with their own corporate peers on the course, their HR departments and those above them within corporate hierarchies sponsoring the course, and with the faculty and support staff of the HEI itself. Aggregating these relationships allows the impact that the overall programme has on the corporation to be measured, which is not possible with a more individualistic and self-selected MOOC. Table 3.1 sets out these contextual differences.

Table 3.1. Contextual Differences between Customised Executive Education and MOOCs.

Aspect	Customised Executive Education	MOOCs
Origination	Commissioned by the client's HR department (or equivalent) for delivery to a selected group of executives	Developed by faculty for a wide, self-selected audience
Tailoring	Highly tailored in terms of the tools and technologies used, delivery method and content	Generic, determined by the faculty
Relationship	An ongoing relationship with the client's commissioning team, with the possibility of generating future revenue from the company	No parallel to this
Pricing	Significant fees charged to the corporate client, which may then be passed down to the participant's budget code	Generally, no fee for the course, although participants can pay for add-ons
Motivation	Individuals attend the programme as part of their job	Individual participants make their own choice to attend the course
Completion	Completion is compulsory for the participant	Traditionally high drop-out rate
Network	Peer-to-peer interaction with people from the same company, with whom participants can expect the ongoing contact	Peer-to-peer interaction, generally transient, with strangers
On-selling	No ongoing commercial relationship with participants after the programme (although there could be ongoing contact)	Possibility of on-selling qualifications or more courses to generate revenue

3.3. The Role of Technology in Course Commissioning and Design

It is now taken for granted by corporate clients that any course will include elements of TEL. At the very least, participants will access administrative details through a bespoke portal; however, the vast majority of programmes are blended, with some being totally online.

Chronologically, customised executive education begins with the request to tender, but the main impact of technology is at the design stage. Here, the difference to MOOCs is very clear. In MOOCs, the participants could well have very different levels of aptitude with technology, but this is not necessarily known beforehand and may not influence course design or delivery. By contrast, in the customised executive education world, courses are co-created with clients to achieve the agreed contractual, learning, behavioural and/or organisational development outcomes for the target participants, with the extent of TEL integration in the course design subservient to these outcomes.

Course objectives and design reflect contextually dependent variables such as aptitude with technology, client (and HEI) preference for technology platforms, client policies with regard to bring-your-own-device, and internet access regulations (and availability) for internet-connected devices: overall, this presents a highly ambiguous starting point. This technology-related ambiguity is amplified when set against the ideological contrasts inherent in the respective end-goals of a corporation versus an HEI, such as between the priority of earning over learning, for instance. Given this complex set of variables, working with clients with different levels of sophistication and with lecturers who may be more or less comfortable with TEL creates a number of challenges in co-creation, as illustrated in Table 3.2.

Table 3.2 focuses on the individual academic rather than on the institutional level of TEL ability. This illustrates another facet of the customised executive education world. In the MOOC environment, academics largely self-select to deliver online education because of their interest, prior experience and level of comfort with the technology. However, in the customised environment, the client company may select a specific academic or team on the basis of profile or subject expertise, and may then ask for online delivery modes. It could be that the requested academic, whilst an expert in their field, is less familiar or comfortable with the technologies and techniques required for online learning.

Another important consideration that will affect the individual academic's participation is the HEI's cultural norms regarding attitudes to the displacement of physical teaching time-space towards virtual teaching time-space. For example, systems of faculty reward based mainly on classroom-hours could discourage all but the most ardent devotees of TEL from designing more creative learning programmes. We discuss this later in the chapter.

Choices made at the institutional level may also affect the corporate online environment, as the platform tech tools available may be predetermined by institutional choices made elsewhere in the university. In this respect, these choices

Table 3.2. How Client and Academic TEL Skills Influence Course Design.

	Academic TEL skills high	Academic TEL skills low
	1 – Mutual High Tech	2 – Client Lead
Client TEL sophistication high	High TEL 'conciliation' means increased productivity in design and delivery, as the available tools are well-understood and the focus is on the most appropriate TEL and design. The danger is that design and execution may suffer from TEL 'whizz bang' at the expense of desired outcomes	In a sophisticated client environment, low-tech delivery may lack credibility with the commissioning client and the participants. The client will push for more relevant TEL and academics may face an uncomfortably steep learning curve. This could limit some academic participation
	3 – Academic Lead	4 – Mutual Low Tech
Client TEL sophistication low	Course design process is driven by the academic, who might need to educate the client on what is possible and appropriate. The outcome could be a move towards box (1) or, if not successful, closer to box (4)	Education solution is most likely to be traditional face-to-face. A blended or online course could be designed and delivered, but it is unlikely to be effective. Often, it will not even be considered as an option

become 'external factors' (Whitaker, New, & Ireland, 2016) since the individual academics have little or no influence over them.

3.3.1. Co-creation of Course Design

Course design is an iterative process in the executive education world, and particularly so when considering online or blended provisions. Customised online executive education courses are co-designed with the client (and often with the participant), who may or may not make explicit their company's technological, ideological and cultural variables. To support andragogic learning (Knowles, 1990) in post-experience executive learners, we advocate constructing online or blended executive education in several modules with inter-module work that may include project and group work as well as coaching or other inputs from the teaching team.

Typically, content and course design discussions will involve several key stakeholders, such as the client company's HR team and technical experts and/or the company's finance director or CTO. Considerations will include whether or how client experts should co-deliver part of the course, or how the organisation's bespoke versions of models can be introduced and used. The 'textbook' examples employed in MOOCs are often rejected early in the design stage, even if they are the academic's preferred choice.

During this co-creation process, the consideration of which mode of TEL is most appropriate for that client and context plays an active part in course design. Discussions will take place around how various elements of the curriculum can be rendered and delivered in an online format. For instance, how learners are expected to collaborate online with each other, and with the HEI; what form learner support should take within the course; and the role that the corporation's own learning management systems, enterprise social media and dedicated learning support systems have in mediating the eventual course design. Case study 3.1 illustrates two different clients and their approach to co-creation with us.

Case Study 3.1. Co-Creation in Course Design

Co-creation works differently depending on the client experience and need:

Mutual High Tech: In Client 1, a multinational company for whom we had been running courses for many years, the brief was very specifically to bring in TEL as a substitute for face-to-face delivery. The driver for this was not educational but, rather, to minimise travel time and cost for the participants. Here, the client was technically adept and the long-standing relationship meant that we understood the participant needs and skills very well. Consequently, the co-creation focused on exploring the most appropriate delivery methods for the different types of content. The danger was that some outcomes might have been compromised by the client's insistence on TEL for non-educational reasons; many of the discussions were about how to avoid that.

Academic Lead: For Client 2, a new client in the public sector, the emphasis was more on the content than the delivery methods. The client commissioning team believed that the organisational culture meant that target participants would be unwilling to accept much TEL. So, despite the academic lead having strong TEL skills, the client sought a course design that focused mostly on classroom delivery. Here, therefore, both the perceived sophistication and the appetite for TEL on the part of the client were relatively low and the danger was that the client would be uncomfortable with the proposed TEL components. The co-design team agreed to test these perceptions, so the brief was received from the commissioning team and then tested with potential participants in detailed interviews and focus groups to ensure relevance of content and delivery method.

3.3.2. Roles in Executive Education Course Design

Up to this point, we have considered the role of technology in the course design process as though the course were designed by a single academic. Whilst this might be true in a classroom-only context, it is not so in the online education world where course design is carried out by a combined team of academic and education technologist. In the customised executive education field, course design is also influenced by two sets of clients: the commissioning client (especially in the design stage) and the participant client (during each delivery iteration). Some universities, our own included, have a business development team who may also be involved in course design. Figure 3.1 illustrates the involvement of the various parties.

The HEI academic delivery team will comprise education technologists and academics: each role is necessary and neither is privileged. If the academic team is accustomed to working with TEL, they might have clear ideas on what will work and will discuss with the education technologists the most effective way to deliver. In other circumstances, the design process is driven by the education technologist, continually questioning and challenging the academic about learning objectives and content, to establish the most appropriate learning structure. For example, in Client 1, the case study above, the course design process was led by the education technologists, with the academics being guided through the

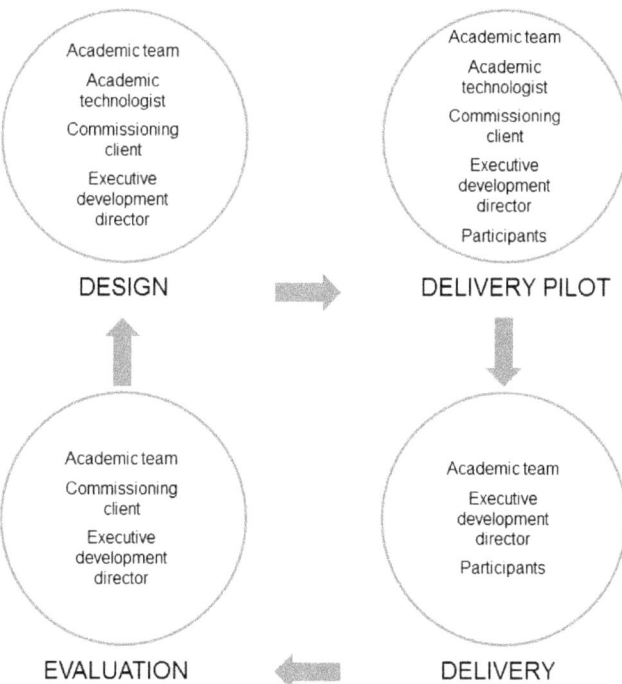

Figure 3.1. Co-creation at Each Stage of the Process.

large range of technologies available and encouraged to think more widely about how the learning objectives could be delivered. In Client 2, the design process was led by the academic team, with input sought from the education technologist at specific points. These examples illustrate the difficulty of characterising technical sophistication in TEL at the organisational level (c.f. Table 3.2), when it might well differ markedly between different parts of both the client and the academic partner organisation.

Case Study 3.2. TEL is Not Always the Solution

The matrix in Table 3.2 suggests that the combination of sophisticated client and sophisticated academic will lead to a course rich in TEL. However, this is not always the case.

Client 3 is a UK-based multinational. The brief was for an extensive and transformational leadership development programme for middle and senior managers. The client was highly sophisticated in respect to TEL, and most of the participants were equally TEL-savvy, a fluency which arose from the nature of their work. To complement this, the academic team responsible for design and delivery were experienced in this area.

In the design stage, the commissioning client placed considerable emphasis on building and maintaining a sophisticated online platform to support and to run the programme. This included an online component to provide expert knowledge between face-to-face sessions, programme overview webinars run at the start of each cohort, and online coaching sessions delivered by Skype, to maintain development momentum.

As it turned out, contrary to the client/HEI expectation, the online aspects of the programme became increasingly occluded as the true benefit of the eventual programme design came to prominence: namely the deeply personal, highly impactful 'realisations' that emerged, for each participant, from the developmental exercises on each module. The commissioning client benefited enormously from the exercises and projects framed by the individual participants and from the positive impact that the transformed middle managers had on their direct reports.*

Several conclusions can be drawn from this. Firstly, that a reconciliation of high TEL sophistication in both the client and HEI is no *prima facie* guarantee of eventual enhancement of the learning on a customised executive development programme via technology. Secondly, neither is the commissioning client's expectation of inclusion of TEL mediation a guarantee of TEL inclusion on the programme. Thirdly, it is not possible to attribute purely learning intentions or outcomes to the so-called 'enhancements' via technology, not when cultural, organisational and contextual forces – i.e. non-learning forces – are at play.

*The revised programme was a great success, winning for Cranfield the 2016 Excellence in Practice Gold Award for Executive Development, run by the European Foundation for Management Development.

It is worth noting that sometimes the co-creation process drives the programme in the opposite direction to that expected. Case study 3.2 provides such an instance.

3.3.3. Course Design – TEL or Don't TEL?

As discussed earlier, although it doesn't always work as anticipated, corporate courses which until comparatively recently might have been delivered in the classroom now routinely adopt TEL. There is no simplistic dyad of *either* face-to-face *or* online delivery in this market; instead, there are complex design considerations that are influenced by the commissioning and participating clients, the academics, the academic technologists and possibly by other contextual factors such as chosen technology platforms, academic workload and recognition, and client costs and culture.

We do not start with the assumption that 100% online delivery will be the right answer. Unlike MOOCs, which are designed for purely online delivery, customised executive education is rarely just online but includes a blend of delivery methods reflecting its complex balance of contextual variables. Course design includes several different considerations:

(1) Which elements of the jointly designed curriculum would best be delivered in the classroom and which would work online?
(2) Which aspects of the course should be presented by the academic and which should be done peer-to-peer?
(3) Which are best done synchronously and which can be done asynchronously?
(4) Which learning is appropriate for the individual, and where might group learning be more appropriate?
(5) For all course elements, which, if any, technology(ies) might be the most appropriate to use?

The primary driver for selecting any particular TEL component comes from the learning aim(s) moderated by contextual factors such as client sophistication.

Our university espouses the blended method for executive education, adopting different techniques for different aspects of learning.

For skills where repetition and private practice are useful, or where ability and familiarity vary substantially from participant to participant (e.g. finance and accounting skills for managers), we advocate the use of TEL and flipped classroom. However, skills that benefit from interaction (such as problem-solving and project managing) are best delivered through small-group working, projects and classroom sessions. Finally, in the development of personal and leadership skills (e.g. mindfulness), we urge our clients to use coaching, facilitation and consultancy-type interventions, some of which may be online and some of which may be face-to-face.

Of course, many of these decisions had their counterparts in executive education even before the regular use of TEL, but TEL, as we will discuss later, provides an exciting flexibility that can enhance the learning and engage the learner. A simple example of this is the learning teams that we set up, to work on specific issues or projects within their organisation. Setting these up as private groups online with shared virtual whiteboard and document sharing facilities now enables internationally mixed groups to work together with ease. This facilitates learning projects that are far more complex and potentially more useful to the client organisation than was ever possible in the face-to-face environment.

Another feature of customised online executive education at the pre-delivery phase is the 'freeze point' both of learning-material production and of the design process. Online executive education tends not to have content strongly frozen in advance. Given the multiple stakeholders who may comment on the content, re-engineering of the course continues up to and beyond the course launch point: otherwise, the promise of a 'customised' course becomes mere rhetoric. For this reason, we advocate 'pilot' versions of each component (both material and the TEL), where we positively invite clients to comment and critique; and we commit to detailed pre-launch testing and discussion with clients and to in-course adjustments if required by participants. This is another point of contrast with MOOCs, as we prefer to sacrifice consistency between cohorts in the interests of tailoring to each cohort as we go. Indeed, with many of our clients, the course development process continues throughout the whole engagement (as illustrated by Client 3). Building this into the education culture means that our academic and technology teams learn to expect and accept change and respond to participant feedback.

Timing is another factor that differentiates customised executive education. Blended courses involve face-to-face elements, which need to be diarised rigorously. In theory, dates are co-determined based on client, participant and academic availability. In practice, corporate clients tend to expect their academic providers to 'flex' in response to their changing needs. Inevitably, this leads to tensions where the client's preferred academic(s) have long-established commitments for other teaching. Where TEL has been disruptive is in the way it can ease this tension, allowing flexibility to be built in pre- or post-launch for on-demand learner support from academics, or ad hoc virtual collaboration tool sessions involving academics or other support staff involved in the customised online executive education course. Examples of this include 'out of office-hours consultations' or 'project team webinars', enabling coaching and consultation internationally but requiring flexible hours of the academics involved.

3.4. The Role of Technology in Course Delivery

The discussion so far has demonstrated that the design phase of an executive education course is not clearly separated from its delivery. However, once delivery starts, there are some additional uses of technology that may disrupt the 'standard' educational model. In this section, we consider the disruptive impact of participants' experience with technology, collaborative learning and learner engagement.

3.4.1. Participants' Experience with Teaching and Learning

Corporate executive education is characterised by participants who commonly have at least 10 years' managerial experience, often within a variety of corporate contexts, from a range of sectors. As such they are highly confident with respect to their fields of expertise, but may not have recent (or any) experience of formal or HEI-based courses of learning. Also – and perhaps related to this – they will have different levels of prior experience and commitment to the education process.

Furthermore, they may be less than confident with the modes of teaching and learning delivered via contemporary educational technologies. In theory there is huge diversity of ways in which learners and lecturers can interact and engage with each other (for example: e-learning, Google hangouts and webinars, instant messaging, eBooks, virtual business simulations, online peer-assessments). However, in practice, the lecturer may need to adjust their delivery using these mechanisms to a point that is comfortable to a 'digital immigrant' learner. One way to do this is to include short tutorials or crib sheets on 'how to use XYZ' in the pre-course preparation and on the course portal, so that learners who may be in senior roles but struggling with new (to them) technologies can inform themselves privately. It is also wise to consider phasing the introduction of new tools if the participant sophistication is low, rather than introducing an avalanche of new technologies up front, which could overwhelm and disengage participants. Gamification can be useful, here – learning to use a new tool in a fun game situation, rather than formally, can work well. We routinely use a gamified learning management system (LMS) on our customised programmes as a means to manage the online aspects of the programme, for the benefit of both the participants and the commissioning client. Alongside all the quantitative benefits of such a system, the LMS uses the more qualitative gamification function to encourage participants to engage both with the material-downloads from the programme, as well to engage in the chat and collaborative portions that constitute the ongoing 'developmental conversations' that take place throughout the programme.

3.4.2. Tailoring to Learning Styles

Education theory advocates that delivery should be influenced by the learning styles of the participants. In face-to-face classroom teaching the styles may not be known in advance, but in executive education environments where the participants are known in advance, their learning styles can be profiled (possibly in a pre-course assessment centre) and this this information used to shape course design and delivery.

Adjusting for different learning styles is arguably easier in a blended customised education context as more tools and techniques are available, and there is much more flexibility.

3.4.3. Collaborative Learning

Unlike either the conventional classroom face-to-face environment or the MOOC environment, the online or blended executive education context requires multi-way collaboration between the lecturer, the participant and the corporate sponsor and between participants. A commonly-used and highly effective method of online collaboration is the web-based seminar, or webinar. The most successful webinars are where the technology empowering the virtual collaboration of the dispersed participants disappears into the background of the actual content of the collaboration: this relegation demands higher levels of technology fluency than the typical cultural norms encountered in business schools or HEIs, but when achieved can become a significant differentiator between customised online executive education and MOOCs.

In classroom delivery, time is an obvious constraint – conventional lectures have to be delivered within the scheduled time slot. Online, exercises can be enriched by tasking the participants to search for additional resources. Interestingly, this requires the lecturers to be confident enough and knowledgeable enough to react to new materials that participants may bring to the discussions, so there is less lecturer 'control' of the teaching experience than in classroom delivery. This places greater demands on the lecturers themselves, a point we return to later. Case study 3.3 gives an example.

3.4.4. Peer-to-Peer Learning

Peer-to-peer learning is not just a derivative benefit that emerges from interaction with the multiple TEL components but, as with MOOCs, becomes the medium in which the learning takes place. The mutually supportive interaction between learners and learners, and learners and lecturers, can be mediated via text chat, FaceTime™, video, the business simulation platform and discussion forums, as well as email, Skype, WhatsApp and phone and corporate

---

Case Study 3.3.   Enhancing Learning Using TEL

In a face-to-face finance and accounting course this lecturer distributed financial data and tasked participants, working in syndicate teams, to analyse it and to report back to the rest of the class with their views. Taking this finance course into the online arena, with virtual teams and asynchronous engagement, provided an opportunity to enhance this exercise. The syndicate teams are no longer restricted in the amount of data they access – the whole internet is available to them. Nor need they be constrained by the standard timetable – the report-back can be scheduled for any time in the future. And they are no longer limited in their methods of report-back – technology enables sophisticated spreadsheets, slide packs or the creative use of videos in the way they record and present their findings. This also means that the findings can easily be preserved on a course portal for participants to refer back to in the future.

Exercises like this can take place during the course itself or can be used as inter-module work between different elements of a programme.

conferencing systems[3]. As such, in the online educational environment, the channels for feedback from learners to lecturers are rich and diverse. This becomes particularly relevant when dealing with executive participants, whose experience and contributions can, if handled correctly, be of great value to their colleagues.

3.4.5. Participation and Engagement

Levels of participation and learner engagement are more important in the executive education environment than in MOOCs. As we have mentioned, dropping out of a client course could have a career implication for the participant. It may also have an impact on the university, since the client may treat this as poor delivery. Thus, lack of engagement by participants could have unfortunate consequences.

In a face-to-face setting, the teacher has the luxury of being able to gauge engagement by looking at body language and other signals. In many online educational channels, this is not normally possible (although new technologies are beginning to change this). The fact that it is more difficult for teachers to judge learner engagement and understanding in the online setting challenges the prevailing ideology of teacher 'control' of the classroom, to which the academics must adapt.

Some presenters rely on technology solutions to help evaluate whether the learners are engaged with the learning intervention. For instance, in the case of live webinars, technology solutions exist to show the lecturer whether or not the learners have the appropriate screen open, or whether they are engaged with other material on their devices. However, this is an unreliable indicator and one that sits uncomfortably with the emphasis of andragogy on self-directed non-didactic approaches (c.f. Jarvis, 1985). A better solution is for the HEI lecturer to adapt their teaching/facilitation style to adapt to both the technology and the learner's attention span. This can be done, for example with icebreaker exercises to promote cohort engagement and peer-to-peer learning at the start of live webinars. It can be improved by promoting learner engagement prior to virtual face-to-face webinars with self-testing; and the use and application of learner analytics. (That said, learner analytics rely for their accuracy on larger numbers of learners in replicated learning so may be considerably less reliable in small-cohort adaptive executive education settings.)

The interaction between participants in executive education differs from the MOOC environment in which students rarely know one another. In executive education, participants may already know (or know of) one another but, even if they do not, they share a common corporate history and context, as well as possibly having likely future interaction with respect to a (mostly homogenous) corporate goal. For example, many tailored executive education courses are aimed at developing the next generation of senior managers and leaders. The participants may well know this and may use the courses and associated social

---

[3]This is not an exhaustive list of examples.

interactions as an opportunity to build some useful informal networks as well as to interact with and impress any leaders who are present. These effects frame the interactions between them, and smaller cohort numbers mean that individual participation is easier to judge and a lot more visible than on a typical high-numbers MOOC.

3.5. Evaluation and Outcomes

Post-course evaluation and outcomes in executive education need to address outcomes for both clients: the individual participants and the commissioning company. The company, in turn, may frame its required outcomes in terms of improvement in the performance or promotion potential of the individuals; or it may consider outcomes in terms of organisational efficiency and performance; or both.

Evaluation of individual benefits from executive education courses is fraught with difficulties. Firstly, the company may find it difficult to articulate exactly what it wants to achieve for individual participants. Careful scoping can take a client requirement such as 'we need more people who can run a business unit for us' and turn it into a suitable brief for use by an assessment centre, but effective outcomes measurement is still going to need the client company to agree to and fund, pre- and post-course assessment.

A second major issue with individual outcomes-based evaluation is a political one about how the company intends to use individual outcomes data and what the implications might be. During- and post-course, online and blended executive education may include both formative and summative assessment. The former is largely self-testing for learner engagement and not reported to the client; the latter may be for assessment, but there may be a substantial career risk where a participant 'fails' an end-of-course assessment. The implications for this need careful discussion with client companies, many of whom are keen to build in assessment or even accreditation but are dismayed when the possible downside risk is explained to them. We know of cases where very senior managers have struggled with summative assessments for various reasons including unfamiliarity with the assessment type, length of time out of formal education, lack of time to prepare, dyslexia and overconfidence. High-profile failures by senior people may have difficult consequences for the organisation; and failures by more junior high-flyers may be damaging both to the view that senior managers have of them, and to their own confidence. In one case, working with a professional services firm, we had set a post-module summative assessment that consisted of a planning exercise. We had agreed with the client that the feedback would consist of a grade mark plus detailed qualitative feedback for each section of the submitted document. The highest-marked plans would be the ones that would be featured in future modules and used as exemplars for the company. The grade mark caused furore amongst this group of ambitious high performers, who all expected to achieve top marks in everything that they did. Eventually, the client asked that we quietly drop the mark and provide purely qualitative feedback.

As discussed above, learner analytics are less effective in measuring progress here than they are in MOOCs or large-scale conventional award-bearing courses. Often, smaller groups mean that informal rather than statistically reliable progress and attainment measures are all that are available. Informal measures might be perfectly acceptable if, for example, the education is about developing a small cadre of managers or a top team where the core requirement is behaviour or culture change, rather than knowledge transfer. If so, it is worth making this explicit up front and also agreeing the appropriate time frames for measuring outcomes. Knowledge transfer is reasonably easy to gauge by the end of a module or course, but behavioural change may take some months to become evident.

The second area of evaluation and outcomes that needs attention in delivering customised executive education is the possible impact of the education on the company's own performance. Organisational impact is notoriously difficult to judge since there are so many other variables, both endogenous and exogenous, that can affect it. Here, the use of inter-module and/or post-course project work is a really valuable tool, since results such as cost savings or efficiency improvements are more easily attributable to defined projects. One of our clients works with us each year to define a number of profit improvement projects that will be undertaken by their delegates during and after the course, supervised by our academics. Money saved by these projects is reinvested in education and development for the following year, and the net financial impact is reported to the company's Board. The company views the education we provide as 'free' because the identified project savings more than cover the cost of the courses.

3.6. Business Model and Inhibitors

We have established that online and blended customised executive education as a context differs considerably from the more customary work of an HEI. In this section, we consider some of the inhibitors to adopting this type of course, and some of the ways in which the HEI business model needs to change to accommodate it.

3.6.1. Cross-functional Teams

The first issue challenging standard university business models is the need for cross-functional teams, discussed earlier. In MOOC development, it can be the case that the academic plans the course and content and then 'throws it over the fence' to the TEL team to develop. In the executive education environment, successful suppliers have cross-functional teams comprising academics and education technologists who work together throughout the project. A challenge of this model is the re-engineering of the power relationships within a university, which have traditionally privileged the academic. For this business model to succeed, a more equal relationship is required.

3.6.2. Cost

The high specificity of customised executive education, and the commercially-sensitive content and difficulties in replicating it from client to client mean that this provision is inherently more costly than 'standard' undergraduate or postgraduate education. Furthermore, the need for cross-functional teams means that course design using TEL becomes even more costly. And, unlike in the MOOC environment, the material can rarely be re-used for different clients. (Indeed, given the ongoing nature of tailoring, it is sometimes possible that the TEL will need to be re-engineered between modules.)

This obviously increases the cost base of executive education, which has implications for the business model, as more resources will need to be put into course design and delivery, and this must be recovered from the client. Given that the common perception of 'online' is that it can save costs, clients are not always willing to accommodate this.

3.6.3. Academic Resistance

There are several reasons why academics may resist adopting TEL in customised executive education, and these need to be addressed by the HEI.

One issue is academic attitudes and perception of risk. Many academics are concerned about putting their educational collateral into an online format, as they consider that this will lead to a loss of their intellectual property (Redpath, 2012). The HEI needs to have clear policies in place that will deal with this equitably.

The second area of concern is how the academics need to adapt their delivery mode. We argue that customised executive education already involves a very different mode of delivery to graduate teaching, but the use of technology disrupts this further. For example, the academic will need to understand how to use the different tools that might be needed (which could also differ between clients). Also, as discussed earlier, they will have to develop skills to engage participants in this new environment.

There is also the fact that delivery using TEL is more risky for the academic. The example was given earlier of a finance and accounting course where participants could access and analyse corporate information from a wide range of sources. This inevitably implies a loss of control for the academic. No longer are they the sole source of information. Perhaps more worryingly, if the participants access and analyse novel data, the academic will have to react very quickly to put their findings into the course context: the first few times they have to do this can be very stressful.

On top of all of these issues is the fact that in many cases, the HEI reward model is inadequate in acknowledging and rewarding the commitment and effort needed to create successful blended executive courses. Traditionally, universities reward research and they reward classroom time. For this business model to be successful and equivalence needs to be developed that incentivises client development, course design and creation of TEL.

3.7. Conclusion

Customised executive education differs from the normal provision of universities, and the use of TEL makes it yet more different. The need to involve client and participant in course design provides a unique context. Many of the perceived advantages of TEL, such as its replicability and (sometimes illusory) cost-saving potential disappear in an environment of extreme tailoring and perpetual co-creation, with each course being unique.

The disruptive impact of TEL in these courses is seen in their design and delivery, but also in their impact on the client company. When properly designed, online and blended courses can be highly tailored to achieve business outcomes; they can also provide excellent value for money if suitable organisational impact projects are incorporated into their design and delivery.

That said, HEIs participating in this market need to develop a culture and processes which will encourage academics and technologists to work together. They need systems in place to upskill the academics and they need reward systems that do not stand in the way of this. A substantial problem area remains the lack of recognition that technology-enhanced learning is not cheap and that it requires not just technology inputs but also considerable academic time and development resource. Faculty workload management systems that still reflect a traditional classroom-hours' view of teaching may be holding back academics from committing themselves to new blended learning approaches.

Ultimately, technology has the power to make in-company programmes hugely rewarding for the client and for the contributing academic. We have argued that maximising the positive impact that technology can have on customised executive programmes requires a systematic approach that 'designs in' the appropriate use of technology from the outset. This, in turn, demands a vision of the possible academic benefits of technology and a clear-sighted evaluation of the technological capability of the client company, the delegates and the academics involved. Finally, this only works 'on the ground' if there is a close working relationship between the academic and the educational technologist and an open and honest dialogue with the commissioning client.

References

Jarvis, P. (1985). *The sociology of adult and continuing education*. Beckenham: Croom Helm.

Knowles, M. S. (1990). *The adult learner. A neglected species (4e)*. Houston, TX: Gulf Publishing.

OCR. (2016, August 1). *State of the MOOC 2016: A year of massive landscape change for Massive Open Online Courses*. Retrieved from http://www.onlinecoursereport.com/state-of-the-mooc-2016-a-year-of-massive-landscape-change-for-massive-open-online-courses/

Redpath, L. (2012). Confronting the bias against on-line learning in management education. *Academy of Management Learning and Education*, *11*(1), 125–140. doi:10.5465/amle.2010.0044

Reich, J. (2014). *Reconsidering MOOC completion rates: The intention factor.* Retrieved from http://harvardx.harvard.edu/files/harvardx/files/reich_reconsidering_moocs.pdf

UNICON. (2014). *Minding their business by flexing our minds: A guide to corporate university partnerships.* Retrieved from http://uniconexeced.wpengine.com/wp-content/uploads/2016/04/Maybar-Plaxe_Allen_Renaud-Coulon-UNICON_Corporate-Universities-2014.pdf

Whitaker, J., New, J. R., & Ireland, R. D. (2016). MOOCs and the online delivery of business education: What's new? What's not? What now? *Academy of Management Learning and Education*, *15*(2), 345–365. doi:10.5465/amle.2013.0021

Chapter 4

Internationalisation of Online Learning: A Double Degree Model

Charles Krusekopf

Abstract

Two of the most important trends in higher education have been the emergence of online learning and efforts to internationalise the curriculum and student body. While most universities embraced both these trends, insufficient attention has been paid to how the two approaches might be mutually supportive. Online education offers the opportunity to bring together students living in different countries in common courses and programmes, but cross-border enrolments remain low and new models and approaches are needed to build educational offerings that bring students and faculty from different countries together in sustained educational engagement online. This paper highlights a case study of an innovative blended double degree business masters' program between Royal Roads University (RRU) in Canada and the Management Center Innsbruck (MCI) in Austria that allows mid-career, blended learning students to build international competencies and networks while continuing to work full-time. Through this double degree program, students can complete a Master of Global Management (MGM) at RRU and an MBA at MCI in approximately 24 months. Mid-career students have traditionally had limited opportunities to participate in an international education due to work and family constraints, but the pairing of two blended programmes creates an opportunity for these students to engage in a rich cross-cultural learning community. The paper highlights the challenges of integrating online learning into internationalisation strategies and explains how double degree programmes such as the RRU-MCI collaboration provide advantages that help overcome the challenges associated with online programmes that enrol students from different countries.

Keywords: Internationalisation; online learning; non-traditional students; double degree; MBA; cross-border collaboration

4.1. Introduction

Two of the most important trends in higher education in recent years have been the shift toward online and technology-enhanced learning and moves to internationalise education (Altbach, Reisberg, & Rumbley, 2009; Sursock, 2016). Universities around the world have adopted globalisation strategies to internationalise their curriculum, student bodies and staff (Altbach et al., 2009; CBIE, 2016; Knight, 2012; Sursock, 2016). For example, 93% of European universities surveyed have internationalisation strategies in place or in development, and almost all have embraced online learning (Sursock, 2016). 87% of universities worldwide report that globalisation is included in their institutional mission statement, with 78% reporting that globalisation has been increasing in strategic importance (Green, Marmolejo, & Egron-Polak, 2012).

At the same time, online learning has been growing in importance but has remained focused on domestic students. In 2015, 30% of higher education students in the US took at least one distance learning class, up from less than 10% in 2002 (Allen & Seman, 2013). Despite the potential for unlimited global access, almost all online learning enrolments within university programmes and courses come from students living in the country where the course is offered, with the majority of students enrolled in the institution offering the course. For example, studies show that less than 1% of students taking an online course from a US university live outside the United States and global online programmes have struggled to find a market (Seaman, Allen, & Seaman, 2018; Ziguras, 2018). Online programmes that enrol students across borders remain relatively rare but offer the potential to expand internationalisation efforts among university programmes and widen the set of students who can benefit from globalised learning and interactions.

This paper offers an overview of an innovative blended learning double degree programme launched in 2016 that allows mid-career students to earn an MBA in International Business at Management Center Innsbruck, Austria (MCI) and a Master of Global Management at Royal Roads University (RRU) in Victoria, BC, Canada. The programme includes short residencies on both campuses and online courses connecting students and faculty from both institutions. It provides an example of how online education and internationalisation can be mutually supportive, with each enhancing the other. The paper first reviews how double degree programmes and online education can be combined to expand access to international education to under-served populations. It then provides an overview of the background and structure of the MCI-RRU double degree program and its benefits to students, faculty and the institutions involved. The paper discusses lessons learned and how a double degree framework, such as the one adopted by RRU and MCI, can be used to overcome some of the challenges that have limited the use of online education approaches within internationalisation efforts.

4.2. Internationalisation and Double Degree Programmes

Universities have pursued a variety of strategies to internationalise teaching, learning and research in an effort to improve intercultural competence and knowledge of international issues among students who will live and work in an increasingly globalised world (Altbach et al., 2009; Green et al., 2012; Knight, 2012). Institutions have worked to internationalise 'at home' by expanding the international content within courses and programmes, recruiting international students and faculty and promoting international research and extra-curricular activities with a global focus (Altbach et al., 2009). These internationalisation efforts occurred on the university's home campus and provided benefits by diversifying the curriculum and population of students and faculty at the school.

Institutions recognised the need to extend internationalisation efforts beyond the home campus, and therefore sought out partnerships and opportunities for student and faculty outside their home country. These 'cross-border' internationalisation efforts have been increasing in scope and scale in recent years and include efforts such as opportunities for students to study or complete internships or projects abroad, faculty exchanges, research partnerships, double degree programmes and branch campuses (Green et al., 2012). Such programmes promote mobility among students and faculty, allowing them to have an immersive experience in another country.

However, while short-term study abroad programmes allow students to build their global knowledge and personal skills, visiting students often do not fully integrate into the institution they are visiting and short exchange programmes are less likely to lead to sustained cross-border institutional collaborations. Due to these shortcomings, in recent years there have been a growing number of collaborative degree programmes, such as double degrees, among institutions in different countries (Council of Graduate Schools, 2010; Knight & Lee, 2012). Double degrees allow students to earn two individual qualifications at equivalent levels from partner schools, and allow deeper, more sustainable partnerships at a student, faculty and institutional level (Knight, 2012). The MCI MBA-RRU MGM partnership described in this paper is a double degree partnership as it allows students to obtain two separate masters degrees, including a Master of Global Management from RRU and an MBA from MCI.

Double degrees benefit students because they are able to complete courses and programmes that may not be available at their home institution, connect more deeply with international students and faculty as a regular student in a university outside their home country, and obtain an international degree that will enhance their career prospects (Corno, Lal, & Hassouna, 2016; Council of Graduate Schools, 2010; Culver, Puri, Spinelli, DePauw, & Dooley, 2012). At an institutional level, compared to short-term student exchange arrangements, double degrees are seen as beneficial because they facilitate a deeper level of commitment and interchange among faculty and administrators. Faculty have the opportunity to work closely with counterparts at a partner institution to develop new curriculum, to serve as visiting lecturers and to develop new research programmes and resources (Hall, 2012). Schools see double degrees as a way to support academic internationalisation while also enhancing their global brand and aiding in the recruitment of international students (Henard, Diamond, & Roseveare, 2012).

Government funded programmes, such as SOCRATES, the EU-US Atlantis Program and Erasmus Mundi, played a key role in the development of double degree programs, which are most common among European and North American universities compared to universities in other parts of the world (Kuder & Obst, 2009). A survey in 2008 identified 805 collaborative degree programs (primarily double degrees, but also including joint degrees) offered by European universities, and 291 offered by US institutions, with business and engineering the most common disciplines of focus (Council of Graduate Schools, 2010). Most European double degrees were at a masters' level with partner schools in Europe or North America, while US schools most often partnered with European institutions and offered a mix of undergraduate and graduate double degrees (Obst, Kuder, & Banks, 2011).

Studies indicate a growing interest among universities in expanding double degree programmes in the future, with over 85% of institutions in the US and the EU planning additional collaborative programmes, with a focus on new double degree offerings (Helms, 2014; Kuder & Obst, 2009). The growing interest in double degrees has led to call for the development of new, innovative double degree models that incorporate online learning, consortium-based approaches and innovative program pairings (Knight & Lee, 2012). The increasing number of online educational programmes creates new opportunities for schools to explore cross-border partnerships that allow faculty and students to engage in new international experiences, expand the range courses and programmes available and expand the number of students who engage in international education.

4.2.1. Expanding Access to International Education through Online Learning

Despite university efforts to expand cross-border educational opportunities through programmes such as study abroad and double degrees, overall participation in international education remains low. For example, only 2% of students at US and Canadian institutions studied outside their home country in 2014–2015, despite the fact that 93% of North American academic institutions indicated that it was a priority to promote out of country experiences for their students (CBIE, 2016). In Europe, despite substantial financial support from Erasmus+ and other programmes and widespread participation among institutions, in 2010–2011 fewer than 10% of students in EU universities spent all or part of their studies outside their home country, well below the goal of 20% adopted by the Bologna Mobility Strategy (European Commission, 2014).

While the numbers of students participating in cross-border educational activities in almost all Western countries have been increasing in recent years, the percentage of students participating has remained low overall and important groups of students, including adult, working and low-income students, have been excluded from most study abroad activities. Almost 90% of the Canadian and American students who study abroad are undergraduate students participating in traditional face-to-face courses at a foreign university (CBIE, 2016). Adult and working students have been consistently underrepresented in internationalisation efforts due to the challenges they face in terms of the financial and time costs of most existing study abroad programmes (CBIE, 2016). On the other hand, these students would benefit from greater exposure to the skills and knowledge offered by international education due to their exposure to globalisation and cross-cultural interactions in their workplaces and communities (Merriam & Bierema, 2014).

Online education offers a unique opportunity to increase the participation of non-traditional students in international education because it fits the interests and circumstances of this student group and makes international education more accessible and affordable in terms of time and money (Green et al., 2012). Adult and working students make up the majority of participants in online education, and these students are looking to expand their skill sets and knowledge in ways that can be directly applied in their careers and lives (Altbach et al., 2009; Merriam & Bierema, 2014; Stavredes, 2011). Online learning can contribute to internationalisation at home for adult students who do not have the opportunity to travel to other countries by introducing them to global topics and issues, and by connecting them to information sources, teachers and students abroad through courses or joint exercises that involve students in different countries (Edwards & Teekens, 2012). This form of internationalisation offers benefits because it is flexible and accessible to a wider range of students.

Concerns have been raised, however, about internationalisation efforts that focus on one-time or short-term online interactions due to the lack of direct contact and short duration that deprives students of sustained engagement with international partners (Knight & Lee, 2012). Longer-term engagement, such as through the completion of a series of courses or a full online degree program that enrols students from a variety of countries, is seen as preferable to allow the development of deeper understanding and sharing among students (Knight, 2012). However, while fully online degree programmes have been growing in number in recent years, most online programmes enrol only students from the country where the host university is located (Seaman et al., 2018). This is most pronounced in the US, where only 37,788 of the 2.8 million students taking online courses in 2014 were based outside the country (Merola, 2017).

The one country that has attracted relatively large numbers of cross-border enrolments in online courses is the United Kingdom (UK), which utilises its network of branch and affiliated campuses worldwide to attract international students into online learning offerings from UK institutions (Merola, 2017). However, most of the courses are supported and offered through local teaching institutions located in the home country where the students reside and enrol only international students (Ziguras, 2018). As a result, these programmes and courses are not well integrated with internationalisation efforts that connect UK-based students and faculty with counterparts in other countries. Online education itself has been growing in acceptance around the world, but cross-border collaborations in online education that bring together students from different countries in one integrated program remain rare. As highlighted in the next section, despite a number of benefits, several barriers have hindered the development of cross-border collaborations in online education.

4.2.2. Benefits and Barriers to Cross-border Online Education

There is a growing recognition of the potential benefits of more closely aligning online education efforts and efforts to develop students who are globally aware and cross-culturally capable (Green et al., 2012; Sursock, 2016). Students who have participated in online education courses together with students from different countries gain an understanding and appreciation of other perspectives and gain new knowledge and understanding of the context of issues in their home country and abroad (Gemmel, Harrison, Clegg, & Reed, 2015). International education also improves students' ability to work well with people from other countries and cultures, and which improves employment prospects and long-term success in both business and social environments (Gemmel et al., 2015; Leask & Carroll, 2011; Sanderson, 2011). Employers have highlighted global awareness, cross-cultural capability and online proficiency as key skills in need of development to meet twenty-first-century workplace demands, and the globalised nature of business enhances the need to develop cross-border teams that can work together in virtual formats (Fearon, Starr, & McLaughlin, 2011).

Despite these potential benefits, due to administrative barriers and personal preferences students who study outside their home country almost always enrol in traditional on-campus face-to-face programmes. As a result, cross-border enrolments in online remain limited even in programmes designed to attract a global cohort of students. For example, many top schools developed online MBA programmes that were expected to attract a diverse cohort of students from around the world. However, studies have shown that among universities that offer a choice, the proportion of international students in online MBA programmes is much lower than the proportion of international students enroled in that university's on-campus programme (Ortmans, 2018). In the US, only 4% of international students opt for online programmes, and worldwide less than 20% of students in the top 20 online MBA programmes are international, much lower than the proportion of international students in top on-campus MBA programmes (Ortmans, 2018).

Some educational offerings, such as MOOCs, have attracted significant global enrollment, however the courses and programmes with the largest numbers of international enrollees tend to be offered on a non-credit or non-degree basis (Online Course Report, 2018; Ziguras, 2018). International online collaborations within university courses and programmes have been focused on using tools such as video conferencing or discussion boards to foster sharing of information and views on global or cultural issues among students taking similar courses at universities in different countries (Edwards & Teekens, 2012). These international collaborations are often on a one-time basis, with no structure or plan to sustain the cross-country engagement of students across several courses or a full program. The collaborations often require a substantial commitment of time to coordinate and administer as the students and faculty remain enrolled in their home institutions and lack a common university platform where they can connect. The interactions also lack depth as they typically last for just one session or a few sessions during a course, and do not lead to deeper engagement with peers from other countries across an extended time period or series of courses.

Cross-border enrolments in online degree programmes offered by institutions outside their home countries have been hampered due to concerns about degree recognition, cost, technical and administrative challenges and issues related to language and culture. For example, while online degrees have gained recognition and large enrolments in certain countries such as the United States, a bias against online learning remains among students, employers and governments in many countries (Allen & Seman, 2013; Merola, 2017). This bias is often strongest against online degrees offered by foreign universities because those universities may not be well known in the students' home country or they may be perceived as diploma mills (Shirvani, Scorza, Alkhathian, & Garcia, 2011; Ziguras, 2018). Many governments, such as those in China and India, refuse to acknowledge or accept online degrees taken at foreign institutions, limiting the utility of such degrees for students who plan to work in their home country (Allen & Seman, 2013; Merola, 2017; Ziguras, 2018).

Technical challenges and costs are also often cited by students as barriers to enrollment in cross-border online education (Rye & Stokken, 2012). Online education offered by foreign institutions is often as expensive as face-to-face offerings from the same institutions, and significantly more expensive than online or face-to-face offerings from universities in the students' home country (Ziguras, 2018). Financial aid systems in most countries do not support cross-border enrolments, and therefore students must bear the full costs of online programmes offered by a foreign university. Technical and administrative barriers also create challenges for the enrollment of students from different countries in online courses and programmes. For the course to work effectively, all students must have access to the required equipment, a reliable, high-speed network connection and be familiar and proficient with the learning platform. These issues are of particular concern in developing countries, where online education has been hampered due to technological challenges such as lack of affordable access to computers and high-speed internet (Rye & Stokken, 2012).

Differences in culture, language and educational approaches across countries have also created challenges for the full inclusion and integration of international students in online education (Rye & Stokken, 2012; Shirvani et al., 2011; Simm & Marvell, 2017). Students often vary in learning style and background, leading to challenges with regard to expectations for participation by students, differing understandings of academic standards and potential cultural misunderstanding (Shirvani et al., 2011). Most cross-border programmes adopt English as the language of instruction, which can create challenges in terms of language fluency and the equal inclusion of students in course discussions and activities (Simm & Marvell, 2017; Spiro, 2014).

Because of these challenges, students who want to take a study program from a foreign university almost always opt to participate in face-to-face programmes or courses on the home university campus. Online cross-border programmes remain relatively rare but have been recognised to offer great promise to help universities expand their internationalisation efforts and create new educational opportunities for under-served populations including working and adult students (Shirvani et al., 2011). The following section highlights an innovative cross-border educational partnership between Canadian and Austrian universities that utilises online education and a double degree format to enhance global awareness and exposure for students working full-time in international business careers. While the outlined approach is one of many potential models that might be used to connect internationalisation efforts and online education, the lessons learned from this case study can be helpful to practitioners and institutions that are seeking to develop new programmes or partnerships.

4.3. RRU-MCI Double Degree

In 2015, Management Center Innsbruck and Royal Roads University began to explore opportunities to create a double degree programme between two blended degree business master's programmes, the MBA in International Business at MCI and the Master of Global Management (MGM) programme at RRU. The programmes were offered in English and enroled mid-career students with a strong interest in global business who were working full-time while completing their academic studies. Both were offered in a cohort-based blended learning format, with a limited number of short residency periods on-campus and online learning courses. The double degree partnership was embraced by both institutions as a way to create richer and deeper international exposure for programme students, to differentiate and promote the programmes to prospective students and to build stronger institutional ties between RRU and MCI. This section offers an overview of the two institutions, a description of the double degree programme and its benefits to students, faculty and the institutions and a discussion of how online double degree partnerships such as the RRU-MCI arrangement offer a viable model to expand cross-border online education opportunities.

4.3.1. RRU and MCI Profile

Royal Roads University (RRU) was a Canadian public university founded in 1995 and located in Victoria, British Columbia. The university focused on applied and professional programmes for learners who were already in the workforce. RRU offered more than 50 blended and online degree programmes including bachelors, masters and doctoral programmes that included a combination of short-term residencies on-campus and longer terms of online study. While the university also offered some programs in a more traditional on-campus, face-to-face format, more than 70% of students at RRU continued to work full-time while completing their studies through blended or fully online learning. RRU programmes were designed to build learning communities among a cohort of peers who participate together in both on-campus residencies and online courses.

The Management Center Innsbruck (MCI) was founded in 1996 and offers graduate, non-graduate and post-graduate educational programmes to senior and junior managers from all management levels and branches. MCI offered the majority of its programmes on its campus in Innsbruck, Austria, but was expanding blended and online programme offerings. In fall 2018, it offered 8 online programmes and planned to add new programmes and online options to increase the proportion of students in online learning offerings (MCI, 2018).

RRU and MCI both adopted a global orientation and sought to internationalise both their programme curriculum and student body. MCI was one of the most internationally oriented schools in Europe, and by 2018 had created 11 international double degree programmes and student exchange agreements with more than 250 partner schools around the world (MCI, 2018). At the same time, RRU hosted more than 400 full-time international students studying at its campus in Canada, while also offering RRU degree programmes together with partners in several other countries. However, as was true at other institutions, most of the participants in international programmes at both RRU and MCI were students studying full-time in traditional face-to-face programmes. Very few students from outside North America or central Europe enroled in the online or blended degree programmes offered by the schools, and few opportunities existed for students in these programmes to engage in international studies because they were working full-time while studying online. A blended dual degree programme partnership was therefore seen as a way to enhance learning and expand internationalisation opportunities to students who might not otherwise be able to study with learners from around the world.

4.3.2. RRU-MCI Double Degree Program Development and Design

RRU and MCI began actively working together on the development of a double degree programme between the MCI MBA and the RRU MGM programme in spring 2015. The partnership developed rapidly based on the past experience at both institutions with double degrees, and the willingness of programme champions to work out academic and institutional details in collaboration with the wide set of university departments that needed to be engaged in the development and implementation of the programme.

The development of the double degree programme was supported by both prior experience and the existence of a clear process and written guidelines that specified programme requirements for double degrees. The existence of clear guidelines and procedures within an institution that guided the development of collaborative degrees has been found to be very important to facilitate cooperative development efforts (Hall, 2012; Helms, 2014). The online aspects of the double degree partnership required some special consideration with regard to administrative details, but the basic guidelines and process for the development of an online double degree fit well with the established frameworks. For example, the guidelines specified that students need to complete at least two-thirds of the credit requirements for each programme. This guideline ensured that the double degree was not a 50% plus 50% arrangement where students could complete two degrees while only doing the work required of one, which is important to maintain the programme quality and integrity in the development of double degrees (Knight, 2011).

The programme design of the MBA-MGM double degree ensured that students complete the core course requirements in their first programme before transferring to the partner university. Both the MBA and MGM programmes begin in the fall with an on-campus residency of one to two weeks where students and faculty build close bonds through participation in active learning and team building exercises. After residency students return to full-time work and take online courses together with their cohort. This design helps to build a strong learning community where students have the experience of meeting and working face to face with the other members of their cohort before engaging in online courses. The online components allow students to directly apply their learning within their workplaces and share experiences and hold discussions with other cohort members.

After completing approximately 11 months in their home university programme, students in each programme then decide whether they will complete a single degree at their home university, or transfer to the partner university to start the double degree programme with the incoming cohort at the partner school. Students who opt for the double degree transfer and become full members of the partner university programme, participating in both the first programme residency and online courses. They are able to shorten the time to degree completion by avoiding repetition of common core courses such as accounting and finance that are included in both programmes. The double degree can be completed in 24 months, approximately 6 months longer than the completion time of a single programme due to the elimination of overlapping courses.

A key consideration in the development of the double degree was the establishment of administrative details and processes including working out arrangements for admissions, registration and credit transfer and tuition payments. To ensure compatibility of students within the two programmes and a smooth transfer process, it is recommended that both programmes have similar admission standards (Chevallier, 2013), which is true of the MGM and MBA programmes that both require significant and relevant work experience in addition to an undergraduate degree. Tuition payments with the MBA-MGM double degree were simplified through an agreement that allowed students to pay tuition only to their home university. The two schools agreed to compare student numbers and payments every two years and transfer funds among the institutions to ensure that tuition revenues match the number of students taking each degree programme.

Key factors that supported the success of the RRU-MCI collaboration included the level of institutional compatibility between the two schools and highly committed personnel who were able to work collaboratively to address any concerns or issues that arose. Studies have shown that institutional compatibility and mutual commitment are necessary for successful double degree partnerships (Hall, 2012; Tarazona, 2013). As the programme was the first of its type for both institutions, it was necessary to review and update the administrative and academic aspects of the programme after the first year of operation. For example, adjustments were made to application dates to make the transfer process between universities smoother and to the timing of courses to allow double degree students to complete their thesis research alongside their expanded course requirements. While these adjustments require staff resources to monitor and address, the benefits from the programme for students, faculty, staff and the institutions helped sustain the commitment of both key personnel and the institutions.

4.3.3. Benefits to Students, Faculty and Institutions

Several benefits for students, faculty and the institutions have been identified through the development and implementation of the blended double degree programme between MCI and RRU. First, the programme expanded global learning opportunities for students who are working full-time and who would not otherwise be able to deeply engage in international learning. This benefit is felt most directly by the students who opt to take the double degree programme at the partner university, but it extends to all the students in both university programmes due to the additional diversity the double degree students from the partner university bring to the home university cohort. Therefore, all students in both programmes gain new skills and cross-cultural competencies through the opportunity to get to know and study with students from other backgrounds and countries. These skills have been shown to be beneficial in both academic and work environments (Corno et al., 2016; Culver et al., 2012).

The double degree programme expands the range of courses and experiences available to students. For example, MGM students who took the double degree were able to take advantage of MCI's strength and courses in entrepreneurship, while MCI students were able to take advantage of RRU's focus and courses in the area of sustainability. The students also gained important experience working and communicating across borders. The double degree students were required to navigate the systems and requirements of a new university in a foreign country, thereby demonstrating their ability to work successfully across borders and in online environments. Students who participate in double degree programmes gain confidence in their ability to effectively work in a global and cross-cultural environment (Culver et al., 2012).

The online aspects of the double degree programme provide skills that are valuable in the workplace and overall career development. Through its blended format, the RRU-MCI double degree programme was designed to meet a critical need for managers with cross-cultural and management skills in both face-to-face and online settings. Firms operating in a global environment often rely on teams of people located in different parts of the world who interact primarily online. The MGM-MBA double degree programme required students to engage with a diverse range of participants from different countries and different industry sectors in both face-to-face and online settings. These skills are in increasing demand as companies build collaborations and supply chains that span the globe (Neeley, 2015).

Second, in addition to the benefits that accrued to students, university faculty and programmes benefited from the double degree programme as well. For faculty, the double degree programme created new learning opportunities by helping to internationalise the student body and offered the opportunity to teach at the partner university and explore new pedagogical approaches. The double degree partnership has allowed faculty from both institutions to teach online or face-to-face courses in the partner university, and MCI learning technologists have participated in training sessions related to online learning offered by RRU. These teaching and professional development opportunities allowed faculty and staff from both institutions to learn from one another and apply new knowledge and lessons to home institution approaches and courses.

Third, the double degree partnership between MCI and RRU created several advantages for the institutions involved, including the ability to recruit new students and explore new avenues of cooperation. Enroling students from a partner university offered a low-cost way to recruit additional high-quality students into a programme. Before transferring, double degree students must both meet the admission requirements of the partner programme and successfully complete all the courses in the first year of the partner university programme. This helps to ensure that the students taking the double degree will be able to meet the special academic demands of a cross-border programme. Both MCI and RRU have also been able to utilise the opportunity created by the blended double degree programme to expand the potential pool of programme applicants within their domestic markets. The double degree serves as a market differentiator for the programmes involved, creating a competitive advantage for the schools in an increasingly crowded marketplace for online business degrees. Both institutions prominently highlighted the double degree partnership on their programme websites, and the double degree was a key topic raised by prospective students at recruitment presentations.

4.3.4. Lessons Learned from the RRU-MCI Online Double Degree Partnership

The experience gained by RRU and MCI in the development and implementation of their online double degree programme offers insights for other institutions considering ways to connect university internationalisation efforts together with online learning and highlights the advantages of using a double degree arrangement to facilitate cross-border learning opportunities. First, an international double degree ensures that students have the opportunity to engage in a sustained series of courses and experiences with a diverse cohort of students. Using a blended format for the double degree programme opens this opportunity up to a wider range of students, many of whom would not otherwise be able to engage in study abroad or an international experience, especially one that allows them to engage with a cohort of peers across a range of courses and activities. Most existing cross-border online collaborations offer students a one-time opportunity to work with students from another country, but do not allow students the opportunity to build stronger networks or richer understanding. Longer-term student engagement through the completion of a series of courses has been shown to support deeper collaborations among learners in a cross-cultural environment (Knight, 2012).

The double degree model ensures that students are full members of the learning cohort at the international partner university, and a blended learning approach supports the development of learning communities by allowing students to meet and study together before moving into online courses as a cohort. The cross-cultural and knowledge benefits of having students from the international partner school participate in the full programme extend to all students in the program, even those not taking the double degree, as the programme cohort gains additional diversity and new perspectives through the inclusion of students living and working in another country. The online double degree partnership allows all programme students to enhance key skills and knowledge such as developing cross-cultural capabilities, recognition of multiple perspectives, global awareness and the ability to work in an international online environment.

One benefit of the blended double degree model is that students have the chance in the first year of the programme at their home school to meet and work with students from the partner university. These students have already completed their courses at their home university and can offer insight and counseling to the partner school students on the content and format of the courses that will be required for the double degree. This interaction provides students important information about the requirements and content of the partner school programme and helps them make an informed choice about whether to participate in the programme and prepare for studies at the partner university if they choose the double degree option.

Second, the blended double degree model helps to overcome technical and cultural challenges cross-border online collaborations often experience. As students complete at least one year of an online programme at the partner school before entering the double degree, they have demonstrated that they can successfully access and utilise the required technology and engage in online learning activities such as discussions, live sessions, teamwork and individual assignments. While RRU and MCI use different learning platforms (Moodle and Sakai), the format of online learning classes is very similar and students have been able to easily transition from one platform and learning environment to another. Students in online learning programmes, especially those for mid-career learners, often experience challenges balancing work, school and family commitments. From the experience of RRU and MCI, students who have successfully completed the first year of their home university programme have been found to be highly committed to online learning and able to successfully address the additional challenges of an international online programme.

In addition to fostering a smooth technical transition, the similarities in the backgrounds and interests of the students in the MGM and MBA programmes helped develop culturally diverse, yet cohesive learning communities. Both programmes attract students with similar backgrounds and interests related to international business, and therefore students are able to relate to one another and share relevant experiences with a peer group. They share English as a common language across programmes, and many have global experience outside their home countries. However, the backgrounds and perspectives of the students differ, creating opportunities for deeper learning and sharing. As is true of most online programmes, the learners in each programme come primarily from the home country of the university. The double degree programme, therefore, brings together students from Europe and North America in a shared learning experience that would not occur within the context of a single university programme.

Third, a significant benefit of the double degree arrangement is that it is sustainable for the institutions and faculty involved because it pairs already existing programmes and does not require the development of new curriculum or special technical and administrative solutions. Students who participate in the double degree programme between MCI and RRU are fully enroled in a programme at each university, ensuring that they have access to the all the online and on-campus resources at each school. Short-term online collaborations, such as joint classes or exercises by students at different universities, are often hard to manage and sustain because they must be organised on a case-by-case basis and students and faculty located at different schools are often unable to access the online systems of the other school. While the MCI-RRU double degree partnership required resources and staff time to develop and implement, once established it was relatively easy to maintain and administer as it required no new courses or programme arrangements. It maintained strong institutional support due to the benefits for students and faculty, and a business case that highlighted the low costs to the institution and the recruitment of additional students into the programmes.

4.4. Conclusion

Online learning has experienced tremendous growth over the past 20 years but has yet to play a significant role in the internationalisation strategies of universities. Online education offerings to date focus primarily on domestic students, and cross-border enrolments in online programmes remain very low. Very few examples exist of online education programs that are designed to support international education and bring together students from different countries in a shared learning experience. New thinking and models are required to expand the role online education might play in fostering global understanding and engagement.

International education programmes, in particular off-campus international learning and study abroad opportunities, have been primarily focused on students enroled full-time in traditional, on-campus educational programmes. Adult and working students have limited opportunities to engage in international education due to time constraints and the lack of appropriate programme offerings, but also represent the largest group of learners participating in online education programmes. Therefore, a special opportunity exists to create programmes that allow adult and working students to access international learning through online education.

Several challenges have limited cross-border enrolments in online programmes, including skepticism of online degrees, administrative and technical hurdles and difficulties integrating students with different learning styles within one programme. While MOOCs and other non-degree courses have attracted cross-border enrolments, online university degree programmes continue to almost exclusively enrol students from the home country of the university. While over time internationally recognised online degree programmes are likely to emerge, in the short-term an easier approach to the development of online degree programmes with an international student body is through the linking of existing online programmes offered by universities in different countries.

This paper highlighted one example of how this might be done using a double degree model, which offers several advantages compared to short-term exchanges or other approaches such as one-time shared classes. While there are unique aspects to the partnership between RRU and MCI and the double degree programme that was developed, the concept presented can be applied in a variety of formats. For example, rather than involving just two schools and two programmes, an online double degree partnership might involve multiple schools and programmes located in different countries. Students would be able to choose to complete a second degree in a country or programme of special interest rather than being limited to only one partner school or programme option. This would lead to a more diverse set of students at any one institution and enhance the aspects of student choice. However, a multiple school consortium approach would also require careful selection and coordination among partner schools to ensure that students from different programmes were compatible, schedules were coordinated and course offerings met academic standards.

Other opportunities also exist outside double degree partnerships to expand international online collaborations. The growing list of online courses create opportunities for students to take specialty courses not offered at their home campus in an online format. While students currently often cross enrol in online courses at other institutions within their home country, they rarely enrol in courses offered by institutions in other countries. Many universities have student exchange agreements with international partner schools, but these agreements are almost always focused on face-to-face exchanges. Partnership agreements and cooperation might be expanded to create new opportunities for students to take online courses at international partner schools. These online course offerings might be paired with exchange opportunities that allow students to meet face to face and build personal bonds, enhancing the international learning potential of the online interactions.

Online learning has great potential to support internationalisation efforts by universities and expand the student population that can engage in global learning. The globalisation of the economy has increased the demand for people who can work effectively in an online, cross-border environment. To date, few university programmes have been explicitly designed to facilitate cross-border engagement by students online, but opportunities exist for universities to continue to develop new online educational offerings that meet the needs of students and society.

References

Allen, I., & Seaman, J. (2013). *Changing course: Ten years of tracking online education in the US.* Babson Park, MA: Babson Survey Research Group.

Altbach, P., Reisberg, L., & Rumbley, L. (2009). *Trends in global higher education: Tracking an academic revolution.* Paris: UNESCO.

CBIE. (2016). *World of Learning: Canadian post-secondary students and the study abroad experience.* Ottawa: Canadian Bureau of International Education.

Chevallier, A. (2013). *A process for screening and authorizing joint and double degree programs.* New York, NY: Institute for International Education.

Corno, F., Lal, R., & Hassouna, S. (2016). Building bridges: Enabling intercultural competences within double degree programs. *Turkish Online Journal of Educational Technology (Special Issue for INTE 2016)*, 398−405.

Council of Graduate Schools. (2010). *Joint degrees, dual degrees and international research collaborations.* Washington, DC.

Culver, S., Puri, I., Spinelli, G., DePauw, K., & Dooley, J. (2012). Collaborative dual-degree programs and value added for students: Lessons learned through the evaluate-e project. *Journal of Studies in International Education*, 16(1), 40−61.

Edwards, J., & Teekens, H. (2012). Leveraging technology and the international classroom for cross-cultural learning. In D. Deardorff, H. de Wit, J. Heyl, & T. Adams, *The Sage Handbook of International Higher Education* (pp. 267−282). Los Angeles, CA: Sage.

European Commission. (2014). *The Erasmus impact study: Effects of mobility on the skills and employability of students and the internationalisation of higher education.* Brussels: European Commission.

Fearon, C., Starr, S., & McLaughlin, H. (2011). Value of blended learning in university and the workplace: Some experiences of university students. *Industrial and Commercial Training*, 446−450.

Gemmel, I., Harrison, R., Clegg, J., & Reed, K. (2015). Internationalisation in online distance learning postgraduate education: A case study on student views on learning alongside students from other countries. *Innovations in Education and Teaching International*, 137−147.

Green, M. F., Marmolejo, F., & Egron-Polak, E. (2012). The Internationalization of higher education: Future prospects. In D. Deardorff, H. de Wit, J. Heyl, & T. Adams, *The Sage Handbook of International Higher Education* (pp. 439−455). Los Angeles, CA: Sage.

Hall, F. (2012). *Best practices regarding international dual/double and joint degrees.* Canadian Association for Graduate Studies.

Helms, R. M. (2014). Mapping international joint and dual degrees: US program profiles and perspectives. *American Council on Education, Center for Internationalization and Global Engagement.* Washington DC: American Council on Education.

Henard, F., Diamond, L., & Roseveare, D. (2012). *Approaches to internationalisation and their implications for strategic management and institutional practice.* Paris: OECD Higher Education Program.

Knight, J. (2011). Doubts and dilemmas with double degree programs. *Revista de Universidad y Sociedad del Conocimiento, 8*(2), 297–312.

Knight, J. (2012). Concepts, rationales, and interpretive frameworks in the internationalization of higher education. In D. Deardorff, H. de Wit, J. Heyl, & T. Adams, *The Sage Handbook of International Higher Education* (pp. 27–42). Los Angeles, CA: Sage.

Knight, J., & Lee, J. (2012). International joint, double and consecutive degree programs. In D. Deardorff, H. de Wit, J. Heyl, & T. Adams, *The SAGE Handbook of International Higher Education* (pp. 343–357). SAGE Publications.

Kuder, M., & Obst, D. (2009). *Joint and double degree programs in the transatlantic context: A survey report.* New York, NY: Institute of International Education.

Leask, B., & Carroll, J. (2011). Moving beyond wishing and hoping: Internationalisation and student experiences of inclusion and engagement. *Higher Education Research & Development*, 647–659.

MCI (2018, September 6). *Website of the Management Center Innsbruck.* Retrieved from https://www.mci.edu/en/

Merola, R. (2017). What does data tell us about cross-border online learning. *International Higher Education*, 21–23.

Merriam, S., & Bierema, L. (2014). *Adult Learning: Linking theory and practice.* San Francisco, CA: John Wiley & Sons.

Neeley, T. (2015, October). Global teams that work. *Harvard Business Review*.

Obst, D., Kuder, M., & Banks, C. (2011). *Joint and double degree programs in an international context: Report on an international survey.* New York, NY: Institute of International Economics.

Online Course Report. (2018, March 8). Online Course Report. Retrieved from www.onlinecoursereport.org/state-of-the-mooc-report/

Ortmans, L. (2018, March 4). UK business school takes top spot in 2018 FT online MBA ranking. *Financial Times*.

Rye, S. A., & Stokken, A. M. (2012). The Implications of the local context in global online education. *The International Review of Research in Open and Distributed Learning*.

Sanderson, G. (2011). Internationalisation and teaching in higher education. *Higher Education Research & Development*, 661–676.

Seaman, J., Allen, I., & Seaman, J. (2018). *Grade increase: Tracking distance education in the United States.* Babson Park, MA: Babson Survey Research Group.

Shirvani, H., Scorza, J., Alkhathian, K., & Garcia, F. L. (2011, November 27). *The Challenges of Global Online Education.* University World News.

Simm, D., & Marvell, A. (2017). Creating global students: Opportunities, challenges and experiences of Internationalizing the geography curriculum in higher education. *Journal of Geography in Higher Education*, 467–474.

Spiro, J. (2014). Learning interconnectedness: Internationalisation through engagement with one another. *Higher Education Quarterly*, 65–84.

Stavredes, S. (2011). *Effective online teaching: Foundations and strategies for student success.* San Francisco, CA: John Wiley & Sons.

Sursock, A. (2016). *Trends 2015: Learning and teaching in European universities.* European University Association.

Tarazona, M. (2013). Influences on the sustainability of joint and double degree programs: Empirical findings from programs with German participation. In M. Kuder, N. Lemmens, & D. Obst, *Global perspectives on international joint and double degree programs.* New York, NY: Institute of International Education.

Ziguras, C. (2018). Will global higher education ever take off? Retrieved from http://www.universityworldnews.com/article.php?story=20180116150633478

PART II
CHANGING CLASSROOM DYNAMICS IN THE DIGITAL TEACHING SPACE

Chapter 5

Engagement in Online Learning: It's Not All About Faculty!

Kathy Bishop, Catherine Etmanski and M. Beth Page

Abstract

In this chapter, we, the authors Bishop, Etmanski and Page, argue for the need to disrupt the traditional notion of faculty solely as expert. We redefine the online faculty role to be that of a facilitator who creates the space for students to engage with both content and other students in the class. We discuss the adult learning principles behind our practices and our attention to building community. To illustrate what our online teaching work looks like in practice, we begin by providing a creative script on what online learning could look like. We then speak to utilising the specific strategies of online forums, behind the scenes outreach, synchronous meetings and assignments to create rich engagement in the online environment for higher education and learning.

We place a strong emphasis on building community among our students from the start of course and throughout. Recognising that people respond differently to different scenarios and have different learning preferences, we seek to offer a diverse range of options for experiencing community, with the intention of offering the possibility of belonging for everyone. The intention to create space for engagement in online learning has challenged us to continually ask ourselves how we can adapt or create new activities and experiences for the online learning environment, so as to enhance engagement.

Keywords: Learning communities; adult learning; constructivism; belonging; omnidirectional mentorship; creativity

5.1. Introduction

Online or blended (online and face-to-face) graduate degrees are becoming increasingly popular options across the globe. As the title of this collection suggests, these distance options not only have the potential to disrupt, but already are disrupting traditional notions of education and learning. Although these distance degrees are increasing in popularity (Christensen & Erying, 2011, p. 8), the attitude that online learning is a lesser alternative to face-to-face classrooms remains part of the common discourse in higher education. This belief may be bolstered by non-credentialed organisations offering non-legitimate credentials via spam email messages. However, we argue that in cases where dedicated educators from verified degree granting Universities (or other institutions of higher education) are involved in teaching, the myth that online learning is a second-class option is no longer valid. Furthermore, we concur that the time is 'ripe for disruption-and innovation' (Christensen & Erying, 2011, p. xix) in online learning.

Drawing primarily from our experiences teaching in various university settings and, in particular, a Canadian Master's of Arts in Leadership programme where we three authors teach, in this chapter we speak to creatively cultivating engagement in online learning environments. In order to do so, we argue for the need to disrupt the traditional notion of faculty solely as expert and redefine the role to be that of a facilitator who creates the space for students to engage with both content and other students in the class. Similarly, Featherman (2014) identified that in this time of disruption, successful universities enable meaningful degrees through focussing on student-centred education (p. 13). Therefore, as faculty, we seek to skillfully raise the quality of student experience through creatively cultivating engagement and community online.

To illustrate what our online teaching work looks like in practice, we begin with an engagement script of a presentation we offered at the Western Association of Management (WAM) conference in March 2016. In this presentation, rather than giving a standard lecture on the topic of engagement in online learning communities, we made a conscious choice to disrupt the traditional notion of a conference presentation in the same way that this book suggests that online learning has disruptive potential. To this end, we created a theatrical sketch (Belliveau, 2006) of an online teaching experience in our virtual classrooms. This script highlights both tips and lessons we have learned about how to engage learners in an online environment, for example through a range of discussion forums, activities that elicit heart-felt responses, the ways in which the instructor responds to the needs of different learners both on the online Learning Management System (in our case, Moodle^{TM}) and behind the scenes through personalised email correspondence. Just as we intentionally disrupted the usual approach to giving conference presentations, we are similarly intentional in our choice to include a script as the introductory part of this chapter. In the same way that online learning can disrupt education and calls upon our creativity for better engaging learners, alternative writing styles can also be powerfully disruptive to the ways in which we understand scholarship. We draw from scholars such as Cynthia Chambers, Erica

Hasebe-Ludt, Carl Leggo and Anita Sinner (2012) who promote creative and/or narrative writing as a way of knowing that 'comes from the body, the heart and the imagination, from having our feet planted in the humus of day-to-day, lived experience' (pp. xxiii–xxiv). This approach also appeals to readers who learn from more expressive ways of knowing, as described by Davis-Manigaulte, Yorks, and Kasl (2006).

Following our engagement script, we discuss the adult learning principles behind our practices and our attention to building community and then speak to utilising the specific strategies of online forums, behind the scenes outreach, synchronous meetings and assignments to create rich engagement in the online environment for higher education and learning. The following is our collective narrative account of our approach to online learning and teaching.

5.2. Engagement Script

5.2.1. Week 1 Online Forum: Welcome/Orientation

Instructor (played by Kathy) *typing into computer:* Welcome to 'Engagement in online learning 101: It's not all about faculty!' It is not all about faculty but faculty do have a critical role to play in cultivating engagement with and between learners in online learning. I am your instructor and I am delighted to be teaching this course and share in this stage of your learning journey. You will notice we have a variety of discussion forums. For example, Our Weekly Posts Forum, Our Learning Community Forum and our Q&A Forum. If you run into a question regarding anything during the course, feel free to first post it to the Q&A Forum. For those who may find online learning challenging, since it is a different way of being and doing, I have pre-scheduled a few Collaborate™ sessions for us to spend some real, face-to-face time dialoguing; albeit in cyberspace!

In this forum, please take a moment and introduce yourself to our community.

> **Student 1** (played by Catherine): Hi everyone. My name is AAA and I'm a student of life and a lifelong learner. I'm delighted to be joining this online course and I look forward to learning with you all.
>
> **Student 2** (played by Beth): My name is BBB. I teach on contract at our local University as associate faculty. I'm interested in belonging. I think learning is easier face-to-face.
>
> **Student 1:** Hi BBB! Great to e-meet you! I love face-to-face learning as well, but this is my fourth course now and I'm getting into the swing of online learning. I hope we can engage in some great conversations throughout the course.
>
> **Student 2:** (*No response, but thinks to herself: "Oh brother, what a keener!"*)

Instructor: Beautiful all! What are some of the benefits of online learning?

Student 1: I love that I can login at any time of the day or night and fit this coursework into my busy schedule.

Student 2: The benefits of online learning are I get on when I can because I do a variety of consulting work. And I love that I can post in my pyjamas.

Learning Community Forum

Instructor: Welcome to the Learning Community. The Learning Community Room is a place to discuss the activities and course assignments. For me, it is another space which creates a real opportunity to grow our learning community. I invite you to consider: How do you want to show up here in your learning? How will you support others in their learning? I am sharing a link to a three min YouTube video:

http://www.youtube.com/watch?v=kZlXWp6vFdE

To me, this video epitomises so many belonging values: inspiration, overcoming obstacles, determination, responding in the moment, servant leadership, support, [...] found in Olympian Derek Redmond's story. This may also give you a glimpse into a bit of how I think and what moves me. What might this video tell you about who I am as an instructor in this course?

Student 1: Wow! What an incredible story. I admit it brought a tear to my eye. The agony on his face was so hard to see. I wonder how the other athletes felt passing him by, seeing that he was in pain, yet needing to stay focused on their own race. Sometimes competition can push us toward our own personal best so there is an opportunity to love our competitors for their role in bringing out the best in us.

Also touching, of course, was the incredible support from his father. Even though he lost the race, I think the crowd witnessed an amazing victory for humanity! I love stories like this that remind us of our capacity as humans to truly support and love one another in our moments of vulnerability as well as our moments of strength. I think this video shows that you will break through security to help me across the finish line, even when I'm struggling!

Student 2: It was a powerful moment of persevering to the finish.

Instructor: Awesome! I love hearing your responses and seeing the different lenses we can view one story from, and love the connections to human capacity and the value of support and persevering. Indeed, I am here in support of your learning and am committed to supporting everyone finishing strong in this course!

I tend to be on online courses daily to see how things are going. If things are going fine, I may just smile and revel in your individual and collective capacities. Alternatively, I may offer thought-provoking questions or coaching suggestions to deepen your learning. I am conscious, though, to allow you the space to grow your learning community rooted in omnidirectional mentorship and support[…]. Enjoy a super day of learning!

Week 2 Online Forum: Learning and Belonging in Community

Instructor: Welcome to this Week's Forum on learning and belonging in community. Please read the assigned readings and make 1 online post and 2 responses to your colleagues around, the question: Why is belonging important in online learning? Note: This is a great opportunity to practice referencing skills for your first assignment. Please be sure to refer to your American Psychological Association (APA) publication manual, sixth edition (2010).

Student 1: Peter Block suggested that community cannot exist without people experiencing a sense of belonging. Moreover, Stallard and Pankau identified that 'people have six psychological needs that they expect will be met in the workplace: respect, recognition, belonging, autonomy, personal growth and meaning' (p. 20). Furthermore, Pearce and Pearce noted that in belonging to a community, people gain an (a) understanding that one's own stories and (b) [realise] the value of remaining in the tension between standing one's own ground and being profoundly open to the other. As a result, the act of belonging is co-created through people sharing their stories and expanding their self-understanding.

Student 2: *thinks to herself, 'Wow! That was articulate! Hmmmm, I don't know what to say[…]' She does not post anything.*

Instructor: Excellent point about belonging! I wonder, what are your thoughts about how this understanding of self – in relationship to other – enables effective online learning? Just a quick note about referencing too. According to APA (2010) authors are cited followed by the year. So correctly you would say, Block (2008) suggested […] and Stallard and Pankau (2008) identified […] and Pearce and Pearce (2003) noted. Make sense?

Instructor continues to look through the course site then says: Hmmm, Student 2 has not been online posting. She's been online but no posts [...] (*Looks at watch – Pauses*[1]) 10 hours, still no post. (*Looks at watch – Pauses*) 20 hours still not online posting. (*Looks at watch – Pauses*) two hours past the deadline. I think I'll drop her a private email. *(Begins typing)*

Dear BBB, I'm just checking in. I have noticed that you have been online, but you have missed the deadline to complete this week's activity. I know that it can sometimes take students time to understand the Course site and also to rearrange their work/life schedule in order to have enough space to engage in the online learning community. So I wanted to check in and see how you are doing? Participation is critical. Sharing your reflections on readings, responding thoughtfully to others posts and participating in building our learning community are all important aspects of online learning. Looking forward to hearing from you.

Student 2: Thanks so much to reaching out via email. To be honest, I'm not sure what to say in response to this week's activity. AAA is so articulate and I feel a little intimidated sharing my ideas in this online forum. When I speak in class I can just go with the flow of ideas, but typing seems so permanent. I feel as though the limitations to my knowledge will be on display for all to read! That said, I signed up for this course so I will muster up some courage and give it a shot.

Instructor: Thanks BBB. I know that it sometimes takes students time to get used to the online learning environment. Many students feel the way you do. I appreciate how you are willing to muster up the courage and give it a shot. I am hunching that you are a deep thinker, and I am interested in what you have to say. Without a doubt, others will too. Perhaps there might be some strategy you could put into place, such as you talking into a tape recorder to let your ideas flow and then transcribe it with the caveat that your ideas are still in process. It is in the dialogue that we can really learn and grow! I encourage you to have fun with this new form and let me know if there's something I can do to support you. See you online!

Student 2 *writing in the online forum:* Hello all, I guess what I've been thinking about this week is that in order to really feel like I belong, I need to feel like people accept me as I am, *warts and all!* I'll take a little risk here and say that I'm really feeling out of my comfort zone in this online learning environment so I'm

---

[1] Note this is staging direction within this performance script to show the passing of time.

feeling quite vulnerable. When I watched that video the instructor posted last week I thought to myself, 'oh no, I don't want to be seen hobbling across the finish line on anyone's shoulder—especially not in front of all these strangers online!' But I guess if I'm going to learn, I need to be willing to fall (metaphorically speaking). Maybe belonging means finding a place where it's OK to fall. P.S. No APA this time, but I'll try again next week!

Instructor *continuing the thread in the online forum*: I appreciate your honesty and openness BBB, and indeed this is a place where it's OK to fall! I love how everyone is showing up, authentically, questioning, wrestling with the content and deeply thinking about belonging. As we wrap up the week, please post an image of what belonging in the community looks like to you.

Student 1: *I'm not sure what the instructor means. I think I'll send her an email.* About this week's Learning community activity, I wondered if it is a personal picture I have or is it one from the internet?

Instructor: Hi AAA. Thanks for your email. Great question! It's your choice, any image you would like. Also, this is a great question to post in our Q&A forum because if you have the question likely others may have it as well. Could you please post it there and I will respond for us all to dialogue on it? Thank you!

Student 2: I love this activity! My image is of a carrot. There's a great quote by Paul Cezanne that says, 'The day is coming when a single carrot, freshly observed, will start off a revolution!' After struggling all week to figure out how to join this conversation, I now feel as though I'm seeing online learning differently and think there might be a place for me to belong here. There's hope for me yet!

Student 1: Thanks for your patience. I was a little uncertain about where to begin this week. Here is a picture of our farewell party for a colleague who had been with the organisation for 10 years. I love this picture because we are all so happy, celebrating this person's next move and honouring how much we are all connected.

Instructor: Excellent work this week. I appreciate AAA's question in our Q&A forum, and such great images on Belonging. Very striking! As Kouzes and Posner noted, 'you can't get extraordinary things done by yourself'. Onwards in our learning journey!

PS. I have been calling you on APA this week, and for a bit of fun, I thought I'd let you call me on it too. Did you notice what one APA mistake I made?

Student 1: *I'll take a stab at this.* Is it that you didn't follow Kouzes and Posner with the year (2012)?

Student 2: And, shouldn't you have included the page number (p. 242) after the quotation marks?

Instructor: *What? Two mistakes? I said I only made one!*

5.3. Online Teaching Principles Demonstrated in the Script

Once the role-playing aspect of our Western Academy of Management (WAM) conference presentation was over, we debriefed with the audience for deeper dialogue around the topic of engagement in online learning communities. We asked them which strategies were modelled through the script, what they learned and what other strategies they themselves use. The debrief questions centred on strategies for co-creating community and engagement for both students and faculty.

During this dialogue, we drew upon our individual and collective experiences teaching in different University settings and in particular, in the Master's of Arts in Leadership programme at Royal Roads University (RRU). In 2016, the School of Leadership Studies in which we work celebrated its 20th year of offering leadership degrees for professional adult learners in a blended format (which combines face-to-face and online learning). Created as a special purpose University for working professionals, RRU primarily offers two-year graduate degrees that include at least two on-campus learning experiences (typically one to three weeks in length) with the remainder of the learning happening online. Having refined its learning and teaching model over the past two decades, scholars at RRU have now identified several principles that underpin the success of this model (Grundy et al., 2016; Royal Roads University, 2013). These include, but are not limited to creating learning communities (i.e., students stay together as a cohort to support one another through a whole programme) and fostering engaged learning (i.e., employing learning techniques that require the active participation of students) (Royal Roads University, 2013, p. 15). In addition, this learning and teaching model recognises that adult learners bring a wealth of knowledge and experience to the classroom and therefore applies constructivist notions to co-create knowledge between and among faculty, learners, concepts and theories.

Because the programme in which we teach is blended, members of the audience during this conference presentation raised important questions about whether or not a sense of engagement and belonging to community was possible in a strictly online setting. Since all three of us have taught in online-only classes, we do indeed believe that it can along with other scholars (Austin, 2013; Luppicini, 2007). Underpinning our belief in cultivating engagement in online learning is the desire to disrupt the traditional notion of faculty as expert as advocated by Freire (2005) and redefining the role to be that of a facilitator who creates the space for students to engage with both content and other students in the class. We will now showcase examples of how these ideas are put into practice and demonstrate successful strategies for cultivating engagement. We begin by discussing the adult learning principles behind our practices and our attention to building community and then speak to utilising the specific strategies of online forums, behind the scenes outreach via email, synchronous meetings and assignments (individual and team) to create rich engagement in the online environment for higher education and learning.

5.3.1. Applying Adult Learning Principles

Students frequently come into the online classroom environment with notions of learning based on a more traditional, top-down, teacher-centred model of education, (i.e., Freire's infamous 'banking model'; see Freire, 2005). However, they quickly find that our classrooms, involving adult learning principles and experiential group processes, create bonds among student colleagues and enable them to engage more deeply with the material and one another. From our experience, successful online classrooms are rooted in the principles of andragogy. Specifically, Malcolm Knowles (1970) introduced the European term andragogy in 1968 as adult educators focussed their attention on theory building and learning for adult education, which was a field in the process of differentiating itself from the theory associated with how children learn. According to Merriam (2001), several principles underpin andragogy which includes someone who: can direct their own learning; comes with life experience and learning needs; is seeking immediate application of their learning; and is motivated from their own internal source. As a result, we seek out ways to enable personally meaningful application within the classroom.

We have found that constructing online learning activities according to Kolb's (1984) experiential model of learning is a way to engage students in personally meaningful ways. Course activities are designed to address all four components of Kolb's experiential learning cycle, namely, concrete experience, reflective observation, abstract conceptualization and active experimentation. Students are asked to consider a particular experience, reflect on it by discussing their thoughts and feelings, draw connections to theory, and, put new behaviours into practice and report on their experience. Therefore, in addition to requiring students to read and apply theories, we also require them to actively learn from their experiences throughout the course, which enables them to engage deeper with the course materials.

Furthermore, as adult educators, we are always seeking to find new and innovative means to engage learners. There are five major ways of making meaning: through number, word, image, gesture and sound (Norris, 2000, p. 40). In education, we tend to privilege word, whereas in the arts, image, gesture and sound are recognised as different ways of coming to understand and know the world. Therefore, wherever possible, we tend to blend in creative and/or arts-based practices into the online environment. Arts-based practices are not simply for engaging in artistic processes but are also different ways of knowing that we can draw upon to engage learners. We might suggest activities that incorporate music, photographs, poetry or drawings. Symbolism is utilised to elicit meaning and engage learners in rich conversations. We start with the symbol and elicit meaning that way, rather than starting with the written word alone (e.g., an article or book) to generate meaning.

5.3.2. Building Community

In addition to creating a personally meaningful learning environment as a way to engage students, we also recognise the importance of building community as a way to engage students. As two of us have discussed in a previously published chapter (see Page, Etmanski, & Agger-Gupta, 2016, pp. 159–160), in the existing literature, the concepts of Communities of Learning (CoL) and Communities of Practice (CoP) are frequently conflated. Although CoLs are at times narrowly defined in the educational literature specifically 'as a formal cross-disciplinary approach, involving the restructuring of the curriculum to enhance active, collaborative learning' (Wastawy, Uth, & Stewart, 2004, p. 333), they are typically associated more generally with the sharing and co-creation of knowledge. Likewise, the concept of a CoP is typically associated with Wenger's (1998) work (see also, Lave & Wenger, 1991; Wenger, 2000; Wenger & Snyder, 2000). Described as "groups of people informally bound together by shared expertise and passion for a joint enterprise" (Wenger & Snyder, 2000, p. 139), CoPs have become part of organisational and educational discourse for the past two decades.

The concept of CoP has become more nuanced over the years as new technologies have emerged and the body of related literature has expanded. However, in his original association of *community* with the idea of *practice*, Wenger (1998) claimed that the association of these two words 'yields a more tractable characterisation of the concept of practice – in particular, by distinguishing it from less tractable terms like culture, activity, or structure [and] […] defines a special type of community – a community of practice' (p. 72). Wenger went on to assert that the three characteristics of CoPs were mutual engagement (i.e., people doing things together in the midst of complexity and diversity), a joint enterprise (i.e., in the context of heterogeneity, mutual responsibility and diverse interpretations) and a shared repertoire (i.e., of stories, artifacts, historical events, concepts, and discourses) (pp. 73–85). Moreover, Hydle, Kvalshaugen, and Breunig (2014) have added to Wenger's original conception to assert that 'a view of CoP that extends beyond the local understanding to consider relational ties in terms of spatial and relational proximity is needed' (p. 610). In other words, the more traditional understanding of community as only comprising a place-based group of people has evolved and communities are now understood to exist in virtual settings as well. As such, the Learning Communities (both CoL and CoP) we discuss in this section extend beyond place-based communities of more typical, localised classrooms and into the online setting.

The Learning Communities we seek to create are rooted in omnidirectional mentorship (Clapp, 2010). Omnidirectional mentorship can be thoughtfully introduced to students so that they realise that they can learn with and from each other as well as the faculty. Furthermore, this can create a stronger sense of belonging in the classroom. We recognise that people learn better and engage more when they feel that they belong. As Block (2008) suggested, community cannot exist without people experiencing a sense of belonging. For this reason, we continue to place a strong emphasis on building community among our students from the start of the course and throughout. Recognising that people respond differently to different scenarios and have different learning preferences (Kolb, 1984), we seek to offer a diverse range of options for experiencing community, with the intention of offering the possibility of belonging for everyone.

5.3.3. Strategies for Engagement

In the opening script above, we demonstrated several strategies for facilitating online engagement, namely through online Forums and behind the scene outreaches. In addition to expanding on these strategies, we will also elaborate on synchronous meetings, and course assignments (individual and team).

Online Forums

We highlighted three key forums in our script: weekly forum, learning community and Question and Answer (Q&A).

5.3.3.1. Weekly Forum

Within the first week, we immediately set our role with some type of activity or video which engages learners and demonstrates that in this classroom environment we will be learning from one another and that students need to step up to contribute to make it a personally meaningful experience for all. For one of the authors, Beth, when onboarding people into the course, whether a brand new course or into a pre-existing class, she asks students 'what is the contribution that you are making to our new community to create an inclusive learning environment?' Also at the beginning of a course, we might extend individual welcomes to each student, connecting some element of their introductory post to something we have experienced or something that they have suggested that relates to the learning. This strategy allows us to connect individually with each student and models the way for others to see how they might show up in community. Other strategies that we employ include, posing a curious question that will deepen or further dialogue. In another author, Catherine's online courses, she will often assign students the role of facilitator for the week. This means that students themselves (individually or in pairs or small groups) will be responsible for facilitating the discussion around the week's assigned readings. She often asks them to engage their fellow students in a creative way and this has opened the door to all kinds of possibilities. For example, in their role as weekly facilitators, students have asked their colleagues to post a photograph or come up with a tweet that summarises the article assigned to that week. Sometimes students have used a word cloud generating online tool called, Wordl^{TM} (see: http://www.wordle.net/) to summarise the week's discussions. Regardless of the strategy they use to engage their classmates, the very fact that the conversation has been designed by their classmates creates a sense of accountability to one another and a desire to participate in others' activities so that others will likewise participate in theirs when the time comes.

5.3.3.2. Learning Community Forum

Participation in this particular forum is not mandatory, and acts as a communal space for the class to connect and continue to engage with and among one another in an informal way, thus, fostering further means to engage and co-create community. Students can utilise it to discuss the activities and course assignments, and/or explore different ideas above and beyond course material. As identified in the script included at the outset of this chapter, the author Kathy has used it as a place to speak to her role as an online instructor through posting the Redmond video (URL included above as part of the script). Often after hearing different people's perspectives, she will identify some of the common themes among the students. She will also reiterate her role to create a space for learners to run with the course material and that she will be on the sidelines watching and waiting to offer support and guidance and cheering them on. In the past, the author, Beth, has invited students to adopt a 30-day challenge related to some aspect of the course. We have witnessed students offer a variety of resources, such as TED Talks^{TM} (a free speaker series where videos of short, powerful speeches are posted online; for more information, see: https://www.ted.com/talks), relevant websites or literature, along with quotes of encouragement, cartoons to offer humour and invitations to post pictures of their favourite workspaces, personal adventures or family fun.

5.3.3.3. Q&A Forum

The power of this forum is that students feel they have access to the faculty member as the need arises. Often students will complain that a faculty member is not online and so this is a way to ensure that their needs are met. More often though than not, another student has the answer and responds in the forum before the faculty member. Often students express that they were glad someone posted the question as they had wondered about the same thing and no longer feel alone.

5.3.3.4. Behind the Scenes Outreach

As shown in the vignette above, we email students behind the scenes. In the first week of a programme launch, a check in email will be sent to students who have not shown up online, to reinforce the value of participation and contribution and to offer support if the student is struggling. We do not offer the possibility that anyone will be an outlier. We make sure to round everyone up, and do so sooner than later. If students are not online every few days, we email. If students miss a deadline, we send a personal email checking in. Essentially, the thread of being in community and belonging gets pulled through everything we do.

5.3.3.5. Synchronous Meetings (Formal and Informal)

Technology, such as Collaborate™, Skype™ and Zoom™, allows students to connect virtually through both formal and informal means. Both formal and informal methods are necessary to operate successfully as an organisation (Hydle et al., 2014, p. 620). We as faculty organise virtual synchronous sessions at strategic points, but we also leave our course site Collaborate™ rooms open so students can self-organise as well. For example, we tend to set a synchronous session in the first two weeks of a course to have a virtual face-to-face with the class as a way to get to know one another, go over the course expectations or assignments, and answer any questions that students might have. With the open Collaborate™ rooms, we have witnessed students at their discretion booking informal synchronous check-ins throughout the online portion of their coursework. Catherine once coined this kind of a check-in call as 'a Collaborate Wine and Cheese', which students enjoyed and the term stuck (informal). As well, one of our colleagues sets up an Open Space dialogue, which allows students to experiment and go into different rooms, depending on their topic of interest. Finally, in many online courses, we encourage a synchronous meeting where students can celebrate their learning and completion of the course.

5.3.3.6. Assignments (Individual and Team)

Online there is also the opportunity to build of engagement through assignments both on an individual level and as a team. Similar to the example of author Catherine's example above who assigns students to be weekly facilitators, author, Kathy, builds engagement by requiring learners to implement a student-led seminar as one of the course assignments. For this assignment, each student is expected to lead one asynchronous seminar, by offering a one-page synopsis of a selected topic from a particular textbook and engaging the class in whatever creative means to engage in dialogue (e.g., video, presentation, sound bite, creative questioning). Upon completing the seminar, each student is expected to submit a two-page reflective paper summarising the key learnings resulting from her/his seminar presentation and the class dialogue. Thus, although an individual assignment it requires engagement with other students. Likewise, we build in peer review as part of individual assignments. We ask students to post a draft of their assignments and engage in a discussion with learning partners or triads where they are to pose curious questions and give substantive feedforward (Goldsmith, 2002) to deepen their own learning and that of others. After they engage in this process, they polish and submit their final assignment to faculty for review.

Another way of creating more structured engagement is through setting team assignments. Team assignments are created to offer the opportunity for learners to engage with others, either in partners or small groups. A variety of different technological tools can be built into the team assignments as a way to foster different ways to engage with others. For example, a team assignment can be set up for groups to put together an annotated bibliography by using a Wiki™, which is a tool that can be added to the online Learning Management System similar to a Google Doc™, which everyone can edit.

5.4. Conclusion

In conclusion, our online students have benefitted from our intentional disruption of the traditional view of faculty as an expert. This intention to create space for engagement in online learning has challenged us to continually ask ourselves how we can adapt or create new activities and experiences for the online learning environment, so as to enhance engagement. In this chapter, we contended that engagement in online learning is about how educators create a space for learners to engage with one another by cultivating engaged learning and communities of learning. Grounded in adult learning theory principles and drawing primarily, but not exclusively, from our experiences teaching in a variety of university settings we shared case study examples and strategies for engagement—namely through online forums, behind the scene outreaches, synchronous meetings and assignments. This chapter promotes the possibility that online learning has the potential to disrupt traditional educational approaches through creatively cultivating engagement online and building community. In doing so, online learning may continue to grow and thrive as a viable alternative mainstream option for education in the twenty-first century.

References

American Psychological Association. (2010). *APA publication manual of the American Psychological Association* (6th ed.). Washington, DC: APA.

Austin, R. (2013). *Online learning and community cohesion: Linking schools.* Routledge research in education, 98. New York, NY: Routledge.

Belliveau, G. (2006). Collective playbuilding: Using arts-based research to understand a social justice drama process in teacher education. *International Journal of Education & the Arts*, 7(5), 1–16. Retrieved from http://ijea.org/v7n5/index.html

Block, P. (2008). *Community: The structure of belonging.* San Francisco, CA: Berrett-Koehler.

Chambers, C., Hasebe-Ludt, E. Leggo, C., & Sinner, A. (Eds.), (2012). *A heart of wisdom: Life writing as empathetic inquiry.* New York, NY: Peter Lang.

Christensen, C., & Eyring, H. (2011). *The innovative university: Changing the DNA of higher education from the inside out.* San Francisco, CA: Jossey-Bass.

Clapp, E. P. (2010). Omni-directional mentorship: Exploring a new approach to inter-generational knowledge-sharing in arts practice and administration. In D. D. Schott (Ed.), *Leading creatively: A closer look 2010* (pp. 66–69). San Francisco, CA: The National Alliance for Media, Arts, and Culture. Retrieved from http://namac.org/sites/default/files/images_upload/NAMAC-Leading_Creatively.pdf

Davis-Manigaulte, J., Yorks, L., & Kasl, E. (2006). Expressive ways of knowing and transformative learning. *New Directions for Adult and Continuing Education, 109*, 27–35.

Featherman, S. (2014). *Higher education at risk: strategies to improve outcomes, reduce tuition, and stay competitive in a disruptive environment.* Sterling, VA: Stylus Publishing.

Freire, P. (2005). *Pedagogy of the oppressed (30th anniversary edition).* New York, NY: Continuum. (Original work published 1968).

Goldsmith, M. (2002). Try feedforward instead of feedback. *Leader to Leader, 25*(Summer), 11–14.

Grundy, S. L., Hamilton, D., Veletsianos, G., Agger-Gupta, N., Márquez, P., Forssman, V., & Legault, M. (Eds.). (2016). *Engaging students in life-changing learning: Royal Roads University's learning and teaching model in practice.* Victoria, BC: Royal Roads University.

Hydle, K. M., Kvalshaugen, R., & Breunig, J. K. (2014). Transnational practices in communities of task and communities of learning. *Management Learning, 45*(5), 609–629. doi:10.1177/1350507613500881

Knowles, M. S. (1970). The modern practice of adult education: Andragogy vs. pedagogy. *New Directions for Adult and Continuing Education, 89, Spring 2001.* San Francisco, CA: Jossey Bass.

Kolb, D. A. (1984). *Experiential Learning: experience as the source of learning and development.* Upper Saddle River, NJ: Prentice-Hall.

Kouzes, J., & Posner, B. (2012). *The leadership challenge: How to make extraordinary things happen in organizations.* (5th ed.). San Francisco, CA: Jossey-Bass.

Lave, J., & Wenger, E. (1991). *Situated learning: Legitimate peripheral participation.* Cambridge: Cambridge University Press.

Luppicini, R. (2007). *Online learning communities.* Charlotte, NC: IAP.

Merriam, S. B. (2001). Andragogy and self-directed learning: Pillars of adult learning theory. In S. B. Merriam (Ed.), *The new update on adult learning theory* (pp. 3–22). San Francisco, NC: Jossey-Boss.

Norris, J. (2000). Drama as research: Realizing the potential of drama in education as a research methodology. *Youth Theatre Journal, 14*(1), 40–51.

Page, M. B., Etmanski, C., & Agger-Gupta, N. (2016). Cultivating belonging: Living leadership in communities of learning. In, S. L. Grundy et al. (Eds.), *Engaging students in life-changing learning: Royal Roads University's learning and teaching model in practice* (pp. 154–173). Victoria, BC: Royal Roads University.

Pearce, W. B., & Pearce, K. A. (2003). Taking a communication perspective on dialogue. In R. Anderson, L. A. Baxter, K. N., & Cissna (Eds.), *Dialogue: Theorizing difference in communication studies* (pp. 39–56). Thousand Oaks, CA: SAGE. Retrieved from http://www.pearceassociates.com/essays/comm_perspective.htm

Royal Roads University. (2013). *Learning and teaching model.* Victoria, BC. Retrieved from http://media.royalroads.ca/media/marketing/viewbooks/2013/learning-model/

Stallard, M. L., & Pankau, J. (2008). Strengthening human value in organizational cultures. *Leader to Leader, Winter*, 18–23.

Wastawy, S. F., Uth, C. W., & Stewart, C. (2004). Learning communities: An investigative study into their impact on library services. *Science & Technology Libraries, 24*(3/4), 327–374.

Wenger, E. (1998). *Communities of practice: Learning, meaning and identity*. Cambridge: Cambridge University Press.
Wenger, E. (2000). Communities of practice and social learning systems. *Organization, 7*(2), 225–246.
Wenger, E., & Snyder, W. (2000). Communities of practice: The organizational frontier. *Harvard Business Review*, 139–145.

Chapter 6

Social Collaborative Learning Environments: A Means to Reconceptualise Leadership Education for Tomorrow's Leaders and Universities?

Anja P. Schmitz and Jan Foelsing

Abstract

During the past decade, fast-paced changes created a new environment organisations need to adapt to in an agile way. To support their transformation, organisations are rethinking their approach to learning. They are moving away from traditional instructor-centred, standardised classroom-based learning settings. Instead, learning needs to be tailored to the individuals' needs, available anywhere at any time and needs to enable learners to build their network. The development of digital tools, specifically network technology and social collaboration platforms, has enabled these new learning concepts.

The use of these new learning concepts in organisations also has implications for higher education. The present case study, therefore, investigates how universities can best prepare future employees and leaders for these new working environments, both on a content level and a methodological level. It also investigates if these new learning concepts can support universities in dealing with a changing environment.

The investigated case is a traditional face-to-face leadership lecture for a heterogeneous group of students. It was reconceptualised as a personalised and social collaborative learning setting, delivered through a social collaboration platform as the primary learning environment. Initial evaluation results indicate positive motivational effects, experience sharing and changes in perception of the student – lecturer relationship. The findings also supported previous challenges of computer-supported collaborative learning settings, such as the perception of a higher cognitive load. The implications of these results for the future teaching and business models of higher education are discussed. In addition, the potential of these computer-supported social collaborative learning settings is outlined.

Keywords: Social collaboration; collaborative learning; leadership; disruption of higher education; social learning; social enterprise network

6.1. Introduction

During the last decades, globalisation, economic turmoil, the transformation in technology and digitalisation led to unpredictable changes as well as disruption in many industries (Bennett & Lemoine, 2014; Christensen, 1997). Additionally, organisations are facing a new internal environment due to demographic changes. Employees' values are shifting (Myers & Sadaghiani, 2010) and they have new expectations, for example concerning the provided tools and technologies (Wehner, Ritter, & Leist, 2017). In order to remain competitive, organisations need to adapt to these external and internal challenges (Lawrence & Lorsch, 1967). The ability to continuously adapt to complex, turbulent and, unpredictable environments has been termed organisational agility (Goldman, Nagel, & Preiss, 1995). Agility can only be achieved if an organisation's strategy, culture, processes, structure and competencies are set up to anticipate change, continuously learn as an organisation and provide the resulting knowledge to all of its members (Dove, 1999; Fischer & Häusling, 2018; Robertson, 2016): Agile organisations are striving for fast processes with a clear focus on customer value. They have flatter hierarchies, are organised in (digital) network-structures and focus their culture on sharing information, collaboration and high levels of self-organisation. Leadership focuses on empowering employees and is shared between different people (Amundsen & Martinsen, 2014; Pearce, Conger, & Locke, 2008).

This transformation towards agility also influences organisations' approach to learning and development (Bersin, 2017; Wehner et al., 2017). They are moving away from traditional instructor-centred, standardised classroom-based learning settings. Instead, they are looking for new learning concepts in which learning is collaborative, can be tailored to the individuals' needs, incorporates informal elements, is integrated into work-processes, can take place anywhere at any time and enables learners to interact with others to build their network. This new approach to learning was both, influenced and enabled by technological developments: Network technology and web 2.0 applications. They drove the implementation of Enterprise Social Media or Networks as well as Social Collaboration Platforms (SCPs) (Chui et al., 2012; Kane, 2015; Wehner et al., 2017).

These changes in the global business world also have implications for higher education. The adoption of new technology and learning concepts by companies challenges traditional instructor-centred, standardised, classroom-based learning settings in universities. Additionally, traditional universities are already starting to feel competitive pressure from online educational offers. These developments hold disruptive power for the processes, products and business model of traditional universities (Christensen & Eyring, 2011).

Taken together, the changes in the business world and in higher education, lead to two questions:

(1) How can universities best prepare future employees and leaders for the new working environments, both on a content level and a methodological level?
(2) How can universities adjust their offers and business model to respond to the posed challenges?

This chapter explores these two questions through the case of a reconceptualised traditional lecture-based learning setting: an introductory leadership class for bachelor students. In regards to the first question, the class was reconceptualised to provide a personalised, social collaborative learning setting that seeks to better prepare students for a global work environment from a content and methodological perspective. The content was adapted to include leadership topics related to leading in a global context. On the methodological level, the course was delivered through a SCP as the primary learning environment and included personalised elements. This aimed at fostering students' experience and methodological skills in using new tools because previous research has shown that learners need time to adapt to new learning settings and technologies (Bielaczyc, 2013; Hmelo-Silver, Nagarajan, & Derry, 2006). In regards to the second question, the reconceptualisation was used to explore the potential of social collaborative learning settings as a possible response to the challenges traditional universities are facing.

The chapter first provides a brief overview of the literature, focusing on personalised learning as well as collaborative learning enabled through SCPs. Second, it presents the case of a traditional leadership lecture that was redesigned to incorporate personalised learning and social collaboration. Third, it concludes by discussing the findings of the case study in regards to their potential for preparing students for the workplace and their implications for higher education.

6.2. Background: Learning Beyond Standardised Lecture-based Instruction

Lectures are still frequently used in higher education and the advantages, as well as disadvantages of traditional classroom-based instruction, have been described in depth (Schneider & Preckel, 2017). The following paragraphs thus only give a brief overview of two learning formats beyond standardised lectures, namely differentiated instruction and personalised learning as well as social collaborative learning.

6.2.1. Differentiated Instruction and Personalised Learning

In today's business context, organisations are looking for ways to motivate employees to learn but also want to decrease the time needed for training. One approach to achieve this is tailoring training more specifically to the needs of the respective learner instead of providing the same standard training to all learners.

From an educational perspective, these goals are mirrored in concepts of differentiated instruction and personalised learning (Subban, 2006). Differentiated instruction has been defined as "using strategies that address student strengths, interest, skills, and readiness in flexible learning environments" (Hoover & Patton, 2005, p. 232). Learners are provided with different learning options that can be differentiated on the dimensions of the learning process, content and product. By accommodating the differences in the learners' readiness levels, interests and learning profiles, differentiated instruction seeks to improve student motivation and learning (Tomlinson, 2005, 2014). Its positive effects have been demonstrated in numerous studies (Subban, 2006; Tullis & Benjamin, 2011).

In a similar vein, personalised learning has been defined as learning that is paced to learning needs and tailored more specifically to the learner's individual goals and interests (Alli, Rajan, & Ratliff, 2016; Campbell, Robinson, Neelands, Hewston, & Mazzoli, 2007). Whereas differentiated instruction focuses on the instructor's tasks, personalised learning focuses more on the learner's perspective, as well as his empowerment and self-regulation to drive his own learning (see Bray & McClaskey, 2013 for a detailed discussion).

Personalised learning regained attention as new technology became available to support learning (Dwi & Basuki, 2012; Shaw, Larson, & Sibdari, 2014). One specific method of adapting learning to students' needs and preferences are *learning paths*, in most cases provided through some form of digital courseware (Dwi & Basuki, 2012; Shaw et al., 2014). Learning paths are composed of a specific sequence of the course material. They have been defined as 'flexible groups of content topics that move a learner towards his or her learning [goal].' (Shaw et al., 2014, p. 1192). The paths can contain any type of learning material, such as texts, case studies, videos, etc. (Shaw et al., 2014). In their simplest form, the paths are pre-defined by domain-experts and students can select between different paths based on their preferences (Shaw et al., 2014). In more advanced forms, the sequences are also adaptive to the learner's knowledge level based on the analysis of test results (Dwi & Basuki, 2012). Through the use of web-based learning systems, learner variables can be used as the basis for adaptive learning paths, such as learner behaviour, cognitive traits or styles (e.g., Chen, Huang, Shih, & Chang, 2016; Dwi & Basuki, 2012; Tseng, Chu, Hwang, & Tsai, 2008). Furthermore, personal recommendations can be included based on data collected from previous learners (Shaw et al., 2014).

In addition to tailoring learning to the individual, many concepts of differentiated instruction or personalised learning also emphasise the importance of social processes (Subban, 2006). The following chapter gives a brief overview of collaborative learning and SCPs as the technology supporting it.

6.2.2. Collaborative Learning Enabled Through Social Collaboration Platforms as the Primary Learning Environment

6.2.2.1. Collaborative Learning

Social interaction plays an important role in the development of cognition and many approaches to teaching and learning have been developed to promote social interaction (Bandura, 1977; Lave, 1991; Vygotsky, 1978). Collaborative learning refers to those social interaction processes in which two or more learners actively work together towards a shared learning goal and engage in a process of co-construction (Dillenbourg, 1999). Furthermore, learners provide new knowledge for each other, give feedback, support each other's engagement while also assuming responsibility for their own learning process (Barron, 2003; Walker, Rummel, & Koedinger, 2011).

Many studies indicate the effectiveness of collaborative learning, but also document the challenges related to it (Nokes-Malach, Richey, & Gadgil, 2015; Pai, Sears, & Maeda, 2015; Schneider & Preckel, 2017; Slavin, 1983; Springer, Stanne, & Donovan, 1999). Based on these findings, the respective literature identified a large set of elements that need to be considered when designing collaborative learning settings. Among the most important ones are the following elements: Collaborative tasks need to be complex as well as structured in a way that allows for productive interaction (Cohen, 1994) and an active role of the learner (P. A. Kirschner, 2001; F. Kirschner, Paas, & Kirschner, 2009). Examples are the identification and negotiation of multiple perspectives, including comparing and contrasting results (Akkerman & Bakker, 2011; Jeong & Hmelo-Silver, 2016). Collaboration is specifically beneficial when learners need to access resources of other group members to solve the task, e.g. different knowledge domains (Park, Jeong, Jang, Yoon, & Lim, 2018). Accessing these resources enables learners to explore others' ideas, gain a more complete understanding of the problem and enhances co-construction and critical thinking (Garrison, Anderson, & Archer, 2001; Jeong & Hmelo-Silver, 2016). However, effective and efficient collaboration not only requires different design elements but also different skills and behaviours from learners, such as self-regulation, monitoring and planning skills, initiating and engaging in discussions, giving and seeking feedback (P. A. Kirschner & Erkens, 2013). Although learners may vary in their competence and preference to engage in these behaviours (Barron, 2003), co-construction can be supported by suitable socio-cultural norms and educational contexts (Jeong & Hmelo-Silver, 2016). These norms need to encourage learner empowerment and agency, as well as self-directed learning, critical thinking, the appreciation of different perspectives and a non-threatening feedback-culture based on learning goal-orientation instead of performance goal-orientation (Dweck & Leggett, 1988; Rougas et al., 2015; Tan, Au, Cooper-Thomas, & Aw, 2016). Another important element is the role of the instructor. In collaborative learning contexts, his role changes from being primarily a domain expert to becoming a facilitator of the learning process. The learning process thus becomes a shared experience for both, students and instructors (P. A. Kirschner, 2001).

6.2.2.2. Social Collaboration Platforms

During the last years, new technologies have been developed that focus on enabling social collaboration and on strengthening social connection (Antonius, Xu, & Gao, 2015; Kaplan & Haenlein, 2010; Wehner et al., 2017). They are based on network technology or Web 2.0 platforms and have been researched under different names: Enterprise Social Media, Enterprise Social Networks (Wehner et al., 2017) or *social collaboration platforms (SCP)* (McAfee, 2006). Generally, they contain combinations of social technologies to enable collaboration. Among them are features such as wikis, discussion boards, threaded discussions that support many-to-many communication, chats, as well as distributed communication without direct communication (Wehner et al., 2017). The latter feature lets learners interact via artefacts they create, such as reviews or comments on their work (Antonius et al., 2015; Jeong & Hmelo-Silver, 2016). They have been developed primarily for the purpose of supporting cooperative work but became more and more used in learning contexts, either as stand-alone solutions or as an integral part of larger solutions, such as Human Capital Management systems. Especially in the latter case, they have been included with a learning focus to enhance traditional learning management systems (Bersin, 2017).

In the wake of these technological innovations, collaborative learning regained attention in the business context as well as the educational context. Supported by respective technology, it has been termed *computer-supported collaborative learning (CSCL)* (Stahl, Koschmann, & Suthers, 2014). When computers serve as communication tools collaborative learning is not restricted anymore to physically present small groups but can be extended towards larger learning communities, even on a mass scale (Cress, Moskaliuk, & Jeong, 2016; C. M. Johnson, 2001). These features allow it to be employed in international learning contexts and to take place anytime and anywhere, which added to its widespread use in the business context (Roschelle, 2013).

6.2.2.3. Core Affordances of Social Collaboration Platforms for Collaborative Learning

Providing learners with (new) technology is not sufficient to foster student engagement and learning or to provide an improved learning experience (Prieto, Villagrá-Sobrino, Jorrín-Abellán, Martínez-Monés, & Dimitriadis, 2011). Jeong and Hmelo-Silver (2016) therefore developed a framework of how technology can be used to support collaborative learning. They identified seven opportunities, or core affordances, of technology. These are summarised in the following paragraphs with a focus on those affordances that are relevant for SCPs.

Collaborative tasks: In SCPs learners can easily be provided with joint tasks as well as tools and materials to work on these tasks. The tasks should contain components that need to be worked on together to offer opportunities for checking differences in assumptions and perspectives as well as for developing shared meaning (Jeong & Hmelo-Silver, 2016; Suthers, 2006). The materials may include shared databases, videos, simulations and other multimedia content (e.g., Sinha, Rogat, Adams-Wiggins, & Hmelo-Silver, 2015). When developing these joint tasks, the additional cognitive load created by the use of (new) technology needs to be taken into consideration and the tasks need to be aligned with the overarching learning goals. Furthermore, students need to be aware of why they are using the technology (Jeong & Hmelo-Silver, 2016).

Communication: One of the great advantages of SCPs is their support of two-way communication between a large number of distributed learners through different tools (e.g. chats, message boards, communication streams). Learners can choose their preferred tool for both, synchronous as well as asynchronous communication (Jeong & Hmelo-Silver, 2012, 2016). In addition to making learners more flexible in their communication, asynchronous communication has also been shown to support learners' (self-)reflection (Baker, Andriessen, Lund, van Amelsvoort, & Quignard, 2007).

Sharing resources: SCPs support learners in accessing others' resources for solving tasks by providing a virtual space and the appropriate sub-structures in this space (Jeong & Hmelo-Silver, 2016). However, learners might lack the skills and/or motivation to share information and collaborate (Cress, Barquero, Schwan, & Hesse, 2007; Jeong & Hmelo-Silver, 2016). Encouraging learners to share resources also requires social support, reinforcement and incentives (Kreijns, Kirschner, & Jochems, 2003).

Structuring productive collaborative learning processes: SCPs provide various opportunities for structuring collaboration processes. Online interfaces can, for example, be used to provide collaboration scripts. These scripts can instruct effective collaboration behaviours, such as forming groups and choosing communication modes (O'Donnell & O'Kelly, 1994). Structuring collaboration is more important in computer-supported learning settings than in face-to-face settings. First of all, because learners are likely to have less experience in distributed collaboration. Second, because there might be higher coordination and communication hurdles (Jeong & Hmelo-Silver, 2016). The level of structure should be personalised, that is, adapted to the learners' skill and motivational levels. Both under- and overregulation will have detrimental effects on the learning outcomes, e.g. on the development of learners' self-regulation skills (Jeong & Hmelo-Silver, 2016; Shaw et al., 2014).

Facilitating co-construction: Co-constructive processes enable learners to synthesise information from different group members so that they can develop new knowledge and meaning (Jeong & Hmelo-Silver, 2016). The use of SCPs can facilitate co-construction through the provision of different technological features, such as discussion boards, communication threads or joint workspaces. However, co-constructive processes require social and cognitive skills (Nokes-Malach et al., 2015) and thus need to be supported beyond the provision of tools (Stahl et al., 2014). Rewarding group output as well as individual output, establishing norms of social interaction or asking to build on each other's contributions can be used to support co-construction (D. W. Johnson & Johnson, 1999; P. A. Kirschner, Beers, Boshuizen, & Gijselaers, 2008). Constructivist elements, such as scaffolding and reflection, might also be appropriate to promote meaningful learning experiences but further research is warranted (Cress et al., 2016; Jonassen, 1994).

Monitoring and regulation of collaborative learning: Self-regulation and monitoring demands on learners are higher in CSCL settings than in face-to-face settings (Järvelä & Hadwin, 2013; Lajoie & Lu, 2012). They are increasing with task complexity and group size as well as with asynchronous communication and the number of available communication channels (Jeong & Hmelo-Silver, 2016). SCPs can help to empower learners and support the development of their meta-cognitive skills by providing them access to selected monitoring data, e.g. participation rate, feedback on actions taken or learning analytics (Jeong & Hmelo-Silver, 2016).

Forming and building groups and communities: SCPs allow learners to become part of different communities that support their access to information, introduce them to norms and share experiences (Kling & Courtright, 2003; Lave & Wenger, 1991; Oeberst, Halatchliyski, Kimmerle, & Cress, 2014; Scardamalia & Bereiter, 2014). Groups can be formed by the instructor or with the help of technology and need ongoing investment to be perceived as beneficial (Fields, Kafai, & Giang, 2016). Again, the provision of suitable technology alone is not enough to engage learners and sustain the communities (Kreijns et al., 2003). Communities in SCPs will only become a successful collaborative learning setting when embedded in a suitable instructional design and learning culture that supports interactions and collective learning (Ma, Chen, & Zhang, 2016; Zhang, Hong, Scardamalia, Teo, & Morley, 2011).

In summary, the work by Jeong and Hmelo-Silver (2016) shows that SCPs as a new technology provide specific opportunities for social collaboration. It also shows that the desired learning experience and outcomes can only be achieved through a pedagogically effective orchestration of technology, instructional design and learner support, embedded in an appropriate socio-cultural learning setting (Looi et al., 2009; Prieto et al., 2011).

6.2.3. Summary

Today's market and societal demands have led organisations to employ new approaches to learning. Learning is tailored to the individuals' interest, skills and needs in order to maximise learning motivation and outcomes within the given time period. Furthermore, learning becomes increasingly collaborative: learners interact with each other, assume responsibility and have high degrees of autonomy in their learning. These personalised and social collaborative learning processes can be enabled through SCPs as the primary learning environment. However, it is not enough to provide the technology. The highest learning outcomes will only be obtained when the educational setting aligns technological affordances with conceptual and socio-cognitive support as well as an appropriate learning culture.

6.3. The Case

6.3.1. Course Description: 'Introduction to Leadership'

Bachelor programmes at the Pforzheim University (Germany) contain different elective courses during the 3rd year. Among them is an introductory course to leadership, aimed at providing an overview of leadership concepts in both, theory and practice. The course is taught in English and listed in the course catalogue as a lecture for students from diverse bachelor programmes (e.g. Human Resource Management, Engineering, Logistics). Enrolment is open to students of the Pforzheim University as well as international exchange students. In its traditional format, the lecture was conducted in an interactive teaching style, including questions, class discussion, short exercises and analyses of short case studies.

6.3.2. Encountered Challenges of the Traditional Learning Setting

In the traditional format described above, the course was taught several times and evaluated through standardised student evaluation questionnaires as well as qualitative student feedback. These data revealed the following challenges of the traditional learning setting:

(1) *Language of instruction*
Many students reported that it was more difficult for them to follow the lecture because it was not taught in their native language. This impaired their comprehension of the presented information. The data also showed that the English level of the students was very heterogeneous, reaching from very low experience levels in speaking English to very high levels after spending semesters abroad or because English was the students' native language.

(2) *Class size and participation*
The number of students in the class usually varied from 35 to 50. This class size limited the degree of possible participation from two different perspectives: From the student perspective, it was difficult to ask questions or participate in the discussions due to the combined effect of class size and having to participate in their non-native language. From the course design perspective, the class size limited the type of interactive methods that could be used to activate students. Extended leadership skill-building exercises, such as conducting employee dialogues, could not be included in the course at all. In addition to that, the required time for group work was difficult to gauge due to the different English levels.

(3) *Student background and motivation*
The students attending the course had very heterogeneous backgrounds. Their prior knowledge varied from no knowledge to very good knowledge due to previously attended courses or work experience. Furthermore, they

had very heterogeneous expectations and learning interests in the course. The feedback data revealed three motivation or interest clusters:

- Students who wanted to learn concepts and skills they could directly apply in their first leadership role. Most of these students studied Logistics or Engineering and they are likely to assume a first leadership role after graduation.
- Students who wanted to know about the theoretical concepts of leadership and how they could consult leaders. These were mainly Human Resource Management students, who will most likely work a few years before assuming their first leadership position but might have to act as internal consultants to leaders in their first HR roles.
- Students who were primarily interested in learning about cultural differences and leadership in an international context. These were mainly students with international experience, backgrounds or future plans of studying abroad.

One common topic of interest, however, was mentioned by a high number of students: they wanted to gain practical leadership experience through respective exercises.

(4) *Methodological competencies*

The classic lecture format did not provide ample opportunity for the students to develop methodological competencies. The format was primarily teacher-centred with little demands on the students to further develop their self-regulation, monitoring, planning or collaboration skills. Furthermore, it did not prepare students for learning in complex and unstructured workplace settings where they need to collaborate in international, virtual communities via their own digital persona (Conole, 2014; Solove, 2004).

In summary, the reported data showed that in the traditional lecture format it was not possible to provide a differentiated learning setting to address the heterogeneous levels of learner readiness, needs and interests. The comparison with learning formats currently used in applied settings furthermore revealed that the traditional lecture format did not support students in developing necessary methodological competencies for learning formats they will encounter in the workplace. Based on these findings, the traditional lecture format was redesigned.

6.3.3. Reconceptualisation of the Course: Computer-Supported Social Collaborative Learning Environment with Personalised Elements

The reconceptualisation of the course aimed at overcoming the challenges that had been identified in the evaluation. It was based on the concepts of personalised and computer-supported collaborative learning. Previous findings showed that the use of technology alone will not lead to the expected learning outcomes (Schneider & Preckel, 2017). The instructional design of this course was thus revised based on the theoretical framework described by Jeong and Hmelo-Silver (2016). Since the course was part of an existing curriculum with respective restrictions and guidelines (e.g. assessment, credit hours, instructional format) the lecture format could only be enhanced by additional elements but could not be completely transformed. The following paragraphs describe the elements of the redesigned course that were deducted from the literature and could be implemented within the given curriculum constraints.

(1) *Social enterprise network as the social collaboration platform for the course*
A social enterprise network (Wehner et al., 2017) was used as the SCP for this course. The platform served as the central learning environment for this class and contained all relevant information for the course. The respective tool used in this course was Coyo (https://coyoapp.com). It provided learners with a general course workspace as well as private workspaces, multiple communication options, content pages, lists, a blog, a document repository and a booking tool. It was accessible through any browser or an app on any mobile device. This tool was used so that learners could gain experience in collaborating via their digital persona in learning settings used in the business world. It also aimed at improving their methodological and technological competencies. Learners were supported in using the tool through instructional videos and explanations in class.

(2) *Ongoing communication throughout the course*
The course was redesigned to keep learners continuously engaged through the SCP. Throughout the course, the communication stream tool was used to support the learners' ongoing engagement with the topic of leadership. The course instructors posted additional multi-media material for the students and commented on each other's posts. This was done to model and facilitate co-construction of knowledge and establish norms for collaboration and constructive commenting. The instructors thus also engaged in the collaboration in the role of a learner. The students could also use the communication channels to ask questions or reach the instructors. This new approach to engagement and communication was aimed at creating a supportive learning context.

(3) *Personalised learning through the provision of learning paths*
To better address diverse student interests (Hoover & Patton, 2005), three different learning paths were developed. In this setting, the learning paths were used as an in-depth module, following initial lecture sessions in which all students were introduced to basic concepts and theories of leadership. The learning paths were based on the previously extracted student interests: 'Getting ready for leadership', 'consulting leaders' and 'diversity in leadership'. Through the platform, the students were provided with introductory descriptions to all of the learning paths and could choose the learning path they were most interested in. As elements of cognitive support, each learning path was structured through learning goals and included step-by-step scripts. It consisted of different materials (e.g. readings, videos) the students had to work on. The work on the learning path was self-paced, allowing students to work on their paths of choice according to their own readiness levels. The

learning paths were thus also aimed at increasing students' self-regulatory skills. The time allotted to these equalled the duration of three lecture sessions including the respective preparation time.

(4) *Collaborative tasks*

To promote collaboration, information sharing, synthesis of experiences and ideas, as well as self-regulatory skills, the following tasks were included in the course. All of these tasks were included as mandatory components and needed to be completed in addition to the lecture sessions. Leaners were guided through the completion of the tasks by respective scripts on the platform.

- *Co-constructed summaries:* To start their virtual collaboration, students needed to select a specific leadership theory covered in class, thereby creating different groups of about 4-5 students. They selected the topic through the SCP. Each group had the task to summarise the respective leadership theory in preparation for the exam. They were encouraged to prepare this summary by creating a sub-group workspace in which they could discuss their ideas and compose their summary. The summary then needed to be published in the course workspace. All students could thus access this summary for their individual exam preparation and could also comment on it or ask related questions through the platform. The summaries were also commented on by the instructors.
- *Reflection blog post:* After the initial face-to-face lecture sessions, students needed to pick an individual in-depth learning path and could work on this path at their own pace. Upon completion of the learning path, the students had to compile a reflection on their learning path. They had to summarise their key takeaways, think about their own experiences in regards to leadership and the content covered in their learning path. This reflection also needed to be enhanced by collecting additional material they found helpful or inspiring for their own learning (individual task). These components had to be combined in a short text and then published on the SCP as a blog post.
- *Reflection co-construction:* After publishing their own reflection post, students had to comment two other posts by their fellow students. Each reflection post was also commented on by the instructor.

(5) *Leadership skills training in small-group learning settings*

During the course phase allotted to the work on the individual learning paths, the students also had the opportunity to sign up for one out of three face-to-face leadership skills training session. In the resulting small group sessions with 10–15 people, students were able to apply their leadership knowledge to different practical leadership tasks, e.g. self-presentation in an assessment centre, employee dialogue exercises.

In summary, these instructional design elements were developed to address the challenges contained in the traditional learning setting. They were based on personalised learning considerations as well as on the affordances of CSCL, outlined in Jeong and Hmelo-Silver's (2016) framework. Specifically, the above-mentioned design elements operationalised the affordances of communication, providing collaboration resources and structure, facilitating co-construction, forming and building groups and communities. Not operationalised was the affordance of monitoring student participation. Overall, the reconceptualisation aimed at providing an effective socio-cultural learning setting through the alignment of the employed technology, instructional design, learner support and a changed role of the instructor.

6.3.4. Preliminary Evaluation Findings

Overall, 28 students participated in the redesigned course. As a first and preliminary evaluation step, informal student feedback was gathered in a face-to-face class discussion and student posts on the collaboration platform were analysed to check for emerging themes. The identified themes are reported in relation to the instructional design elements described above.

(1) *Social enterprise network as the social collaboration platform for the course*
   Students' comments indicated that they perceived this platform as very new and did not have any experience working with a similar tool. Among the features they enjoyed were the mobile app, the possibility to comment and like comments of their peers and the opportunity to communicate with the instructors on eye-level, in a fast and more informal way. They also positively commented on the level of instructor engagement and mentioned that the platform appeared much more 'personal' than traditional learning management systems and allowed the learners to establish closer connections with the other classmates. On the negative side, students' comments showed indications of an increased cognitive load: They reported increased effort to get oriented and that the structure and strengths of the platform were only discovered over time. One student also commented that the platform had probably not yet been used to its fullest potential by the participants. Some also reported that it was not as easy to use as consumer apps, such as WhatsApp or Dropbox. Only a few reported not enjoying this new mode of working.
(2) *Ongoing communication throughout the course*
   The learners perceived the multiple communication channels as demanding and needed to get used to their different functionalities, e.g. push-notifications. They also mentioned that a stricter guidance concerning deadlines for posts would have been helpful for spreading the participants' posts more evenly. Not being able to read all of the posts led to feelings of being overwhelmed.
(3) *Personalised learning through the use of learning paths*
   Being able to choose an in-depth learning path was well received by the learners. They enjoyed the mix of learning materials, particularly the videos contained in the learning paths. However, the learning paths were also perceived as an increased workload in comparison to a traditional lecture that only requires learners to review the slides in preparation for the exam.

A recurring theme was the lengths of the included texts and their perceived high level of difficulty.

(4) *Collaborative tasks*

It was positively perceived that the individual work could be shared with fellow students and was not only produced for the instructor. Specifically, the comments and 'likes' for the posts were motivating. One participant also mentioned that it was very positive to be able to engage in these validation behaviours ('likes') for meaningful educational content. On the downside, the group work was perceived as increasing the workload for the course.

The analysis of the student blog posts on the platform showed that their reflections offered more insight into their experiences than their comments and examples shared in class. Even students who did not actively participate in verbal class discussions shared valuable experiences in their blog posts. The comments on the posts also contained first evidence for co-constructed knowledge: some participants built on the others' comments and were able to integrate the different perspectives into their line of argumentation. Many comments were posted on reflections by participants who had already known each other before enroling in this class. However, there were also a number of comments and discussion threads that were carried on between students who had not previously known each other. The affordances offered by the platform also motivated learners to contribute beyond the requirements. One learner even shared the individual study script she had composed for the exam, although this sharing behaviour was not incentivised through the instructional design.

(5) *Leadership skills training in small-group learning settings*

The opportunity to participate in leadership skills training was very positively perceived by the students. They highly valued gaining practical leadership experience for their future work-life.

(6) *General comments on the instructional design*

Concerning the content of the class, learners reported that they enjoyed the topics covered and perceived them as very relevant for their future work-life. Concerning the overall instructional design, the students frequently mentioned that they enjoyed the lectures and discussions in class. They specifically perceived the respectful and appreciative manner of the class discussions as helpful and enjoyable.

6.4. Discussion

Recently, organisations have implemented new approaches to learning in a quest to respond to the societal market as well as societal demands and to increase their agility. They are looking for ways to motivate employees to continuously learn, to maximise the learning outcomes in given periods of time and to support learners in building their network within the company. To achieve this, they tailor learning to the individuals' interests, skills and needs. Furthermore, they focus on collaboration: learners are encouraged to interact with each other and have high degrees of autonomy in their learning. This new approach to learning was enabled by technological innovations, such as social collaboration platforms (SCPs).

Since these changes in the business context also affect higher education, this case study investigated the potential of social collaborative learning environments for preparing university students to work in this new business context. Additionally, the case study's results will be discussed in regards to their potential for enabling traditional universities to better respond to the current challenges they face due to this new business environment, online learning offers and new learner expectations.

6.4.1. *Social Collaborative Learning Environments' Potential for Educating Tomorrow's Leaders*

This chapter described the reconceptualisation of a leadership course from a traditional lecture to a lecture enhanced by social collaboration elements and supported by an SCP as the technological learning environment. The preliminary findings of the learners' perceptions of the new course as well as the analysis of their contributions on the SCP corroborate the affordances and constraints of computer-supported social collaboration learning environments reported in the literature.

The *SCP* and the *ongoing communication throughout the course* were reported to increase learners' perceived cognitive load and at times led to feelings of being overwhelmed. The latter impression mainly resulted from the amount and timing of user-generated content published on the platform. Furthermore, it might have resulted from the combination of functionalities contained in the SCP. Learners might be more used to access different kinds of information in different apps (e.g. communication content, document storage) instead of on one platform. These findings are in accordance with previous results of the effects of technology use (Cohen, 1994) and computer-supported collaborative learning (Jeong & Hmelo-Silver, 2016) and counter more optimistic accounts that computer-supported collaboration and information management come easily to the 'digital natives' (Prensky, 2001a, 2001b). As previous meta-analytic findings indicated, prior experience strongly influences the effectiveness of computer-supported collaborative learning (CSCL): how much students learn in CSCL settings depends on their prior experience and the instructional design elements used (Lou, Abrami, & d'Apollonia, 2001). Enabling university students to gain experience and build competencies in using CSCL settings thus seems a valuable component of preparing them for the future workplace and the learning demands they will face there.

The reports of the increased cognitive load in dealing with the platform might also be an indication that working with SCPs requires more self-regulation. Again, a finding that has been previously reported in the literature (P. A. Kirschner & Erkens, 2013). Learners often perceive these self-regulatory demands as unpleasant. Providing more support for the students decreases the perceived discomfort but is also likely to impair the learning outcome (Hmelo-Silver,

Duncan, & Chinn, 2007). It thus seems more advisable to foster self-regulation strategies in educational settings. This might lead to negative reactions in the short-term but will empower learners for their future careers, especially since the same effects of perceived overload and feelings of being overwhelmed have been described in the workplace (Bersin, 2017). Based on our preliminary data, it can thus be concluded that using SCPs provides learners with much-needed experience in self-regulation. Instructional settings should be designed to support the development of self-regulation skills because these are needed to cope with the demands of continuous, life-long learning in a workplace characterised by informational overload.

Another result that stood out was the perception of the platform as 'personal'. It afforded the instructor to show his/her level of involvement with the class through continuous and eye-level communication. This might have added to the perception of the respectful learning atmosphere, thus supporting the development of a supportive, learning-goal oriented climate (Dweck & Leggett, 1988; Tan et al., 2016). Based on these findings, it can be assumed that CSCL environments support instructors in taking on a more pronounced role as learning facilitators. This new role is of specific importance in a societal and organisational context that values democratic participation, dialogue, relationships, networks and collaboration on eye-level, instead of clear boundaries and hierarchies (Balda & Mora, 2011; McGonagill & Pruyn, 2010; Myers & Sadaghiani, 2010). Through this role, instructors can furthermore serve as role models for a new form of leadership.

The *personalised learning elements through the use of learning paths* were perceived as motivating. However, it also became evident, that the learning paths could not fully unfold their advantages in this setting. Learners predominantly perceived an increased workload instead of a workload reduction through being able to focus learning on their topics of interest. These perceptions might be due to the learners comparing this course to traditional lectures that require them to only study the information contained in the slide set. However, the perceived workload might have also been influenced by the learners' language skills. The elements of the learning paths should thus be revised to include more of those materials that were favourably received, such as videos. However, as this course is an advanced level course aiming to prepare students for their bachelor thesis, the requirement to deal with scientific texts will remain. The inclusion of learning paths thus holds potential for increasing learner motivation in an educational setting but their goals and advantages need to be communicated explicitly.

The use of *collaborative tasks* in the learning setting was, on the one hand, perceived as motivating, on the other hand, as an additional burden. Again, these findings corroborate the reported complex picture of the effects of collaborative learning (Nokes-Malach et al., 2015) and the pitfalls for social interaction in computer-supported collaborative learning environments (Barron, 2003; Kreijns et al., 2003). Based on the findings of the case study and the literature, the use of collaborative tasks with the singular goal of maximising learning outcomes ('instrumental view', Barron, 2003, p. 354) does thus not seem advisable. However, the risks that come with collaboration might be worth taking, if additional goals are pursued in the learning setting, such as introducing students to learning and working formats they will encounter in the workplace. The latter argument is supported by findings pointing out that collaboration in the workplace, e.g. in knowledge-building communities, needs to be practiced (Eberle, 2014). Furthermore, specific tasks and technological features related to the collaborative work, such as 'liking' and commenting on others' work, were perceived as motivating.

Unanimously, the learners gave positive feedback on the practical *leadership skills training elements in face-to-face small-group learning settings.* This underlines findings in the area of leadership evaluation studies indicating the importance of not only building leadership knowledge but also practical skills (Collins & Holton, 2004). University curricula are often dominated by cognitive learning goals (Kuchinke, Ardichvili, Wocken, Seo, & Bovornusvakool, 2018). Among other things, this domination of cognitive learning goals might be due to the curriculum restrictions also faced in the original version of this leadership course. The use of new instructional designs that include self-directed learning parts has in this case been very effective in creating the opportunity to split up the large lecture group and offer these small groups face-to-face practical skills training sessions. The content of these sessions was directly tailored to workplace and leadership tasks students will encounter in selection processes. It thus aimed at producing tangible effects on the immediate employability of the learners.

The positive perceptions of the skills-training sessions are also in line with the *general comments on the instructional design.* The case study and findings in the literature show that time in class and class discussions are still valued by learners. Furthermore, previous research showed not only the positive perceptions of face-to-face small-group learning in the classroom but also the resulting higher achievement (Schneider & Preckel, 2017). The blended approach that was achieved through the redesign of the course was thus able to not only adhere to existing curriculum regulations but also supported recent meta-analytic evidence showing that the combination of online and classroom instruction creates the most effective learning settings (Schneider & Preckel, 2017).

Overall, this case study was thus able to provide preliminary findings that an SCP used as the primary online learning environment can support instructors in dealing with challenges often encountered in university learning settings: a non-native language of instruction, large student groups, diverse learner readiness. It furthermore showed that SCP-supported learning environments afford learning experiences that cannot be provided through traditional lectures. Using SCPs learners can gain experience in using this new technology and can develop the required methodological skills such as self-regulation, monitoring and planning. Possessing these methodological competencies will positively affect their success in the workplace. Knowledge and experience in leadership in virtual environments will furthermore increase their employability (Kuchinke et al., 2018). In accordance with previous findings, the case study also showed that effective learning processes, specifically collaborative learning, can only be supported when the use of technology is aligned with the appropriated instructional design and learning culture (Jeong & Hmelo-Silver, 2016).

6.4.2. Social Collaborative Learning Environments' Potential for Tomorrow's Universities

Based on the preliminary results of the case study, the following paragraphs investigate the power of CSCL settings for dealing with the challenges created by online educational offers and their disruptive power for higher education.

This case study yielded no direct support yet, that students strongly prefer CSCL settings over lecture-based instruction. Although this finding might be due to a number of reasons that need to be investigated in more controlled studies (e.g., weaknesses in course design or lack of technological features, etc.), it is in line with current meta-analytic results. Schneider & Preckl concluded that their data also did not seem to support the conclusion that 'communication technology will revolutionize higher education' (2017, pp. 594–595).

However, as the democratisation of knowledge, social media and other technology, as well as new university models, gain further acceptance in society (Antonius et al., 2015; Mehaffy, 2012) the traditional higher education format and business model might not hold up anymore. Agile companies need to adapt their products and business models very fast. Their employees need to be equally fast in acquiring new competencies. Thus, students, as well as employers, will expect life-long learning offers that are easily accessible and flexible, and provide knowledge- and skill-building on demand. Demand will shift towards 'nano-degrees' that are tailored to specific needs and can be used to secure one's employability in form of 'badges' for very specific skills. Big employers such as IBM are already generating their own badges and their employees add them to their profiles on professional social networks. Universities will have to answer these expectations with concepts that go beyond traditional face-to-face degree programmes and provide a revised approach to teaching and learning.

Personalised and social collaborative learning processes enabled through SCPs as the primary learning environment hold potential for dealing with the challenges faced by traditional universities and their business model for the following reasons.

- They enable universities to redesign traditional teaching settings to cater to the expectations of new student generations concerning personalisation, engagement with peers and facilitators (instructors), as well as on-demand access to learning.
- They provide a framework for preparing learners for new demands in the business context by supporting the development of methodological and technological skills. Students' gain confidence in collaborating beyond boundaries and can engage with members of larger communities (Zhang, Scardamalia, Reeve, & Messina, 2009).
- They are flexible enough to be implemented in different degrees, allowing universities an early response to the possible disruption while still using

traditional and effective face-to-face course elements. They are an advanced tool for offering blended learning settings.
- If used to their fullest extent, social collaborative learning settings provide the unique opportunity to establish sustainable communities of practice. This affordance should be used to create 'knowledge relationships' (Balda & Mora, 2011) between learners and faculty from the beginning. When traditional universities fail to provide this social component, their advantage over full online curricular will vanish. Business organisations are shifting from 'generating knowledge' to 'creating the relationships and connections through which knowledge can flow' (Balda & Mora, 2011, p. 16) and in which different generations are working and learning together 'through relationally driven and technologically [enabled] collaborative processes' (p. 14). Comprehensive social collaborative learning settings allow universities to also create such a relationally-driven environment.
- Successfully sustaining these knowledge communities will open up new business models for universities: They can be used for continuous professional education, enabling universities to provide life-long-learning concepts to their alumni. The university offers a framework and platform for a select student group to learn on demand, informally and with coaching support from professors. The use of technology-supported social collaborative learning environments can thereby support universities' currently 'irreplaceable' functions as mentioned by Christensen and Eyring (2011, p. A72). First: the discovery of knowledge: Social collaborative networks enable pronounced exchanges between scientists and their previous students. The resulting access to the questions currently being asked in the business will inspire science. The networks will provide practitioners with another venue to gain access to research results. Second, they offer a new means to serve as mentoring grounds. The establishment of social collaborative networks, starting in college and turning into a life-long informal learning network, will further help to bridge the scientist-practitioner gap.
- The networks will also enable universities to provide a high-quality learning environment in which shorter, more focused knowledge- and skill-building courses that lead to very specific certificates, can be embedded.

6.5. Limitations

The reported findings are based on preliminary evaluation data only. A more thorough analysis and an experimental design are needed to assess students' reactions, learning, behaviour and results (Kirkpatrick, 1994). The reconceptualisation of this class did not yet include the specific recognition of learner ability for the differentiation of learning paths. Given the importance of ability and other learner variables, the instructional design should be developed further. Additionally, the conclusions concerning the social collaborative learning environments' potential for tomorrow's universities warrant further empirical investigation.

6.6. Conclusion

Personalised and social collaborative learning processes enabled through SCPs as the primary learning environment can enable traditional universities to deal with the disruptive power of online education. They hold the potential to offer a new teaching and business model for traditional universities. Implementing these changes, however, will not be possible without analysing and adjusting organisational structures and culture as well as faculty reward systems.

References

Akkerman, S. F., & Bakker, A. (2011). Boundary crossing and boundary objects. *Review of Educational Research, 81*(2), 132−169. doi:10.3102/0034654311404435

Alli, N., Rajan, R., & Ratliff, G. (2016). How personalised learning unlocks student success. *Educause Review, 51*(2), 12−21.

Amundsen, S., & Martinsen, Ø. L. (2014). Empowering leadership: Construct clarification, conceptualisation, and validation of a new scale. *The Leadership Quarterly, 25*(3), 487−511. doi:10.1016/j.leaqua.2013.11.009

Antonius, N., Xu, J., & Gao, X. (2015). Factors influencing the adoption of Enterprise Social Software in Australia. *Knowledge-Based Systems, 73*, 32−43. doi:10.1016/j.knosys.2014.09.003

Baker, M., Andriessen, J., Lund, K., van Amelsvoort, M., & Quignard, M. (2007). Rainbow: A framework for analysing computer-mediated pedagogical debates. *International Journal of Computer-Supported Collaborative Learning, 2*(2−3), 315−357. doi:10.1007/s11412-007-9022-4

Balda, J. B., & Mora, F. (2011). Adapting leadership theory and practice for the networked, millennial generation. *Journal of Leadership Studies, 5*(3), 13−24. doi:10.1002/jls.20229

Bandura, A. (1977). *Social learning theory*. Englewood Cliffs, NJ: Prentice Hall.

Barron, B. (2003). When smart groups fail. *Journal of the Learning Sciences, 12*(3), 307−359. doi:10.1207/S15327809JLS1203_1

Bennett, N., & Lemoine, G. J. (2014). What a difference a word makes: Understanding threats to performance in a VUCA world. *Business Horizons, 57*(3), 311−317. doi:10.1016/j.bushor.2014.01.001

Bersin, J. (2017). *The Disruption of Digital Learning: 10 Things We Have Learned* (Talent Trends). Retrieved from www.bersin.com

Bielaczyc, K. (2013). Informing design research: Learning from teachers designs of social infrastructure. *Journal of the Learning Sciences, 22*(2), 258−311. doi:10.1080/10508406.2012.691925

Bray, B., & McClaskey, K. (2013). A Step-by-Step Guide to Personalise Learning. *Learning & Leading with Technology, 40*(7), 12−19. Retrieved from http://files.eric.ed.gov/fulltext/EJ1015153.pdf

Campbell, R. J., Robinson, W., Neelands, J., Hewston, R., & Mazzoli, L. (2007). Personalised learning: Ambiguities in theory and practice. *British Journal of Educational Studies, 55*(2), 135−154. doi:10.1111/j.1467-8527.2007.00370.x

Chen, S. Y., Huang, P.-R., Shih, Y.-C., & Chang, L.-P. (2016). Investigation of multiple human factors in personalised learning. *Interactive Learning Environments*, *24*(1), 119–141. doi:10.1080/10494820.2013.825809

Christensen, C. M. (1997). *The innovator's dilemma: The revolutionary book that will change the way you do business. Harper Business Essentials.* New York: HarperCollins.

Christensen, C. M., & Eyring, H. (2011). How to save the traditional university, from the inside out. *Chronicle of Higher Education*, *57*(42), A72–A72.

Chui, M., Manyika, J., Bughin, J., Dobbs, R., Roxburgh, C., Sarrazin, H., Westergren, M. (2012). *The social economy: Unlocking value and productivity through social technologies*. Retrieved from https://www.mckinsey.com/industries/high-tech/our-insights/the-social-economy

Cohen, E. G. (1994). Restructuring the classroom: Conditions for productive small groups. *Review of Educational Research*, *64*(1), 1–35. doi:10.3102/00346543064001001

Collins, D. B., & Holton, E. F. III. (2004). The effectiveness of managerial leadership development programs: A meta-analysis of studies from 1982 to 2001. *Human Resource Development Quarterly*, *15*(2), 217–248. doi:10.1002/hrdq.1099

Conole, G. (2014). The 7Cs of learning design – a new approach to rethinking design practice. In *Proceedings of the 9th International Conference on Networked Learning* (502–509). Retrieved from http://www.lancaster.ac.uk/fss/organisations/netlc/past/nlc2014/abstracts/pdf/conole.pdf

Cress, U., Barquero, B., Schwan, S., & Hesse, F. W. (2007). Improving quality and quantity of contributions: Two models for promoting knowledge exchange with shared databases. *Computers & Education*, *49*(2), 423–440. doi:10.1016/j.compedu.2005.10.003

Cress, U., Moskaliuk, J., & Jeong, H. (Eds.). (2016). *Mass collaboration and education*. Heidelberg: Springer.

Dillenbourg, P. (1999). What do you mean by collaborative learning? In P. Dillenbourg (Ed.), *Collaborative Learning: Cognitive and Computational Approaches* (pp. 1–16). Amsterdam: Pergamon, Elsevier Science. doi:10.1111/j.1600-0463.1999.tb05661.x

Dove, R. (1999). Knowledge management, response ability, and the agile enterprise. *Journal of Knowledge Management*, *3*(1), 18–35. doi:10.1108/13673279910259367

Dweck, C. S., & Leggett, E. L. (1988). A social-cognitive approach to motivation and personality. *Psychological Review*, *95*(2), 256–273. doi:10.1037/0033-295X.95.2.256

Dwi, C. A., & Basuki, A. (2012). Personalized learning path of a web-based learning system. *International Journal of Computer Applications*, *53*(7), 17–22. doi:10.5120/8434-2206

Eberle, J. (2014). Legitimate peripheral participation in communities of practice: Participation support structures for newcomers in faculty student councils. *Journal of the Learning Sciences*, *23*(2), 216–244. Retrieved from https://www.learntechlib.org/p/167897/

Fields, D. A., Kafai, Y. B., & Giang, M. T. (2016). Coding by choice: A transitional analysis of social participation patterns and programming contributions in the online Scratch community. In U. Cress, J. Moskaliuk, & H. Jeong (Eds.), *Mass Collaboration and Education* (pp. 209–240). Heidelberg: Springer.

Fischer, S., & Häusling, A. (2018). Agilität und Arbeit 4.0 [Agility and work 4.0]. In S. Werther & L. Bruckner (Eds.), *Arbeit 4.0 aktiv: Die Zukunft der Arbeit zwischen Agilität, People Analytics und Digitalisierung* [Work 4.0: the future of work between agility, people analytics and digitalization] (pp. 88–107). Wiesbaden: Springer.

Garrison, D. R., Anderson, T., & Archer, W. (2001). Critical thinking, cognitive presence, and computer conferencing in distance education. *American Journal of Distance Education, 15*(1), 7–23. doi:10.1080/08923640109527071

Goldman, S. L., Nagel, R. N., & Preiss, K. (1995). *Agile competitors and virtual organizations: Strategies for enriching the customer*. New York, NY: Wiley.

Hmelo-Silver, C. E., Duncan, R. G., & Chinn, C. A. (2007). Scaffolding and achievement in problem-based and inquiry learning: A response to Kirschner, Sweller, and Clark (2006). *Educational Psychologist, 42*(2), 99–107. doi:10.1080/00461520701263368

Hmelo-Silver, C. E., Nagarajan, A., & Derry, S. J. (2006). From face-to-face to online participation: tensions in facilitating problem-based learning. In M. Savin-Baden & K. Wilkie (Eds.), *Problem-based learning online* (pp. 61–78). Maidenhead: Open University Press.

Hoover, J. J., & Patton, J. R. (2005). Differentiating curriculum and instruction for english-language learners with special needs. *Intervention in School and Clinic, 40*(4), 231–235. doi:10.1177/10534512050400040401

Järvelä, S., & Hadwin, A. F. (2013). New frontiers: Regulating learning in CSCL. *Educational Psychologist, 48*(1), 25–39. doi:10.1080/00461520.2012.748006

Jeong, H., & Hmelo-Silver, C. E. (2012). Technology Supports in CSCL. In J. van Aalst, K. Thompson, M. J. Jacobson, & P. Reinmann (Eds.), *The future of learning: Proceedings of the 10th International Conference of the Learning Sciences: Volume 1, Full papers* (pp. 339–346). Sydney, Australia: Society of the Learning Sciences.

Jeong, H., & Hmelo-Silver, C. E. (2016). Seven affordances of computer-supported collaborative learning: How to support collaborative learning? How can technologies help? *Educational Psychologist, 51*(2), 247–265. doi:10.1080/00461520.2016.1158654

Johnson, C. M. (2001). A survey of current research on online communities of practice. *The Internet and Higher Education, 4*(1), 45–60. doi:10.1016/S1096-7516(01)00047-1

Johnson, D. W., & Johnson, R. T. (1999). *Learning together and alone: Cooperative, competitive, and individualistic learning* (5th ed.). Boston, MA: Allyn and Bacon.

Jonassen, D. H. (1994). Thinking technology: Toward a constructivist design model. *Educational Technology, 34*(4), 34–37. Retrieved from https://www.learntechlib.org/p/171050/

Kane, G. C. (2015). Enterprise social media: Current capabilities and future possibilities. *MIS Quarterly Executive, 14*(1), 1–16.

Kaplan, A. M., & Haenlein, M. (2010). Users of the world, unite! The challenges and opportunities of social media. *Business Horisons, 53*(1), 59–68. doi:10.1016/j.bushor.2009.09.003

Kirkpatrick, D. L. (1994). *Evaluating training programs: The four levels*. San Francisco, CA: Berrett-Koehler.

Kirschner, F., Paas, F., & Kirschner, P. A. (2009). A cognitive load approach to collaborative learning: United brains for complex tasks. *Educational Psychology Review, 21*(1), 31–42. doi:10.1007/s10648-008-9095-2

Kirschner, P. A. (2001). Using integrated electronic environments for collaborative teaching/learning. *Research Dialogue in Learning and Instruction*, *2*(1), 1−9.

Kirschner, P. A., Beers, P. J., Boshuisen, H. P. A., & Gijselaers, W. H. (2008). Coercing shared knowledge in collaborative learning environments. *Computers in Human Behaviour*, *24*(2), 403−420. doi:10.1016/j.chb.2007.01.028

Kirschner, P. A., & Erkens, G. (2013). Toward a framework for CSCL research. *Educational Psychologist*, *48*(1), 1−8. doi:10.1080/00461520.2012.750227

Kling, R., & Courtright, C. (2003). Group behavior and learning in electronic forums: A sociotechnical approach. *The Information Society*, *19*(3), 221−235. doi:10.1080/01972240309465

Kreijns, K., Kirschner, P. A., & Jochems, W. (2003). Identifying the pitfalls for social interaction in computer-supported collaborative learning environments: a review of the research. *Computers in Human Behavior*, *19*(3), 335−353. doi:10.1016/S0747-5632(02)00057-2

Kuchinke, P. K., Ardichvili, A., Wocken, L., Seo, J., & Bovornusvakool, W. (2018). Leadership development for undergraduate students at U.S. universities: The case for HRD research and practice. *Human Resource Development Quarterly*, *15*(1), 549. doi:10.1002/hrdq.21309

Lajoie, S. P., & Lu, J. (2012). Supporting collaboration with technology: Does shared cognition lead to co-regulation in medicine? *Metacognition and Learning*, *7*(1), 45−62. doi:10.1007/s11409-011-9077-5

Lave, J. (1991). Situating learning in communities of practice. In L. B. Resnick, M. J. Levine, & S. D. Teasley (Eds.), *Perspectives on socially shared cognition* (pp. 63−82). Washington, DC: American Psychological Association.

Lave, J., & Wenger, E. (1991). *Situated learning: Legitimate peripheral participation. Learning in doing*. Cambridge: Cambridge University Press.

Lawrence, P. R., & Lorsch, J. W. (1967). Differentiation and integration in complex organizations. *Administrative Science Quarterly*, *12*(1), 1−47. doi:10.2307/2391211

Looi, C. K., Wong, L. H., So, H. J., Seow, P., Toh, Y., Chen, W., Soloway, E. (2009). Anatomy of a mobilized lesson: Learning my way. *Computers and Education*, *53*(4), 1120−1132. doi:10.1016/j.compedu.2009.05.021

Lou, Y., Abrami, P. C., & d'Apollonia, S. (2001). Small group and individual learning with technology: A meta-analysis. *Review of Educational Research*, *71*(3), 449−521. doi:10.3102/00346543071003449

Ma, L., Chen, A., & Zhang, Z.-X. (2016). Task success based on contingency fit of managerial culture and embeddedness. *Journal of International Business Studies*, *47*(2), 191−209. doi:10.1057/jibs.2015.45

McAfee, A. P. (2006). Enterprise 2.0: The dawn of emergent collaboration. *MIT Sloan Management Review*, *47*(3), 21−28.

McGonagill, G., & Pruyn, P. W. (2010). *Leadership Development in the US − Principles and Patterns of Best Practice* (Leadership Series). Gütersloh. Retrieved from http://www.bertelsmann-stiftung.de/cps/rde/xbcr/bst_engl/xcms_bst_dms_30820_30821_2.pdf

Mehaffy, G. (2012, September/October). Challenge and change. *Educause Review*, 24−42. Retrieved from https://er.educause.edu/articles/2012/9/challenge-and-change

Myers, K. K., & Sadaghiani, K. (2010). Millennials in the workplace: A communication perspective on millennials organizational relationships and performance. *Journal of Business and Psychology*, *25*(2), 225−238. doi:10.1007/s10869-010-9172-7

Nokes-Malach, T. J., Richey, J. E., & Gadgil, S. (2015). When is it better to learn together? Insights from research on collaborative learning. *Educational Psychology Review*, *27*(4), 645–656. doi:10.1007/s10648-015-9312-8

O'Donnell, A. M., & O'Kelly, J. (1994). Learning from peers: Beyond the rhetoric of positive results. *Educational Psychology Review*, *6*(4), 321–349.

Oeberst, A., Halatchliyski, I., Kimmerle, J., & Cress, U. (2014). Knowledge construction in wikipedia: A systemic-constructivist analysis. *Journal of the Learning Sciences*, *23*(2), 149–176. doi:10.1080/10508406.2014.888352

Pai, H.-H., Sears, D. A., & Maeda, Y. (2015). Effects of small-group learning on transfer: A meta-analysis. *Educational Psychology Review*, *27*(1), 79–102. doi:10.1007/s10648-014-9260-8

Park, S., Jeong, S., Jang, S., Yoon, S. W., & Lim, D. H. (2018). Critical review of global leadership literature: Toward an integrative global leadership framework. *Human Resource Development Review*, *17*(1), 95–120. doi:10.1177/1534484317749030

Pearce, C. L., Conger, J. A., & Locke, E. A. (2008). Shared leadership theory. *The Leadership Quarterly*, *19*(5), 622–628. doi:10.1016/j.leaqua.2008.07.005

Prensky, M. (2001a). Digital natives, digital immigrants Part 1. *On the Horizon*, *9*(5), 1–6. doi:10.1108/10748120110424816

Prensky, M. (2001b). Digital natives, digital immigrants Part 2: Do they really think differently? *On the Horizon*, *9*(6), 1–6. doi:10.1108/10748120110424843

Prieto, L. P., Villagrá-Sobrino, S., Jorrín-Abellán, I. M., Martínez-Monés, A., & Dimitriadis, Y. (2011). Recurrent routines: Analyzing and supporting orchestration in technology-enhanced primary classrooms. *Computers & Education*, *57*(1), 1214–1227. doi:10.1016/j.compedu.2011.01.001

Robertson, B. J. (2016). *Holacracy: The revolutionary management system that abolishes hierarchy*. New York, NY: Penguin Random House.

Roschelle, J. (2013). Special issue on CSCL: Discussion. *Educational Psychologist*, *48*(1), 67–70. doi:10.1080/00461520.2012.749445

Rougas, S., Clyne, B., Cianciolo, A. T., Chan, T. M., Sherbino, J., & Yarris, L. M. (2015). An extended validity argument for assessing feedback culture. *Teaching and Learning in Medicine*, *27*(4), 355–358. doi:10.1080/10401334.2015.1077133

Scardamalia, M., & Bereiter, C. (2014). Knowledge building: Theory, pedagogy, and technology. In R. K. Sawyer (Ed.), *Cambridge handbooks in psychology. The Cambridge handbook of the learning sciences* (pp. 97–118). Cambridge: University Press.

Schneider, M., & Preckel, F. (2017). Variables associated with achievement in higher education: A systematic review of meta-analyses. *Psychological Bulletin*, *143*(6), 565–600. doi:10.1037/bul0000098

Shaw, C., Larson, R., & Sibdari, S. (2014). An asynchronous, personalized learning platform—guided learning pathways (GLP). *Creative Education*, *05*(13), 1189–1204. doi:10.4236/ce.2014.513135

Sinha, S., Rogat, T. K., Adams-Wiggins, K. R., & Hmelo-Silver, C. E. (2015). Collaborative group engagement in a computer-supported inquiry learning environment. *International Journal of Computer-Supported Collaborative Learning*, *10*(3), 273–307. doi:10.1007/s11412-015-9218-y

Slavin, R. E. (1983). When does cooperative learning increase student achievement? *Psychological Bulletin*, *94*(3), 429–445. doi:10.1037/0033-2909.94.3.429

Solove, D. J. (2004). *The digital person: Technology and privacy in the information age. Ex machina*. New York, NY: New York Univ. Press. Retrieved from http://www.loc.gov/catdir/enhancements/fy0730/2004010188-d.html

Springer, L., Stanne, M. E., & Donovan, S. S. (1999). Effects of small-group learning on undergraduates in science, mathematics, engineering, and technology: A meta-analysis. *Review of Educational Research*, *69*(1), 21–51. doi:10.3102/00346543069001021

Stahl, G., Koschmann, T., & Suthers, D. D. (2014). Computer-supported collaborative learning. In R. K. Sawyer (Ed.), *Cambridge handbooks in psychology. The Cambridge handbook of the learning sciences* (pp. 479–500). Cambridge: University Press.

Subban, P. (2006). Differentiated instruction: A research basis. *International Education Journal*, *7*(7), 935–947. Retrieved from https://eric.ed.gov/?id=EJ854351

Suthers, D. D. (2006). Technology affordances for intersubjective meaning making: A research agenda for CSCL. *International Journal of Computer-Supported Collaborative Learning*, *1*(3), 315–337. doi:10.1007/s11412-006-9660-y

Tan, K. W. T., Au, A. K. C., Cooper-Thomas, H. D., & Aw, S. S. Y. (2016). The effect of learning goal orientation and communal goal strivings on newcomer proactive behaviours and learning. *Journal of Occupational and Organizational Psychology*, *89*(2), 420–445. doi:10.1111/joop.12134

Tomlinson, C. A. (2005). *How to differentiate instruction in mixed-ability classrooms* (2nd ed.). *Merrill education/ASCD college textbook series*. Upper Saddle River, NJ: Pearson.

Tomlinson, C. A. (2014). *The differentiated classroom: Responding to the needs of all learners* (2nd ed.). Alexandria, VA: Association for Supervision & Curriculum Development.

Tseng, J. C. R., Chu, H. C., Hwang, G. J., & Tsai, C. C. (2008). Development of an adaptive learning system with two sources of personalization information. *Computers & Education*, *51*(2), 776–786. Retrieved from https://www.learntechlib.org/p/67330/

Tullis, J. G., & Benjamin, A. S. (2011). On the effectiveness of self-paced learning. *Journal of Memory and Language*, *64*(2), 109–118. doi:10.1016/j.jml.2010.11.002

Vygotsky, L. S. (1978). *Mind in society: The development of higher mental process*. Cambridge, MA: Harvard University Press.

Walker, E., Rummel, N., & Koedinger, K. R. (2011). Adaptive support for CSCL: Is it feedback relevance or increased student accountability that matters? In H. Spada, G. Stahl, N. Miyake, & N. Law (Eds.), *Connecting Computer-Supported Collaborative Learning: CSCL2011 Conference Proceeding Volume I—Long papers* (pp. 334–341). Hong Kong: International Society of the Learning Sciences.

Wehner, B., Ritter, C., & Leist, S. (2017). Enterprise social networks: A literature review and research agenda. *Computer Networks*, *114*, 125–142. doi:10.1016/j.comnet.2016.09.001

Zhang, J., Hong, H.-Y., Scardamalia, M., Teo, C. L., & Morley, E. A. (2011). Sustaining knowledge building as a principle-based innovation at an elementary school. *Journal of the Learning Sciences*, *20*(2), 262–307. doi:10.1080/10508406.2011.528317

Zhang, J., Scardamalia, M., Reeve, R., & Messina, R. (2009). Designs for collective cognitive responsibility in knowledge-building communities. *Journal of the Learning Sciences*, *18*(1), 7–44. doi:10.1080/10508400802581676

Chapter 7

Online, Not Distance Education: The Merits of Collaborative Learning in Online Education

Desiree Wieser and Jürgen-Matthias Seeler

Abstract

As a result of the rapid technological innovation and its disruptive power also on the educational sector, teaching and learning practices changed fundamentally and new forms of education, as well as totally new degree programmes emerged. Today, higher education institutions (HEIs) make use of different online resources and new collaborative tools by integrating digital technologies and the internet fully within the curricula. However, although online education offers numerous advantages and has the power to overcome traditional barriers in education as time and space, many higher education institutions are still struggling with issues such as fostering student collaboration on one hand and reducing feelings of social isolation on the other. In the present case study, we analyse a blended Bachelor degree programme in Management at a European business school with the aim to provide practical suggestions and inspiration for implementing e-learning and online education in higher education. The introduced case demonstrates how collaborative learning aspects, organisational and pedagogical structures, philosophical assumptions and educational settings can be combined to decrease one of the main challenges in online education, namely distance.

Keywords: Online education; blended learning; collaborative learning; distance; social isolation; management education

7.1. Introduction

As online education has become increasingly accessible in the last years, the number of students enroled in online programmes has grown and in turn also pedagogical models and higher education systems have changed with the aim to use the virtual space offered by the internet, transforming it into a social learning space (Harasim, 2000; Liang & Chen, 2012; McKiernen & Wilson, 2014). Indeed, online education is very often no more only adopted as an extension to traditional and common learning and teaching modes in higher education institutions, but even considered a promising alternative for differentiation (Kim & Bonk, 2006; Sursock, 2015). Thus, online education has become reality for many institutions and their students within the last years.

Nevertheless, the effectiveness and success of online educational offers are still doubted from time to time. These doubts result mainly from the higher drop-out rates in online courses compared to traditional courses on campus. Distance and feelings of social isolation are often named as the first causes why students do not complete their online study programmes/courses successfully.

A very popular form of initiating and implementing online education – often claimed as having the power to outbalance issues as distance and social isolation – is blended learning. The blended model combines traditional classroom education with synchronous and asynchronous online teaching (Fearon, Starr, & McLaughlin, 2012) and benefits thus of both modes of content delivery, the traditional face-to-face delivery, as well as the online delivery of content (Allen & Seaman, 2010; Harasim, 2000). The advantages include and combine next to the typical advantages regarding time and space (Harasim, 2000; Liang & Chen, 2012), on one side the personal and regular teacher – learner interaction (which would be lost in full online programmes) and on the other side, the use of different facilitation modes enabled by technologies and ICT like podcasts, discussion boards and online forums (Fearon et al., 2012). Moore (1991), however, sees the key to diminish distance in online education, specifically in an enhanced interaction by fostering and improving collaborative learning.

The introduced case study offers an example for the implementation of the blended mode as a form of online education in management education, emphasising, in particular, the collaborative learning aspect to outbalance social isolation and distance in online education. Hence, the present study seeks to answer the research question how to implement blended learning in management education in order to inhibit one of the key disadvantages in online education namely distance.

Before introducing and analysing the case, the next section will investigate into literature and the distance factor of online education, taking a closer look on interaction and collaborative learning and its influence on distance in online education.

7.2. Distance in Online Education

A major barrier for students to succeed in an online programme, often also termed as a key disadvantage of distance and online learning, is *transactional distance*. This term was developed by Moore (1991) and describes the theory of cognitive space between instructor and learners in an educational setting, which means actually the psychological and communicational distance between instructor and learner. Indeed, many students enroled in online courses or programmes suffer from social isolation caused by a decreased feeling of the social presence of the teacher and their peers. This, in turn, affects motivation and involvement negatively and learning outcomes deteriorate. Social isolation is thus a major danger which increases finally also the likelihood of student dropouts, as various empirical studies claim and proved (Bitzer & Janson, 2014; Eom & Ashill, 2016; Hiltz, 1998; Muilenburg & Berge, 2005; Rovai, 2003; Skinner, Furrer, Marchand, & Kindermann, 2008; Tinto, 1987; Wallace, 2003; Wu, Tennyson, & Hsia, 2010). In turn, it can be assumed that if learning outcomes want to be maximised and drop-outs minimised, transactional distance has to be minimised first.

According to Moore (1991) transactional distance can be minimised among three main factors: dialogue, autonomy and structure. Dialogue implicates the regular interaction and exchange between learner and teacher, and among learners. More interaction and regular interaction reduces the transactional distance sustainably. Furthermore, also the autonomy of the learner plays a crucial role because more autonomous and self-directed learners need less interaction with the instructor and less standardisation and structure than people who are not able to manage to learn on their own. Also, the structure of the programme which can adopt different characteristics from flexible to standardised, to blended or fully online, from collaborative to independent and so on has a huge potential to influence transactional distance (Moore & Kearsley, 2011). Finally, and of crucial importance for the improvement of the overall learning experience within online education, as argued by Moore (1991), are key aspects as personal student support, guidance and encouragement, mutual feedback, criticism and supervision.

Looking at the discourse of Moore (1991) and Moore and Kearsley (2011), 'interaction' is one main factor which seems to have a huge overall impact on the reduction of transactional distance in online education. The next section will, therefore, investigate into collaborative learning within online environments by looking at its benefits and its power to decrease transactional distance.

7.3. Collaborative Learning and Online Education

According to the school of cognitive and constructivist learning theories, collaborative learning plays a central role in understanding and acquiring knowledge, as learning and understanding are seen as processes of interaction where meanings are negotiated and established in social contexts (Piaget, 1982; Vygotsky & Cole, 1978).

When talking about collaborative learning, Dillenbourg (1999) has been one of the most pioneering authors. Dillenbourg (1999, p. 5) explained collaborative learning as 'a situation in which particular forms of interaction among people are expected to occur, which would trigger learning mechanisms, but there is no guarantee that the expected interactions will actually occur. Hence, a general concern is to develop ways to increase the probability that some types of interaction occur.' He identified four critical items that determine collaborative learning:

(1) Defining the situation: Setting up initial conditions;
(2) Defining the interaction: Specification of the collaboration contract with a scenario based on roles;
(3) Defining the process: Ensuring productive interactions by encompassing interaction rules;
(4) Defining the effects: Monitoring and regulating interactions.

To summarise, collaborative learning starts with a situation that generates interaction patterns. These patterns trigger cognitive mechanisms in a second step and produce cognitive effects in the end.

Glaser (1990) defined collaborative learning in a similar way before and claimed that it demands for interaction and collaboration with others and builds on shared understandings. McAlpine (2000) added later that learning from peers and teachers is thereby crucial.

Johnson and Johnson (1992) conducted a longitudinal study where they revealed that the achievement and productivity of learners is higher in collaborative or cooperative settings, compared to individualistic and competitive settings. Indeed, they also proved cooperative learning experiences to foster positive social relationships which positively influences students' self-esteem and strengthens their social ability competences. In this context, they also highlighted the special role of the instructor to actively support learners in their construction of knowledge.

Put into practice, collaborative learning expresses itself through students' active search for information, the engagement in discussion, the asking of questions and the discussing of answers, ideas and problems from different perspectives. According to Morris and Hayes (1997) interaction, group activities and collaboration are considered to enhance deep learning and to improve learning outcomes by the development of transferable skills, communication and interpersonal skills. Furthermore, active collaboration between students is claimed to render learning more realistic because it provokes activity and stimulates motivation (Petraglia, 1998), and as claimed by Bekele (2010), increased motivation is an important criterion for student success and lower dropouts. As a result, students do no longer take on a passive role in the learning process but do actively contribute to the co-creation of knowledge through their prior knowledge and experiences, their beliefs and values and the preparation of activities, as explained by Petraglia (1998).

In turn, instruction becomes more learner-centred, instead of teacher-cantered. Consequently, also the role of the teacher changes. In the new learning process, the teacher often becomes a facilitator in a collaborative environment by supporting students in the creation of their knowledge, whereby knowledge is viewed as a social construct which is enabled through peer interaction, evaluation and cooperation, as explained by Hiltz (1998).

With the diffusion of the internet and the development of new technologies and ICT new opportunities for collaboration, communication, but also for learning have emerged. Collaboration is now also possible among a long distance of space by the use of computer-mediated communication (CMC) systems as Veerman and Veldhuis-Diermanse (2001) explain. McAlpine (2000) claims computer networks, databases and the internet to be important cognitive tools in a collaborative learning environment as they enable the development of shared understanding and collaborative problem-solving. According to him the combination of collaborative learning and online education makes interaction vivid, emphasising the learning process itself which has the power to outweigh the lack of contact and the feelings of isolation in online education (McAlpine, 2000).

Similarly, Harasim (2000) argues that one of the major strengths of online education is social, affective and cognitive interaction and collaboration which can be enabled through the use of CMC.

Indeed, some studies already proved that collaborative learning can be more effective for online learning than traditional pedagogical approaches in some cases, providing evidence for Hiltz (1998) that the advantages of online education can increase over the disadvantages until traditional barriers as social isolation can be finally outbalanced. In the past, it has been already argued by Henri and Rigault (1996) that communicating online can even be more intensive as traditional face-to-face communication in some cases, because of a lack of social pressure and much more freedom to express its own opinion, which in turn allows participants to react to the content in a more reflective and effective way of communicating.

Indeed, Veerman and Veldhuis-Diermanse (2001) claim that technologies and CMC in online education, as for example text-based chats, can facilitate the structuring of interaction and communication, as well as enhance reflection at the same time, offering the possibility of re-reading messages, and the slowness of communication which helps to focus and track.

Summarising the standpoints of these and other authors it becomes clear that interaction and collaboration are very often seen to be integral and substantial parts of online educational environments (Dabbagh, 2007; Goodyear, 2002; Harasim, 2000; Liang & Chen, 2012).

As a result, and out of those collaborative and cooperative learning theories, pedagogies of networked learning emerged, which emphasise especially the learning with information and communication technologies. A prominent and especially relevant networked learning model in the present context is the model developed by Goodyear (1999, 2002, 2005). It builds on the collaborative learning approach by Dillenbourg (1999), and captures the benefits of learning through collaboration (Goodyear, 2002). Goodyear, Banks, Hodgson and McConnel (2004) defined networked learning as a process of learning which uses ICT to promote connections between learners, between learners and instructors and between the learning community and the learning resources.

In his model Goodyear (1999, 2002, 2005) sets the pedagogical framework in relation to the educational activity in a real-world setting. Hence, it is an attempt to describe real-world settings, concrete activities, processes, capturing people and artefacts involved in learning. Both, the pedagogical framework and the educational setting are influenced by the higher education institution itself and its organisational framework. The model builds on the assumptions that learning is always influenced by the learning philosophy (how learning occurs) behind it. The educational setting, however, brings together tasks (brainstorming, discussion, critique, etc.), activities (writing, reading, memorising, developing, etc.), people (students, instructors) and the social environment (chat room, discussion boards, shared folders, etc.).

But not only the networked learning model by Goodyear (1999, 2002, 2005) debates the key relevance of collaborative learning in online education and vice versa, also in practice there is evidence that students enjoy connecting with others, and realise benefits through it. They report that relationships with others, working and learning with peers and in teams, reduce loneliness and motivate them at the same time, in order to be able to learn more successfully in an online learning environment. In turn, other authors conclude that collaborative learning environments have the power to foster learning from a social, as well as an academic perspective by preventing social isolation on one hand and leading in turn to fewer drop-out rates and student success in online education on the other hand (Bekele, 2010; Moessenlechner, Obexer, Sixl-Daniell, & Seeler, 2015; Stanford-Bowers, 2008).

Nevertheless, some other questions remain still unanswered. In particular the statement of Dillenbourg (1999) at the beginning where he emphasises the fact that there is no guarantee that interactions which influence the learning outcome positively actually occur, entails an interesting question: How is it possible to increase the likelihood that the 'desired types of interaction' occur, if collaborative learning in itself is not automatically able to induce the 'expected interactions' which lead to positive outcomes?

Yukselturk and Bulut (2007) would argue that it demands reasonable and efficient instructional strategies which provide effective feedback and monitor performance in online education. At the same time the question also ties up to the three factors developed by Moore (1991) to reduce transactional distance, as mentioned earlier:

interaction/dialogue, autonomy, and structure.

Furthermore, as drawn out by Garrison and Kanuka (2004) blended learning is indeed a fundamental reconceptualization and reorganisation of teaching and learning in an institution. The implementation of blended learning can adopt various differing forms, depending always on the respective institution and its disciplines, resources, mission, etc. Profiting from a one-size-fits-all approach might, therefore, be difficult, if not redundant. Hence, the question appears: *how to actually implement blended learning successfully in order to overcome, at least however to outbalance, one of the key disadvantages in online education namely distance?*

7.4. Method

We apply a case study approach which investigates a blended Bachelor Programme in Management, in a European Business School. A discussion of merits and challenges of case study research is omitted here, but frequent criticism on this kind of inquiry to be anecdotal and subjective is acknowledged. Given the fact that to date little data is available on collaborative learning in an e-learning environment, case study research appears to be appropriate as it allows for investigating a phenomenon in its social context. It is descriptive in nature and aims at displaying certain phenomena on a theoretically informed basis in order to build a foundation for further research. As it is not the goal to generalise from findings, but rather to gain rich understandings and insights on how traditional barriers in online education as distance can be counter or outbalanced, a case study appears to be particularly useful (Yin, 2003).

The primary criteria for the selection of this specific case were the institution's innovative approach which provides insights into alternative modes of delivery and new and creative ways of learning by combining two special approaches, namely collaborative learning and e-learning. In this regard, we were especially interested in a blended degree programme in management which has been realised in an e-learning environment and builds upon collaborative learning principles at the same time. Moreover, it is characterised by some special and unique features, not yet very prominent in the same form in the closer higher education environment.

The study builds first of all upon the experiences and observations of faculty (head of the study, senior lectures) involved in the study programme under research. Also, other perspectives and observations from non-directly related departments and faculty, as well as management have been considered and included in the analysis. Formal blueprints and reports, as well as brochures and publicly accessible data on websites, etc. and related material (study programme brochures, etc.), has been examined to comprehend strategy, goals, learning philosophy and organisational structures. In addition, the study uses the networked learning model by Goodyear (1999) presented earlier, as a conceptual framework for the analysis.

7.5. The Case

At the institution under study, a blended Management Bachelor programme is offered. This programme grants after completing the academic degree of 'Bachelor of Arts in Business', lasts 3 years (6 semesters) and accredits for 180 ECTS. It is officially labelled by the institution as business-oriented, practical study programme with eCampus support, including webcasts, videos, moderated chats, live streams and digital course material. The study programme under research also builds on a cohort-based approach which means that each year a group of students enrols and remains the same until graduation, following a predefined curriculum pathway.

The target group is a separate category of students differing from traditional on-campus students. Those targeted students appreciate especially flexibility in learning and the possibility to study next to outside commitments as family and job responsibilities. Indeed, most of the students enroled in the study programme at hand are full-time workers and 'adult learners' being on average 28–29 years old, and thus older than the traditional on-campus student who starts studying right after high school very often (Dabbagh, 2007; Dutton & Dutton, 2002; Oblinger, Barone, & Hawkins, 2001).

The institution under study does not strive for economies of scale by taking in as many students as possible. In fact, the study programme receives public subsidies for a predetermined number of students. The Bachelor degree programme initially started with 30 study places in 2014. In 2015, 54 student places were offered, and in 2016, the programme was able to allow 84 new students to enrol. In anticipation of potentially high drop-outs, an excess of 20 to 30% was taken in.

These numbers in mind, the institution's strategy in this online programme was optimising active student engagement and participation in their studies. To achieve this objective, collaborative learning has been declared as a key measure.

As in any other study programme offered by the institution, also within the programme under research student participation in lectures is obligatory. Students have to attend at least 75 % of lecturing hours in each subject. This is regarded an essential precondition for effective collaborative learning. Since the launch of the study programme in 2014, a number of 275 students enroled and opted for the blended educational format. The programme by now counts four cohorts (2014/15, 2015/16, 2016/17; 2017/18).

As with typical blended programmes, the programme in question combines traditional classroom education with synchronous and asynchronous online education whereby 80% of the content is delivered online through network classrooms. Hence, students have direct live contact with other students and the instructor, and work independently with online resources and the learning management system on most days. Furthermore, there are mandatory residencies which include face-to-face teaching and examinations.

Looking at the pedagogical framework, a student centred approach, as well as the co-construction of knowledge, is seen as the cornerstones of the overall teaching strategy of the business school which is also true for the study programme in question which is offered in a blended format. In regards to this pedagogy, one of the key features is the institution's unique understanding of collaborative learning. Collaborative learning is part of the business school's overall learning goals, its assurance of learning and the curriculum management. This unique understanding of collaborative learning means, in particular, the facilitation of learning and the learning process through new approaches which go beyond the traditional instructor-student exchange. The same approaches and goals are also fostered within the e-learning environment at the institution.

Collaboration, however, is not simply understood as students working together with peers. This is why it also takes student-instructor interaction into account. Thus, instructors hired into the programme have to commit to high levels of responsiveness to any student queries on the one hand, and to a pro-active approach of supervision and coaching of students on the other. Thus, the importance of hiring sufficiently qualified and motivated instructors must not be underestimated because it is assumed that online facilitation varies considerably from classroom teaching, as far as concerning the initiation of collaborative learning processes. Therefore, instructors who are open to new teaching strategies are seen as a necessity in online education at the institution. Indeed, the institution and its faculty never talk about 'instructors' but use the term 'facilitator' to describe the role of the lecturers in the blended study programme.

To systematically organise collaborative learning in an online programme with students who are not physically represented, the institution relies on its Learning Management System (LMS) *'Sakai'*. In the study programme in question, it is mandatory that all parties involved are entirely facilitated via the LMS, with the exception of classroom lectures. Students and instructors are advised to solely communicate via the LMS (again with the exception of classroom activities). This proved to be a challenge at the beginning. In particular, external faculty was resistant to employing the tools because they were used to communicate via private email accounts and other channels. So the decision was made that instructors, upon their first assignment, have to sign a guideline clearly stipulating the sole use of the LMS for any communication with students. Students, however, were advised to use the LMS for follow-up reasons. It was made clear that employing other communication channels could compromise attempts to give evidence in cases where they felt treated unfairly.

The online degree programme is fully displayed in the LMS and subdivided into courses sites. Each course provides for an introductory video in which the instructor introduces him/herself and presents key elements that are going to be addressed in the course. Thus, students get a personal impression of the instructor and a first idea of the course contents. Course sites then provide for a set of sub-sites e.g. announcements, resources, drop box, assignments, messages, forums, virtual classroom access, etc. Each of these sub-sites contributes to student collaboration, in particular, however, 'Messages', 'Forums' and 'Virtual Classroom Access'.

Using the 'Virtual Classroom Access', students are entering the webinar system which, among other features, allows for live online lectures. Students can participate here via voice or chat. Instructors may also split students up into groups. It has been shown that the more experienced online instructors are, the more they are able to motivate students to extensively use the chat function. Furthermore, instructors are expected to use open questions and to let students generate the knowledge, rather than presenting the entire content directly as in traditional frontal teaching (e.g. flipped classroom and co-construction of knowledge). Given the lack of immediate feedback in online teaching situations, it proved to be helpful for instructors to prepare for this questioning approach well in advance, preferably already by embedding it into the presentation slides. Undoubtedly, there are students who are not actively participating in such activities but experience shows that the percentage of inactive students is not higher than in typical classroom situations. In some online sessions, students were required to work on even more comprehensive assignments (with time allocation of up to 2 hours). Again, most of the students were found to be actively engaged in the activity.

Directly linked with live interaction during lectures is the use of the 'Forum' as an integral part of the LMS. During lectures as well as for any kind of assignments between lectures, students are not only requested to present their results in the forum but in line with the collaborative learning approach, they are especially challenged to comment on other students' works too. Highly relevant is that students understand what exactly they are supposed to do in forum work. Otherwise, students might have a tendency to simply 'manufacture' forum entries by simply agreeing to the works of others (e.g. obligatory commenting – posting at least three comments, etc.). Not only students can profit from this peer-learning approach, but also instructors who would never be able to provide feedback for all statements generated in the forums, especially if student groups are large. As the institution's experience shows it is not uncommon to have also more than 1000 forum posts in a group of 40 students within a week for example. Thus, the instructor benefits in the same manner as students do, as he/she relies on the fruitful exchange between peers, and the co-construction of knowledge, generating inputs and sharing knowledge with students.

Given the lack of face-to-face communication in an online programme, instructors' responsiveness to student queries is of particular importance. In the online department, measures have been taken to assure that students receive answers to their questions well in time. Therefore, instructors must sign-up to a procedural guideline, in which they agree to answer all student queries within 36 hours during an ongoing course. This includes weekends due to the fact that most of the students in the online Bachelor degree programme remain in their professions whilst studying and thus to better cope with their individual needs. Given the structure of the online Bachelor with courses taught in 3-weeks blocks, instructors must be available for questions by students for 21 days overall. As said earlier, emails are supposed to be exchanged via the message-function. This allows for regular checks on response times of instructors in their courses.

After the first three years, a drop-out rate of 20 % is observable, which is comparable to the drop-out rate in regular on-campus programmes in the same local area and the European area in general (Vossensteyn et al., 2015).

Table 7.1 summarises the key features of the blended study programme, building on the networked learning model by Goodyear (1999, 2005).

7.6. Discussion

7.6.1. Strengths

Analysing the present case, it becomes evident that the institution under study strives for a balance between monitoring and supervision on one hand, emphasised by Yukselturk and Bulut (2007) as precondition for collaborative learning and desired types of interaction to occur, and support and co-construction on the other, declared by Dillenbourg (1999) and Moore (1991) to be essential parts in collaborative learning settings. Through this approach the key aspects such as

Table 7.1. Overview Key Features.

Organisational Framework	• European Business School • Blended Bachelor Degree Programme in Management (full programme) • Cohort-based approach • 180 ECTS and 6 semesters • Public subsidies for a predetermined number of students • 275 students by now
Pedagogical Framework	Philosophy: • Student-centred approach • Instructors are seen as facilitators supporting the co-construction of knowledge • Online facilitation varies considerably from classroom teaching, especially concerning the initiation of collaborative learning processes • Unique understanding of collaborative learning – collaborative learning is part of learning goals, assurance of learning and the curriculum management Pedagogy: • Systematic organisation of collaborative learning in an online programme • Delivery through a blended format (80% of the content is delivered online) • Students must attend at least 75% of lecturing hours in each subject • Instructors have to commit to high levels of responsiveness to students and must apply a pro-active approach to supervision and coaching of students • LMS is the core mean for communication between students and instructor
Educational Setting and Student Activity	• 'Virtual Classroom Access' – live online lectures through the webinar system • 'Forums' students not only present their results in the forum, but in line with the collaborative learning approach, they have to give feedback on other students' works • ICT enabled and supported group works, etc.
Drop-out Rate	• Drop-out rate of 20%

student support, guidance, encouragement, feedback, criticism and supervision to counterbalance transactional distance emphasised by Moore (1991) become substantial parts of the programme.

On one side there is a strong focus on the constructivist and cognitive learning pedagogies. The study programme builds upon the assumptions by Piaget (1970) that knowledge is constructed through active and personal experience and observation, and that understanding is a process of interaction. Thus, education, where the learner is constantly challenged to reflect and discuss the learnt content in a social context with others, is provided and students do not take on a passive role but contribute to the co-creation of knowledge through their prior experiences and the exchange with peers and instructors (Petraglia, 1998) or better 'facilitators' as they are termed by the institution itself.

On the other side, the study programme under research fosters the student-instructor interaction in a particular way. Hence, certain measures were established to assure a regular student-instructor interaction, as instructors must be available for questions by students for a certain amount of days and have to sign a procedural guideline where they ensure their commitment to do so. Hence, the role of the instructor changes, as proposed by Hiltz (1998), and he becomes a facilitator in a collaborative learning environment by supporting students in the creation of their knowledge, emphasised as a precondition for a successful collaborative learning environment. Regular interaction is not only assured from the faculty-side, but also from the student side. A precondition here is the mandatory attendance of students. Furthermore, they are encouraged to interact with their peers through obligatory commenting in forums, etc. (e.g. making at least three constructive comments) where they have to review and enrich the work of others, as well as through team-based assignments and assessments. Hence, the institution recognises the importance of active collaboration between students and students and facilitator.

Furthermore, the learning management system and especially its effective and consequent utilisation and application (monitoring and supervision on one hand and guidance and feedback on the other), builds the basis for collaborative learning in the online environment. This special approach differentiates the institution and its blended study programme from other higher education institutions which often limit the use of LMS to provide basic information such as schedules, marks and other learning material.

By a unique combination of different collaborative elements as e.g. group assignments, virtual classrooms, forums, etc., the fostering of interactional aspects can be ensured at all levels, whereby the learning process becomes more vivid and thus more realistic in the end. Hence, the presented learning model is congruent with the assumptions of the authors Dabbagh (2007), Harasim (2000) and Liang and Chen (2012) regarding the importance of interaction within the learning process as an integral and substantial part of online education.

In this context, the blended format has to be highlighted. Through this blended format, key benefits of online education such as the flexibility, the possibility of coaching and interaction and learning through the incorporation of educational technology can be combined with the advantages of on-campus teaching and the personal facilitator-learner and learner-learner interaction, as drawn out by Fearon et al. (2012). Through this blended format, students have the possibility to also meet in person and are thus able to further build and extend relationships in the virtual learning environment afterward. This enhances feelings of social inclusion and strengthens the feeling of belongingness to a group, following the theory of Social Identity (Tajfel & Turner, 1979; Turner & Tajfel, 1986) and the assumptions regarding increased retention outlined by Tinto (1993).

As claimed by Hiltz (1998) and McAlpine (2000), it becomes apparent that through this blended format and through a special combination of collaborative and digital learning elements in the curricula, it is not only possible to better respond to the special needs of the online educational target group in seeking for more flexibility, but it enables vivid and realistic interaction that diminishes, in turn, the risk of social isolation in the study programme.

Considering the organisational frame and the implementation of a whole study programme building on a cohort-based approach, instead of a single course or module might bring further advantages. As student groups are remaining the same over the years (cohort-based approach) they might also be more motivated to build up social contacts, as chances to create lasting relationships are higher. Moreover, this is not only a possibility to strengthen relationships between peers but also between students and instructor or faculty in general. Students will probably be more engaged and motivated to create valuable contacts with faculty and the institution if they know they will spend the next three years with them and not as in single modules some weeks only. Indeed, the study by Abel (2005) found evidence that institutions offering online education successfully clearly preferred full programmes over single courses/modules to be offered online, as they show higher retention rates. Looking at the case at hand, a real integration of ICT (internet, CMC, digital tools, etc.) not only within the curricula, but the overall teaching strategy becomes apparent.

Finally, through this special combination of collaborative learning and e-learning aspects, a strong reciprocal reinforcement between both approaches has been established, rendering the offered online programme more effective. Indeed, after the first three years, it can be observed that student drop-out rates are comparable to the European standards in on-campus programmes, which at least by now, pleads for the institution's implemented e-learning approach.

7.6.2. Weaknesses

The study programme at hand is rather novel and therefore still in a developmental phase. As it has been launched in 2014, findings only refer to three years of experience, observations and outcomes. The sustainable evidence is therefore still absent and it remains to be seen how the programme will evolve over time.

Second, it must be admitted that it will not be possible to fully remove the lack of personal contact, neither within blended learning. Hence, also the amount of autodidactic learning remains still higher compared to traditional on-campus education. In turn, students who are not that autonomous in managing their learning may struggle more to succeed in online education, whereas students who are known to be more autonomous and self-directed learners need less interaction, standardisation and structure, as drawn out by Moore and Kearsley (2011). An option could be to identify those students in order to offer individual and personalised support where needed.

However, from time to time, instructors also have to rely on the self-directed learning of their students as they would never be able to react on every single student activity, even more so in classes with many students, as confirmed in this case. Thus, lecturers actually depend on the collaborative learning elements which should foster the co-construction of knowledge and should ensure a fruitful peer-to-peer exchange. However, the risk remains that this will not occur.

Finally, such an approach to learning as in the present case pushes faculty, instructors and higher education management in general, to their limits. The efforts regarding planning, designing and structuring such learning models and the subsequent implementation, processing and monitoring are excessive. On the one hand, instructors are not able to leave anything to chance as detailed planning is essential for a smooth flow to ensure that learning occurs in the first place. On the other hand, a certain degree of flexibility must be apparent as target students have special requirements. Hence, finding a balance between standardisation and flexibility remains a challenge.

In addition, this particular approach to learning requires for experienced faculty and might therefore be very difficult to handle for inexperienced and freshman instructors or external faculty. Consequently, trainings and briefings regarding the implementation and application of collaborative learning in online education might be necessary, entailing, however, additional costs. In addition, more experienced faculty would probably require a higher salary and will be harder to find. Thus, the implementation of blended learning as a form of online education as illustrated in this case bears also the risk of excessive costs linked to a stressful and exhausting recruiting and personnel training process.

Talking about costs, it must be kept in mind that the programme at hand benefits from public subsidies, which might not be the case for many other higher education institutions. This may be an obstacle, but also a benefit if tuition fees can be adjusted to costs in the absence of subsidies. Therefore, every institution should consider revenue and costs streams, as well as resource allocations when responding to the disruptive power of online education, deciding carefully if online education should be offered and how many study places can be offered. Similarly, also legal and policy aspects should be considered and evaluated, as they may vary considerably among countries. Hence, it has to be kept in mind that the present study illustrates a case within the European area and that implementing a similar programme in other countries especially outside Europe might also be unfeasible.

Table 7.2 summarises the strengths and weaknesses identified, building again on the networked learning model by Goodyear (1999, 2005).

Table 7.2. Strengths and Weaknesses of the Study Programme.

	Strengths	Weaknesses
Organisational Framework	• Offering a whole Bachelor's programme in a blended format with a cohort-based approach – increased and regular contact with peers, deepens and reinforces intensified and close relationships with peers, as well as faculty	• European business school – respective policy and legal conditions have to be considered (implementation in the manner outlined might not be possible, as inadmissible) • Risk of excessive costs resulting from recruiting and personnel training processes
Pedagogical Framework	Philosophy: • Co-construction of knowledge – higher collaboration and decreased the feeling of social isolation • Instructors as facilitators supporting the co-construction of knowledge – new relationship emerges where students and instructors collaborate and co-construct, learning is more effective and social isolation can be decreased • Unique understanding of collaborative learning – transparency among all levels and departments about learning goals	Philosophy: • Instructors are seen as facilitators supporting the co-construction of knowledge. At the same time, they are also supposed to guide, monitor and supervise students. This double-burden for instructors might also be exhausting and requires for experienced faculty • Online facilitation varies from classroom teaching in the initiation of collaborative learning – this assumption requires experienced and well-trained faculty and might also imply additional efforts & costs

Table 7.2. (*Continued*)

	Strengths	Weaknesses
	Pedagogy:	Pedagogy:
	• Systematic organisation of collaborative learning – implying consequent procedures and structures	• Systematic organisation of collaborative learning in an online programme requires for huge efforts, including time and costs affecting all parties involved
	• Delivery through a blended format (80% of the content is delivered online) – ensures that personal contact does not get fully lost	• High levels of responsiveness of instructors and pro-active supervision and coaching – also highly exhausting for faculty and could be an additional burden.
	• Students must attend at least 75% of lecturing hours in each subject – a precondition for collaboration	• Lack of social contact will not fully disappear.
	• High levels of responsiveness of instructors and pro-active supervision and coaching – fosters interaction and diminishes social isolation	• Entire and sole communication via LMS might be an obstacle for external or inexperienced faculty
	• LMS as core mean for communication – reinforces clear rules and transparency for all parties involved	
Educational Setting and Student Activity	• 'Virtual Classroom Access' – live online lectures through the webinar system which makes synchronous interaction possible and fosters interaction thus interaction	• Self-directed learning of students is sometimes also a precondition.

	• 'Forums' – students have to comment on other students' works. This fosters not only interaction and collaboration (reduces lack of contact), but also critical thinking
	• Autodidactic (self-directed learning) has to be higher compared to on-campus programmes
Drop-out Rate	• Drop-out rate of 20% – comparable to on-campus rates in the European region
	• Novel programme (launched in 2014), still in a developmental phase

Key Pillars of the Programme

- Combination of online education and collaborative learning and reciprocal reinforcement
- Full programme, blended and cohort-based approach
- Consequent commitment to LMS in use
- Engagement from faculty and balance between being facilitators and supporting students, and guidance and monitoring

7.6.3. Summary

To sum up, the present case provides an example for the four critical items developed by Dillenbourg (1999) for defining the situation (conditions), interaction (specification), processes (rules) and effects (monitoring and regulating). With the introductory video in which the instructor introduces him/herself and presents key elements that are going to be addressed in the course, conditions and settings are clarified from the beginning. Getting a first sight impression of the instructor and his/her appearance also lays the foundation for building up further relationships, fostering social inclusion. Moreover, through mandatory attendance and group tasks implying a minimum of critical reflection (e.g. mandatory commenting to peer postings), interaction patterns and rules are generated with the specification of collaboration and roles, as proposed by Dillenbourg (1999). Finally, the LMS in use and its consequent utilisation enables the control and the monitoring of those interactions through the tracking of postings, emails, etc. and the recording of student and class activities. Thus, the presented case study may well serve as a prime example on how to imply reasonable and efficient instructional strategies which provide effective feedback and monitor performance in online education and foster the occurrence of desired interactions in an online environment, as proposed by Dillenbourg (1999). At the same time, these conditions emphasised by Dillenbourg (1999), constitute a solid based to reduce transactional distance through dialogue, autonomy and structure as emphasised by Moore (1991).

The first aspect important to reduce distance as claimed by Moore (1991), namely dialogue and so to say interaction, can be reinforced in this case through a collaborative learning approach, as drawn out earlier following the key elements developed by Dillenbourg (1999). This lays the bricks for the following two aspects, autonomy and structure. Autonomy is fostered through the support of those students that are less autonomous learners with guidance, supervision and feedback from lecturers who at the same time act as facilitators, but also from peers who help to co-construct knowledge. Important factors to mention in this context are the availability of instructors and their commitment towards responding in time, as well as group works and the obligatory use of the LMS and connected tools as discussion forums, for communication and interaction. The third factor – structure, is fostered through the implementation of a whole Bachelor study programme in a blended format that builds on a cohort-based approach, building a basis for enhanced social contacts while reducing feelings of social isolation.

Hence, an accurate answer to our research question how to implement blended learning successfully in order to overcome, at least however, to inhibit one central disadvantage in online education, namely distance and the connected feelings of social isolation, can be found. First of all, the secret lies in this special case, within the combination and integration of collaborative learning elements and e-learning in one and the same degree programme. Secondly, the underlying assumptions that learning occurs through interaction, and that online education enhances this interaction and finally facilitates deep learning supports the design, development, implementation and evaluation of the study programme, constituting a guiding mission for everyone involved. Thirdly, through the design as full programme building on a cohort-based approach, and the delivery of the content through a blended format, personal contact between student and instructors and between peers gets not fully lost and builds a basis for deepening virtual relationships at the same time. Finally, the consequent commitment to the LMS in use, as well as the claimed engagement from faculty facilitates and improves the communication and interaction between students, and instructors and students.

The case at hand also demonstrates that not only blended learning/delivery alone has the power to decrease feelings of social isolation, but that it is, in fact, more a matter of combining different factors which reinforce this process even more. Indeed, it is a combination of various organisational determinants, pedagogical and philosophical approaches, educational setting designs and the linked activity and used resources, as drawn out in Table 7.2.

7.7. Conclusion

The present case serves as an example on how educational settings can be embedded in the e-learning context and how organisational and pedagogical frameworks can provide the direction to overcome traditional barriers in online education as social isolation and distance by fostering interaction.

It becomes clear that the cognitive and constructivist approach towards learning, the facilitation of a whole programme through a blended, cohort-based format, the deployment of and commitment to the LMS in use, as well as the embedding of collaborative learning in online education in combination with a strong faculty commitment (striving for a balance between monitoring and supervision on one hand and support and co-construction on the other hand) can be referred as key pillars and at the same time as major strengths of the study programme.

Thus, our study contributes being an example, guiding other higher education institutions in their starting gates to implement and apply online education through a blended mode, while they get the possibility to reflect and are thus able to learn from other HEIs and their implemented online educational approaches.

References

Abel, R. (2005). Implementing best practices in online learning: A recent study reveals common denominators for success in internet-supported learning. *EDUCAUSE Quarterly, 28*(3), 75–77.

Allen, E., & Seaman, J. (2010). *Learning on demand: Online education in the United States, 2009*. Babson: Babson Survey Research Group, The Sloan Consortium. doi:10.1108/13673279710800718.

Bekele, T. A. (2010). Motivation and satisfaction in internet-supported learning environments: A review. *Educational Technology & Society, 13*(2), 116–127.

Bitzer, P., & Janson, A. (2014). Towards a holistic understanding of technology-mediated learning services – A state-of-the-art analysis. In *International Conference on Information Systems* (pp. 1–19). Tel Aviv: European Conference on Information Systems (ECIS).

Dabbagh, N. (2007). The online learner: Characteristics and pedagogical implications. *Contemporary Issues in Technology and Teacher Education, 7*(3), 217–226.

Dillenbourg, P. (1999). What do you mean by collaborative learning? In P. Dillenbourg (Ed.), *Collaborative learning Cognitive and computational approaches* (pp. 1–19). Oxford: Elsevier. doi:10.1.1.167.4896

Dutton, J., & Dutton, M. (2002). How do online students differ from lecture students? *JALN, 6*(1), 1–20.

Eom, S. B., & Ashill, N. (2016). The determinants of students perceived learning outcomes and satisfaction in university online education: An update. *Decision Sciences Journal of Innovative Education, 14*(2), 185–215. doi:10.1111/dsji.12097

Fearon, C., Starr, S., & McLaughlin, H. (2012). Blended learning in higher education (HE): Conceptualising key strategic issues within a business school. *Development and Learning in Organisations, 26*(2), 19–22. doi:10.1108/14777281211201196

Garrison, D. R., & Kanuka, H. (2004). Blended learning: Uncovering its transformative potential in higher education. *Internet and Higher Education, 7*(2), 95–105. doi:10.1016/j.iheduc.2004.02.001

Glaser, R. (1990). The reemergence of learning theory within instructional research. *American Psychologist, 45*(1), 29.

Goodyear, P. (1999). *European Journal of Open, Distance and E-Learning, 2*(1).

Goodyear, P. (2002). Psychological foundations for networked learning. In *Networked learning: Perspectives and issues* (pp. 49–75). London: Springer.

Goodyear, P. (2005). Educational design and networked learning: Patterns, pattern languages and design practice. *Australian Journal of Educational Technology, 21*(1), 82–101.

Goodyear, P., Banks, S., Hodgson, V., & McConnel, D. (2004). Research on networked learning: aims and approaches. In P. Goodyear, S. Banks, V. Hodgson, & D. Mcconnel (Eds.), *Advances in research on networked learning*. Dordrecht: Kluwer Academic Publishers.

Harasim, L. (2000). Shift happens online education as a new paradigm in learning. *The Internet and Higher Education, 3*, 41–61.

Henri, F., & Rigault, C. R. (1996). Collaborative distance learning and computer conferencing. In T. T. Liao (Ed.), *Advanced educational technology: Research issues and future potential* (pp. 45–76). Berlin: Springer.

Hiltz, S. R. (1998). Collaborative learning in asynchronous learning networks: Building learning communities. In *WebNet 98 World Conference of the WWW, Internet, and Intranet Proceedings* (pp. 1–9). Orlando, Florida. doi:10.1007/BF02763577.

Johnson, D. W., & Johnson, R. T. (1992). Positive interdependence: Key to effective cooperation. In *Interaction in cooperative groups: The theoretical anatomy of group learning* (pp. 174–199). Australia: Cambridge University Press.

Kim, K.-J., & Bonk, C. J. (2006). The future of online teaching and learning in higher education: The survey says. *Educause Quarterly*, (4), 22−30.

Liang, R., & Chen, D.-T. V. (2012). Online learning: Trends, potential and challenges. *Creative Education*, *3*(8), 1332−1335. doi:10.4236/ce.2012.38195

McAlpine, I. (2000). Collaborative learning online. *Distance Education*, *21*(1), 66−80. doi:10.1080/0158791000210105

McKiernen, P., & Wilson, D. (2014). Strategic choice: Taking business out of b-schools. In A. Pettigrew, E. Cornuel, & U. Hommel (Eds.), *The institutional development of business schools* (1st ed., pp. 248−269). Oxford: Oxford University Press.

Moessenlechner, C., Obexer, R., Sixl-Daniell, K., & Seeler, J.-M. (2015). E-learning degree programs: A better way to balance work and education? *International Journal of Advanced Corporate Learning*, *8*(3), 11−16.

Moore, M. G. (1991). Distance education theory. *The American Journal of Distance Education*, *5*(3), 1−6.

Moore, M. G., & Kearsley, G. (2011). *Distance education: A systems view of online learning* (3rd ed.). Wadsworth, OH: Cengage Learning.

Morris, R., & Hayes, C. (1997). Small group work: Are group assignments a legitimate form of assessment. In R. Pospisil & L. Willcoxson (Eds.), *Learning through teaching* (pp. 229−233). Murdoch: Proceedings of the 6th Annual Teaching Learning Forum.

Muilenburg, L. Y., & Berge, Z. L. (2005). Student barriers to online learning: A factor analytic study. *Distance Education*, *26*(1), 29−48. doi:10.1080/01587910500081269

Oblinger, D. G., Barone, C. A., & Hawkins, B. L. (2001). *Distributed education and its challenges: An overview*. Washington, DC: American Council on Education, EDUCAUSE.

Petraglia, J. (1998). *Reality by design: The rhetoric and technology of authenticity in education*. Mahwah, NJ: Routledge.

Piaget, J. (1970). *Science of education and the psychology of the child* (Vol. 51). New York, NY: Orion Press.

Piaget, J. (1982). *The child's conception of the world*. London: Palladin.

Rovai, A. P. (2003). In search of high persistence rates in distance education online programs. *Internet and Higher Education*, *6*(1), 1−16.

Skinner, E., Furrer, C., Marchand, G., & Kindermann, T. (2008). Engagement and disaffection in the classroom: Part of a larger motivational dynamic? *Journal of Educational Psychology*, *100*(4), 765−781.

Stanford-Bowers, D. E. (2008). Persistence in online classes: A study of perceptions among community college stakeholders. *MERLOT Journal of Online Learning and Teaching*, *4*(1), 37−50.

Sursock, A. (2015). *Trends 2015: Learning and teaching in European universities. EUA Publications 2015*. EUA European University Association asbl.

Tajfel, H., & Turner, J. C. (1979). An integrative theory of intergroup conflict. *The Social Psychology of Intergroup Relations*, *33*(47), 74.

Tinto, V. (1987). *Leaving college: Rethinking the causes and cures of student attrition*. Chicago, IL: University of Chicago Press.

Tinto, V. (1993). Leaving college: Rethinking the causes and cures of student attrition. In *Toward a theory of doctoral persistence* (pp. 230−256). Chicago, IL: University of Chicago Press.

Turner, J. C., & Tajfel, H. (1986). The social identity theory of intergroup behavior. *Psychology of Intergroup Relations*, 7–24.

Veerman, A., & Veldhuis-Diermanse, E. (2001). Collaborative learning through computer-mediated communication in academic education. In *Euro CSCL*, (pp. 625–632).

Vossensteyn, H., Kottmann, A., Jongbloed, B., Kaiser, F., Cremonini, L., Stensaker, B. [...] Wollscheid, S. (2015). *Drop-out and completion in higher education in Europe – Main report*. European Commission. Luxembourg.

Vygotsky, L. S., & Cole, M. (1978). *Mind in society: The development of higher mental process*. Cambridge, MA: Harvard University Press.

Wallace, R. M. (2003). Online learning in higher education: A review of research on interactions among teachers and students. *Education, Communication & Information*, 3(2), 241–280. doi:10.1080/14636310303143

Wu, J.-H., Tennyson, R. D., & Hsia, T.-L. (2010). A study of student satisfaction in a blended e-learning system environment. *Computers & Education*, 55(1), 155–164. doi:10.1016/j.compedu.2009.12.012

Yin, R. K. (2003). *Designing case studies*. Thousand Oaks, CA: Sage Publications.

Yukselturk, E., & Bulut, S. (2007). Predictors for student success in an online course. *Journal of Educational Technology & Society*, 10(2), 71–83.

Chapter 8

Disrupting Higher Education in Alaska: Introducing the Native Teacher Certification Pathway

Paul Berg, Kathryn Cruz, Thomas Duening and Susan Schoenberg

Abstract

The geosocial divide that separates many rural regions of Alaska continues to present considerable challenges, such as those that have long plagued the Yukon-Kuskokwim region with cultural and value conflicts. Lack of empirical data and improper identification of the root causes of the ongoing socio-political, cultural and economic disparities between rural Alaska and the rest of the country contribute to the general misconceptions of the turbulent nature of life on the tundra today. In this isolated region, the state has built dozens of schools that largely employ non-Natives. Teacher certification requirements have largely alienated Alaska Natives from pursuing careers in their home villages due to cost, lack of access, lack of student support and irrelevant curriculum. Despite rigorous standards and extraordinary funding opportunities, the current model has traditionally underperformed against both state and national norms.

This research targets a project that re-conceptualizes the teacher certification pipeline for remote Alaska Native villages via the utilisation of a competency-based bilingual curriculum, mentoring and interactive learning delivered via hybrid and online formats. The Native Teacher Certification Pathway proposed will be significant both in its local impact on unemployed adults and Yupik youth, and globally as a site for innovation in the application, delivery and assessment of evidence-based student support activities and programmes. Leveraging place, identity, language and values make learning incredibly powerful, increases efficacy and creates a true impact. Universities and business programmes that are sensitive to this fact and tailor their programmes appropriately will likely see a greater return on their investment.

Keywords: Culturally relevant education; online teacher certification; biculturalism; adaptive curriculum; indigenous education models; positive identity formation

8.1. Alaska's Need for Disruption in Teacher Education

Alaska is a land of contrasts and extremes. The central landmass of Alaska extends 870 miles north from the Gulf of Alaska to the Arctic Ocean, and 800 miles west from the Canadian border to the Bering Sea. Nature and international politics have given Alaska two appendages. Southeast Alaska extends south from the central landmass for 500 miles, while the Alaska Peninsula and the Aleutian Islands jut into the Bering Sea for 1000 miles. With these regions added, Alaska's dimensions become truly monumental – 1,400 miles from north to South and 2,260 miles from east to west and a landmass of 586,400 square miles. Alaska is twice as large as France, yet has less than one-hundredth the population (State of Alaska, 2010).

The urban centres of Alaska are similar to towns found in the contiguous United States. But away from the major urban centres of Anchorage, Fairbanks and Juneau; away from the paved roads and shopping malls, another world emerges. Small villages dot the landscape, most accessible only by aircraft or boat. Here, away from the cities, live 70,000 Aleuts, Eskimos and Indians, making up about 78% of the total population. Here the English language still yields in varying degrees to Native languages. The economy changes as one moves away from the population centres. Hunting and fishing emerge as important economic activities as this is the largest geographic region of the world where subsistence is still an essential part of life. Here the Inupiaq, Yupik, Athabascan, Tlingit and Aleut live in homelands they have traditionally occupied. This is bush Alaska – the other Alaska.

Like the geography and climate, Alaska's human condition exhibits the same pattern of contrasts and extremes. One of the most obvious of these is the boom and bust nature of the economy. For the past 150 years, Alaska has experienced a consistent pattern of alternating periods of rapid economic growth followed by periods of steep economic contraction. In the past, mineral development and the gold rushes have spurred on these exaggerated economic cycles. Since the mid 1970s, with the discovery of oil in Purdue Bay, Alaska has experienced a period of unprecedented economic growth. However, with steadily declining oil production and the steep drop in oil prices, Alaska is again experiencing a financial crisis of lean budgets and economic contraction.

But perhaps the most enigmatic contrast and extreme in Alaska is the contrast of the human condition of the immigrant and indigenous residents of Alaska. Most of the wealth of Alaska is derived from the sale of raw materials from the rural areas. However, most of the wealth is concentrated in the urban non-Native communities (Goldsmith, 2008).

In contrast to this unprecedented wealth of the non-Native communities, Alaska has succeeded over the past 35 years in establishing a dismal record in the human condition of the Native population. The negative health and social statistics spike in the rural Native community.

- Alaska Natives make up 16% of the state's population, but comprise 32% of the offender population revealing a potential systemic bias in Alaska's criminal justice system (Alaska Department of Corrections, 2015).
- As of 2012, Alaska was incarcerating 4.1% of all Native males aged 18 years and above. This is the second highest male indigenous incarceration rate in the world, following Australia (Alaska Department of Corrections, 2015).
- Alaska Native males aged 15 to 24 years have the highest rate of suicide in the United States, 1.5 times higher than the national average suicide rate. (Centre for Disease Control, 2015).
- For the second year in a row, Alaska is considered the most dangerous state with the highest per capita rate of violent crimes in the nation. (Department of Public Safety, 2015).
- In 2014, the Congressional Bipartisan Indian Law & Order Commission report singled out rural Alaska law enforcement and judicial processing as being the worst in the United States.
- For the 2014–2015 school year, 23% of students enroled state-wide were Alaska Native. Of that 23%, 38% of high school students drop out state-wide annually (State of Alaska, 2015).

According to the 2014 Native Youth Report prepared by the Executive Office of the President, this problem extends beyond Native Alaska. For example, the report found that:

- More than one in three American Indian and Alaska Native children live in poverty.
- The American Indian/Alaskan Native high school graduation rate is 67%, the lowest of any racial/ethnic demographic group across all schools. Alaska Native and American Indian students are the least likely to finish high school.
- 39% of Native students who enroled in a four-year institution in the fall of 2004 completed a bachelor's degree by 2010, compared to 62% of white students.
- American Indian and Alaska Native youth are the least likely to be offered an Advanced Placement course in their high schools and often are not enroled in rigorous high school courses that are gateways to higher education (Executive Office of the President, 2014).

Education is the means by which cultures perpetuate themselves. For Alaska Natives who live in the Arctic, the subarctic, the interior and the mountainous regions of the state, learning to live in these challenging environments is a life-long process. Their knowledge base and life process are currently excluded from the education system and teacher certification process.

The purpose of this research is to eliminate such educational disparities through the investigation of the feasibility of a new, disruptive teacher certification pathway. An alternative model would prepare Alaska Native teachers of the highest quality, preparing on the Yupik Eskimos of the Yukon-Kuskokwim Delta for life-long careers in their villages. There will be teachers grounded in Yupik language and culture (Yuuyaraq), uniquely able to serve Yupik students. Envisioning new ways of preparing teachers to serve Yupik villages requires a shift in existing administrative assumptions and practices. Such a proposed alternative teacher certification would be based on the recognition of linguistic, cultural, historic and local knowledge skills which are neither taught nor recognised in current teacher programmes. The alternative preparation programme would seek accreditation through the state and the World Indigenous Nations Higher Education Consortium (WINHEC). Pending success, the alternative teacher certification programme could serve as a model for indigenous certification practices worldwide.

An alternative indigenous teacher certification programme has the potential to establish relationships among certified teachers, public school districts, the Alaska university system, the Alaska Department of Education & Early Development (DEED) and tribal entities. Creating an online pathway for certification based on the knowledge and skills in the indigenous culture is a supplement to traditional teacher certification. The online certification aims to redress a basic shortcoming in the rural Alaska education system – the failure to recognise the indigenous education system and values of Alaska's traditional native people who are living in their native homelands.

Unfortunately, empirical research concerning the direct connections between education systems and community health and wellness is spread thin throughout the social sciences. The result of these inconsistencies is that some ideas presented are speculative, whereas others have significant empirical support. At the least, we hope these findings can be used as a springboard for more controlled investigations into the potential of new teaching models in Alaska to equalise the education system.

8.1.1. Crisis in Alaska Native Education

Alaska is at a critical juncture in its educational history as the current rural village school system is serving fewer and fewer students effectively. The state has also been exhausting dwindling economic resources in its attempt to operate a system that in some villages, fails to produce a single high school graduate. Educating Alaska Natives has predominantly relied on non-Native sources, with new teachers and administrators circulating in from the contiguous 48 states each year. Although these teachers meet the requirements mandated by the state, they are oftentimes culturally unaware and ultimately unqualified to work with Alaska Native youth, resulting in high teacher attrition rates. The state's attempts to ignore the consequences of maintaining the status quo coincides directly with high rates of violence, suicide and other alarming health factors currently rising in rural villages. While universities and the state-wide school system practices have adopted the rhetoric of equal educational opportunity for all, data and statistics show that reality continues to fall short of the expectation. Nowhere is this situation more evident than in the Yukon-Kuskokwim Delta and the Yupik people who have resided in the region since time immemorial.

The Yupiit School District consists of three villages: Akiak, Akiachak and Tuluksak. The total population of all three villages is approximately 1,600. During the 2013 – 2014 school year, the state of Alaska spent USD$ 12,600,000 for the education of the children in rural Alaskan villages, or over USD$ 41,000 per child. This figure is representative of the level of expenditure per student in the remote regions of Alaska. (Source: Notes taken during November 21, 2014 Yupiit School Board meeting.)

The single largest expenditure for the school district is teacher and administrator salaries. The majority of the new hires are from the contiguous 48 states. The current superintendent of the Yupiit School District is the only Alaska Native out of 54 superintendents state-wide. The school district bears the expense of recruiting out-of-state staff, including travel to and from Alaska, salaries and subsidised housing. Most of the teachers and administrators save as much of their salary as possible and relocate out of Alaska within two or three years. Of the few non-Native administrators and teachers who do make a career of teaching the Yukon-Kuskokwim Delta, the majority retire to homes out of state:

> Teachers and administrators in rural Alaska schools are mostly Euro-American and short-term, many staying in a village only 1 or 2 years (with a few staying for less than a week). While the villages themselves strongly reflect their particular Alaska Native culture, Euro-American culture dominates the school and the curriculum. In the recent past, Alaska Native students were forbidden to speak their native language in the schools. (Kawagley, Tull, & Norris-Tull, 1998, p. 3)

In addition to financial constraints in operating the current model, there are several factors contributing to a lack of cross-cultural understanding in the district and across the state.

8.1.1.1. Alaska Natives Are Not Immigrants

Minority school performance has long been the focus of extensive research and scrutiny. However, despite decades of investigation into the factors that influence success within our current systems, there remains little agreement among educators and administrators about how to positively increase learner success. John Ogbu, a Nigerian-American anthropologist, developed educational theories based on the concept of how race and ethnic differences affect educational and economic achievement. Ogbu concluded that the educational infrastructure of the United States was designed by and for the *settler society*, a society where the dominant group is made of immigrants that have come here for self-improvement and general conformity. Therefore, the educational system is highly successful in helping other immigrants, minorities or not, 'assimilate,' feel American and find success in schooling.

The other group of minorities Ogbu identifies is those 'who have been made a part of the society against their will'. He defines these two groups as *autonomous, voluntary (immigrant)* and *involuntary (non-immigrant)* minorities. The original peoples of the land, the Alaska Natives and American Indians fall into this 'involuntary' category along with Hawaiians, Mexican Americans and descendants of slaves.

In Ogbu's 1998 research, he discovered, 'involuntary minorities are less economically successful than voluntary minorities, usually experience greater and more persistent cultural and language difficulties, and do less well in school' (Ogbu & Simons, 1998, p. 166). Investigations of the root causes of how the Yupik became a minority group indicate that the encroachment of Western civilisation in the Yupiaq world happened relatively recently, with the first Euro-Americans arriving in the early 1800s, placing Yupik Eskimos in the involuntary minority category.

8.1.1.2. Education's Role in Identity Formation
The American educational dream is inclusive and immigrant minority students from literate cultures, after several years of adjustment, generally do quite well in school. Much of this process of identity affirmation, and even the awareness of the process, take place at an unconscious level. Immigrants have a frame of reference as to where they came from and if what they are experiencing are better or worse than their lives previously. However, the curriculum and educational methodologies which work for the immigrant-based population do not work with the majority of indigenous peoples living in their ancestral homelands:

> Immigrants see school success as a major route to making it in the United States. The community, family, and students believe strongly that the same strategies that middle-class white Americans employ for success, namely, hard work, following the rules, and getting good grades, will also work for them in school and in the future job market.
>
> Involuntary minorities have an ambivalent folk theory of making it. True, they believe that hard work and education are necessary to succeed in the United States. But because they have faced employment and wage discrimination as well as other barriers to making it in a white-controlled economy for many generations, they have come to believe that (1) job and wage discrimination is more or less institutionalized and permanent, and (2) individual effort, education, and hard work are important but not enough

to overcome racism and discrimination. The ambivalence may not be conscious. (Ogbu & Simons, 1998)

Generations of Alaska Native children were taken away from their families entirely and sent to boarding schools in the contiguous states, often to never be reconnected with their families or homes. Eradication of Alaska Native culture was an understood goal of early Alaskan educational systems (Kawagley et al., 1998). 'As a tool of colonisation, education served the dual purposes of imposing European and Euro-American cultures and justifying seizure of Indian land' (Executive Office of the President, 2014, p. 7).

8.1.1.3. Alaska's Educational Model Does Not Foster Bilingualism or Biculturalism

The definition of culture differs amongst scholars and becomes even more of a point of contention in regards to biculturalism. For the purpose of this article, we will refer to a culturally competent individual as someone who would have to:

> (a) possess a strong personal identity, (b) have knowledge of and facility with the beliefs and values of the culture, (c) display sensitivity to the affective processes of the culture, (d) communicate clearly in the language of the given cultural group, (e) perform socially sanctioned behavior, (f) maintain active social relations within the cultural group, and (g) negotiate the institutional structures of that culture. (LaFromboise, Hardin, Coleman, & Gerton, 1993)

How a bicultural individual becomes culturally competent varies, and currently there are five accepted models that explain the transition that is experienced in second-culture acquisition, 'the processes by which an individual from one culture, the culture of origin, develops competence in another culture, often the dominant majority culture' (LaFromboise et al., 1993, p. 396).

(1) *Assimilation*, a model that operates under the assumption that an individual loses their original cultural identity entirely to acquire a new identity, usually perceived as more desirable by the dominant culture.
(2) *Acculturation* refers to the process where 'the member of the minority group is forced to learn the new culture in order to survive economically'. Acculturation differs from assimilation in that through acculturation, the individual will still be identified as a minority, instead of losing their original identity.
(3) *Alternation* models assume individuals can understand two cultures and apply different behaviours as necessary. Through this model, it is possible to feel a part of both cultures without compromise as there is no hierarchical relationship superimposed and the relationship is more bidirectional.
(4) *Multicultural* models address institutional relationships globally.

(5) The final model is the *fusion* model, which proposes that after enough time of sharing institutional structures, 'a new common culture' emerges (LaFromboise et al., 1993, p. 401). The fusion model, however, requires more research as oftentimes, minority cultures lose their identity to blend in with the majority group.

In LaFromboise's study of biculturalism, it was concluded that the combination of having low amounts of contact with Western society, along with a strong desire to identify as the dominant culture, caused the greatest incidences of personality maladjustments and emotional difficulties for the individual. In rural Alaska, students have minimal exposure to Western lifestyles but are developing personally, socially and intellectually within a predominantly Western education system.

Monolingualism and monoculturalism remain the common practice in rural Alaskan school models, despite empirical evidence that shows the current acculturation model is not producing desired educational or socio-health results. The Akwesasne Mohawk collected data on the bicultural curriculum in both segregated and desegregated schools on the reservation. When allowed to learn through the context of Mohawk culture and language until the 4th grade, students were able to develop coping strategies and mechanisms for dealing with cultural dissonance independent of their future school setting. Both schools saw higher retention rates in students who attended Mohawk elementary programmes, and found non-Indian students were 'differentially and more positively influenced by the bicultural curriculum than the Indian students' (LaFromboise et al., 1993, p. 400). LaFromboise's study also examined the long-term effects of bicultural competency and efficacy:

One of the most influential institutions in the rural villages is the village school. Unfortunately, the schools currently are agents of cultural breakdown and change. Ninety-five per cent of the teachers are non-Natives who are not familiar with the local language, culture, knowledge base, history or learning style of the children. The classes are conducted in English. The children are taught with textbooks and materials designed and written for students living in the contiguous United States. Educational assessment is conducted with standardised tests. The local cultural, linguistic and environmental setting in which the children live is marginalised in this system. However, there is an important meta-lesson which the children learn from this arrangement. Students see that the non-Native educators have the best jobs, the best housing, the highest pay and the most status in the community. Currently, education is being delivered by those who do not possess cultural competence for where they are living, and an unintended effect is that young people grow up unsure of their own identity and how to navigate the bicultural world in which they live.

8.1.2. *Barriers to the Success of Previous Programme Offerings*

In 1992, the United States Department of Education's Indian Nations at Risk Task Force submitted their findings to the George H. W. Bush administration at a White House Conference dedicated to Native American issues. Northern Arizona University's Professor, Jon Reyhner, compiled research on factors leading Native students to drop out of school:

- Large schools that present students with an impersonal education.
- The perception that teachers do not care about Native students.
- Passive 'transmission' teaching.
- Inappropriate curriculum designed for mainstream America.
- Use of culturally biased tests.
- Tracking of Native students into low achieving classes and groups.
- Lack of Native parent involvement.

With a lack of Native teachers to model the career choice at the elementary and secondary levels, students struggle to identify with the teachers they interpret as being the instruments of exclusion. Young Alaska Natives are being tasked with developing a sense of persistent identity in a rapidly changing world without key adults modelling to do so themselves.

> Nowhere are the costs associated with failures to achieve a proper measure of individual and cultural continuity more apparent than in the identity struggles of young First Nations persons who are required not only to clear the standard hurdles that punctuate the ordinary course of individual identity development, but to construct a sense of shared identity out of the remnants of a way of life that (as a result of colonisation, ongoing prejudice, and positional inferiority) has been largely overthrown. (Hallett, Chandler, & Lalonde, 2007, p. 394)

Eighty per cent of rural students are Alaska Native but less than 5% of Alaska's certified teachers are Alaska Native (Leary, Tetpon, Hirshberg, & Hill, 2014). Alaska Natives have resisted involvement in formal teacher certification programmes. Despite a number of university endeavours to increase the number of Alaska Native certified teachers, the university system in Alaska has produced an average of only four certified Native teachers per year over the past 40 years (Leary et al., 2014). In Leary's study examining all Alaska Native teacher programmes, she concluded that the programmes were unsuccessful due to three factors (Leary et al., 2014, p. 97):

(1) *Access and cost:* Students, even when enroled in distance programmes, were still required to leave their home villages for at least a part of their teacher preparation.
(2) *Academics:* University programmes certify students in western pedagogy and curriculum instead of incorporating Native ways of teaching and learning.
(3) *Student support:* There is a lack of intensive advising in the areas of navigating all facets of the university system and key certifying exams.

8.2. Native Teacher Certification Pathway

The Native Teacher Certification Pathway (NTCP) is designed to provide support to Yupik teaching candidates through two dimensions: skills based – focusing on technical skill development – and emotional/motivational – focusing on the personal and professional development of each scholar. The initial emphasis must be placed on increasing the amount of Alaska Native teachers certified at the elementary level. The linguistic, cultural and historical identity of the child must be taught and reinforced in the schools at a young age for proper identity formation to occur. The fundamental Native skills and knowledge are found among the indigenous people and teacher certification should reflect this.

The NTCP project will begin this transformational process by establishing an indigenous certification programme for teachers of grades K-5 under the control of specific cultural regions. In other words, the people of the Yupik region would establish certification requirements. Teachers certified by the indigenous communities would additionally be issued teacher certification recognised by the state of Alaska based on their demonstrating competency instead of based on the traditional requirement of seat time.

Candidates for indigenous certification would have to meet regional cultural standards as identified by Native leaders. Such standards may include knowledge of local language, history and culture; successful employment history, character background requirements and demonstrated desire to participate in a transformational educational experience. We propose that the candidates be required to participate in a condensed course to teach basic pedagogical skills in collaboration with the state and university system. The skills would be taught by highly experienced and successful master village teachers, Native and/or non-Native. A list of such skills may include but not be limited to:

(1) *Planning*: creating comprehensive lessons and units of instruction which
   - are grounded in the context of the local culture, local environment and local reality to increase relevancy;
   - integrate core subjects such as reading, writing, math and language;
   - emphasise decision-making, problem-solving, reflective and critical thinking and the formation of values and concepts needed to navigate Yupik and western social norms; and
   - operate under the bidirectional alternation model as opposed to assimilation or acculturation.
(2) *Classroom organisation*: how to plan for materials, orchestrating both group and individual learning centres and time management.
(3) *Discipline*: alignment with administrative expectations and policies based on local norms and Yupik knowledge.
(4) *Local language, culture and history.*
(5) *Project-based curriculum development.*
(6) *Working with elders and cultural resources.*
(7) *Collaborative teaching.*

In addition, candidates would be supported by mentor village teachers, either locally or through distance education, during the first two years of teaching. Scholars will be required to successfully complete two three-week follow-up summer training sessions and participation in continuing online classes and social forums before receiving final certification.

Each scholar in the programme will also need to participate in working with or mentoring secondary high school students. This intervention programme is designed to help Yupik youth persist, advance and graduate high school with the hope and expectation that they will continue on to the NTCP higher education programme.

High tech interventions will utilise the internet, mobile applications and web-based culturally relevant content and technology to deliver a wide range of curricular and co-curricular support to each student on an individualised basis. Utilising live online problem-solving and materials based on Yupik culture, students will have extensive opportunities beyond the classroom for practice, observation and learning that honours Yupik teaching, which can occur in a variety of settings.

The project will develop its curricular and co-curricular support using an evidence-based strategy. That is, all of the supporting materials will be derived directly from research into Alaska Native student persistence and factors associated with success and expertise development such as identity formation and positive psychology. Current research in identity theory highlights the importance of identity formation to undergraduate students. Identity theory is concerned with questions such as 'who am I?' and 'how should I act?' (Cerulo, 1997). Ashforth and Mael (1989, p. 135) conceived social identity as 'perception of oneness with or belongingness to some human aggregate'. Positive psychology 'is about identifying and nurturing [a person's] strongest qualities, what they own and are best at, and helping them find niches in which they can best live out these strengths' (Seligman et al., 2000, p. 186).

It is necessary for individuals to develop grit and resilience in order to face down obstacles to positive affect and positive outcomes. The NTCP programme will be based in large measure on ensuring that Yupik Scholars develop the emotional and motivational tools to persist through the inevitable challenges of teacher fields of study and undergraduate life in general.

(1) *The Positive Power of Culturally Responsive Curriculum and Technology*
    With the possibility of an indigenous certification pathway that integrates local language and culture, comes the possibility to reverse this catalyst of cultural breakdown. The University of Oxford examined what community-level markers had the most influence on 'cultural continuity' in a 2007 study on Aboriginal language knowledge and youth suicide. The study discovered the following:

    > The common theme that cuts across all of these research efforts is that any threat to the persistence of personal or cultural identity

poses a counterpart threat to individual or community wellbeing.
(Hallett et al., 2007, p. 393)

Results indicated that, at least in British Columbia, tribes with higher levels of language knowledge, defined as more than 50% of the village reporting use of conversational language, suicides declined at a statistically significant rate. Villages that reported that less than half of the community members spoke conversational language experienced suicide rates six times greater. The results of this study demonstrate indigenous language use is a strong predictor of health and wellbeing in tribal communities (Hallett et al., 2007).

Hallett's research was preceded by a literature review conducted by Demmert, Grissmer, and Towner (2006) that searched for factors contributing to the effectiveness of culturally based education programmes serving American Indian, Alaska Native and Native Hawaiian students. Their research found that successful cultural programmes included the following:

- recognition and use of Native American languages;
- pedagogy that stresses traditional cultural characteristics;
- adult-child interactions as the springboard for education;
- pedagogy built around traditional culture as well as contemporary ways of knowing ;
- curriculum based on traditional culture, including Native spirituality;
- strong Native community participation in educating children and in the planning and operation of school activities; and
- knowledge and use of social and political mores of the community (Hattori, 2014).

Geneva Gay, author of the seminal book, *Culturally Responsive Teaching: Theory, Research, and Practice*, defines culturally responsive teaching as 'using the cultural knowledge, prior experiences, frames of reference and performance styles of ethnically diverse students to make learning encounters more relevant to and effective for them' (Gay, 2013, p. 50). She says that culturally responsive teaching enhances academic success is critical to developing a sense of individual self-worth and 'validates, facilitates, liberates and empowers ethnically diverse students'. The Equity Alliance gives the key features of culturally responsive teaching as including getting to know the cultures represented by the students in order to anchor the curriculum in the everyday lives of students. The Equity Alliance recommends presenting multiple viewpoints, actively engaging students in their learning, building scaffolding based on what students already know and using learning structures that are familiar to students culturally (Kozleski, 2010).

The Native Teacher Certification Pathway Programme (NTCP) is designed both to help teacher trainees provide culturally responsive education to their K-12 students and to model this by providing culturally responsive education to the teacher trainees themselves. The programme will consist of:

- A blended-learning course on pedagogy and teaching skills.
- A virtual course to help new and existing non-native teachers learn how to develop project-based learning units based on local culture and place.
- A virtual community that will provide support during and after the courses.
- The creation of a new bilingual, bicultural teacher certification pipeline.

(2) *Blended-learning Course: Twelve Skills of Master Teachers*
'Twelve Skills of Master Teachers' is a blended-learning course on pedagogy and teaching skills, specifically customised for the Yupik culture. This course will enable native language teachers and cultural bearers who currently have Type M certification to earn an initial K-5 teaching certificate. Type M certification is given to those who do not have bachelor's degrees to be 'cultural specialists' or 'native language teachers' in the school districts of Alaska. Often, they have 20 or more years of teaching experience but are not able to get a teaching certificate without a bachelor's degree. The course will be completed mostly online, with one in-person workshop to provide the students with the opportunity to observe and try out various teaching techniques. The online portion of the course will present pedagogy within the Yupik context. Native instructors will provide mentoring to the learners, and learners will interact with one another via social media.

(3) *Virtual Learning Course: Culturally Responsive Project-based Learning*
'Culturally Responsive Project-based Learning' is an online course that will walk teachers through the process of creating a culturally responsive project-based learning unit. Teachers will learn by doing and will build one or more projects that draw on a native culture that they can immediately use with their students. This course will also include mentoring by native instructors and student interaction via social media.

(4) *Cohort Model and Virtual Community*
Cohorts are research-based boosters of success for NCTP students as they foster positive relationships with peers, mentors and master teachers. This scholarship criterion is evidence-based and supported by research. To help enhance and maintain the cohort, students in the NCTP programme will also participate in a virtual learning community. Learning communities are similar to affinity spaces, a term first coined by Paul Gee (Gee & Hayes, 2009). Gee and Hayes noted that affinity spaces encourage and enable people who use it gain and spread knowledge, and act as a 'learning system'. According to the 2014 National Survey of Student Engagement annual report, 'Learning-directed uses of social media were systematically and positively related to engagement in effective educational practices' (NSSE, 2014). Similarly, studies on both community college students and four-year-college students have found a relationship between social media usage and students' persistence and success, as well as learning outcomes and ability to adapt to university culture (Fagioli, Rios-Aguilar, & Deil-Amen, 2015; Yu, Tian, Vogel, & Kwok, 2010). The virtual community will consist of social media groups connecting the students, a blog that the students themselves will write, discussion threads monitored by teachers and mentors, and space

for students to showcase their work and ideas. An additional intervention designed to foster community will be sending students periodic motivational texts. A recent study (Chande et al., 2015) found that a simple intervention of sending encouraging text messages to students increased class attendance and student retention.

(5) *Bilingual, Bicultural Teacher Certification Pipeline*
In the final phase of this project, we aim to help create a bilingual, bicultural teacher certification pipeline. The pipeline will be supported by online teacher certification and continuing education courses, social media, online mentoring and virtual communities. The use of technology will enable personalised learning for each student, and allow students to learn from within their communities. Students can utilise their own culture and background in both their own learning and their subsequent teaching. The NTCP programme will provide concrete skills, focusing on developing teaching skills and using culturally relevant material, and will also provide emotional and motivational support, focusing on the personal and professional development of each teacher.

Today's educational technology is uniquely suited to provide many of the culturally relevant factors. Online learning communities can be used to help students who are geographically isolated, but who share a culture, to connect with one another. They can also be used to promote sharing across cultures. Social media in online courses can be used to allow students to share their culture with each other and with the instructor. Personalised learning systems can help present differentiated learning to students based on learning styles, current knowledge and skills, culture and language. Digital systems can be used to provide culturally relevant videos, interactive activities, experiential learning and online collaboration tools. Competency-based models allow for students to excel at their own pace, displacing traditional seat time requirements that are a barrier to subsistence-based lifestyles. Technology can also be used to help provide mentors and role-models from a similar cultural background. Finally, translation software helps to break down language barriers and make learning more accessible for a variety of students, or in the case of Alaska Native interests, helps to preserve and promote local languages. In this way, educational technology can be used to provide the culturally responsive teaching that has been shown to enhance academic success.

The NTCP programme addresses all three of the factors Leary identified as barriers to Native student success – access and cost, academics and student support – by providing inexpensive online access so that students can remain in their home villages and participate in an affordable programme, using a culturally responsive curriculum and providing an online system for intensive student support. Culturally responsive higher education can offer Native students an opportunity to share the opportunities of the larger society, and can also provide social and economic mobility. University policies and programmes aimed at decreasing indigenous attrition are typically oriented toward helping the students make the transition from their home culture to the culture of the university (Kirkness et al., 1991). For a post-secondary institution to truly serve Alaska Natives requires a paradigm shift away from viewing higher education as a tool to synthesise, reproduce and integrate its members toward social norms. Achieving positive disruption via a bicultural, bilingual online certification requires viewing the pursuit of higher education as more than just obtaining a university degree to teach in local schools, but instead the pursuit of education to address Yupik communal needs as a self-determining society. An alternative model needs to be humanised and framed around respect, relevance, reciprocity and responsibility to preserve Yupik cultural integrity throughout the entire education process (Kirkness et al., 1991).

NTCP also directly aligns with current research and the latest recommendations reported by the White House. To reverse the failures of the past and transform future opportunities, the Executive Branch recommends collaborations between tribal nations, as well as the private and public sectors, to create and maintain transformative programmes that directly:

- strengthen tribal control of education;
- provide comprehensive student support systems;
- integrate Native culture and language into school climate and classrooms;
- support the creation of new, high-quality teacher pipelines and programmes to strengthen the skills of current instructional staff by infusing cultural competency training into professional development;
- promote twenty-first century technology for tribal education;
- strengthen and expand efforts targeting suicide prevention;
- improve community systems of care to address the behavioural health needs of Native youth (Executive Office of the President, 2014).

As an alternative to the current situation, we propose that Alaska recognise the skill and knowledge which exists within the Native cultures of Alaska. An important first step in this process is to recognise that there are, and have been for millennia, 'teachers' in the Native villages. We can begin to recognise this reality by creating a process which includes, rather than excludes, Native teachers in the certification process.

This programme seeks to support Yupik community members in their pursuit of teaching degrees throughout the duration of their studies. This objective extends beyond mere degree acquisition, into the realm of metacognitive awareness, increasing self-efficacy, professional development and career placement in rural villages. The NTCP curriculum is designed to be dynamic and continuously reviewed for effectiveness, with observations about best practices inside and outside of the classroom shared with other professionals to promote educational equality and innovation in teacher education. There is also a great emphasis on career-centric pedagogy to help students with identity construction. By allowing high school students to internalise teacher virtues and discover career attributes, the programme gives students the time to focus their concentrated teacher studies on the professional path that best fits with their sense of self. (Duening & Metzger, 2015)

With advanced mobile delivery technologies, a highly motivated Yupik school board, and the recent international attention to Indigenous rights, coupled with dwindling economic resources in Alaska and climbing rates of violence and student drop outs, Alaska is well-positioned to integrate an alternative teacher certification model. The proposed NTCP model would be directly adhering to Article 14-1 of the 2007 United Nations Declaration on the Rights of Indigenous Peoples which states:

> Indigenous peoples have the right to establish and control their education systems and institutions providing education in their own languages, in a manner appropriate to their cultural methods of teaching and learning.

Finally, educational funding can be re-conceptualised as a community and regional developmental resource. High unemployment rates in cash-poor tribal villages should not be viewed as a challenge solely for the government. Alternative teacher certification has the potential to allow entry-level workers to move from public assistance into career positions. The creation of pathways to higher education for members of the Native community, in addition to salaries, will allow pensions to stay in Alaska, contributing to further economic development.

8.2.1. International Models of Success

Global awareness of the rights of Indigenous nations has caused positive disruption to educational models around the world. Norway, Nunavut in Canada, Greenland and Hawaii all provide evidence of success where organisational transformation of the education system has resulted in significant improvement in the quality of life for indigenous people. Success has come from the recognition of the need for genuine local control of education, and the balanced blending of both the indigenous and Western education systems.

Historically, Norway utilised schools to systematically unite the country in an effort to Norwegianise its citizens. A consequence of this action was the loss of the indigenous Sámi language and identity. Sámi people are one of two classified Indigenous Caucasian people of the world. A combination of Nazi occupation and Sámi cultural breakdown led Norway to rewrite the Norwegian constitution in 1987 to include opportunities for Sámi and non-Sámi students to have access to Sámi curriculum and language through immersion schools (Hornberger, 2008). Today, Sámi students have the opportunity to learn through their language and culture from Pre-K through higher education. The Sámi University of Applied Sciences offer advanced degrees in language preservation and indigenous journalism, for example:

> The Sámi School, as part of the common school, is founded on the principle that education must be common and equal and start from and be based on the nature and needs of the Sámi society. In terms of content and quality, education must provide basic skills which bring the cultural heritage to life, motivate students to make use of the local culture, and provide children and young people with the desire to become active and innovative in both the Sámi and Norwegian societies. Education must enhance a positive self-esteem in each pupil. (Hornberger, 2008, p. 21)

A recent United Nations Educational, Scientific and Cultural Organisation Report (UNESCO, 2010) investigated the educational and social impact of the *kōhanga reo* (Māori language nests) movement in New Zealand. The summary found that Māori students who participated in *kōhanga reo* followed by Māori immersion schools 'have recorded significantly better achievement rates than their Māori peers in English-medium schools' (Skerrett et al., 2010). Even the English-medium schools that some Māori attend are still required to operate in a bicultural curriculum frame. In 2006, the New Zealand Ministry of Education found that nesting schools were rated stronger if they had teachers fluent in *te reo Māori* (the Māori language) and access to strong professional development.

The differentiating factor between other models and NTCP is that the proposed programme targets youth identity-formation and provides support for a seamless transition into the higher education realm through online education. The programme extends beyond language and culture revitalisation to educational autonomy and pedagogical leadership. Previously, there has been insufficient research conducted on the power of utilising online education as a strategy to weave together professional development and culturally responsive teacher certification. NTCP builds upon the knowledge generated by previous international models, best practices and various online technologies to foster the development of a culturally responsive teacher certification.

8.3. Conclusion

Root causes of educational disparities amongst Alaska Native students stems from complex historical and contemporary factors including lack of genuine tribal control, lack of comprehensive student support, challenges in recruiting and retaining highly effective teachers and school leaders, lack of native languages and culture in schools and insufficient funding (Executive Office of the President, 2014). Alaska, however, recently signed into law House Bill 216, officially recognising 20 Alaska Native languages. The passing of the language bill could have effects on education and social policy throughout the state. Multilingual social policies open up ideological spaces for multicultural education.

Research indicates that teachers who are Native speakers of the language of their students, and who are deeply familiar with their culture, produce better educational outcomes than their non-Native peers. It is therefore imperative for Alaskan tribal villages, and for similar communities around the world, to certify teachers from the respective regions. As such, there is a compelling need to disrupt the current model of teacher development and certification, and to re-imagine what is possible for Alaskan Native students aspiring to become teachers, and for their communities. The results and efficacy of NTCP are dependent on the degree of Alaska Native influence on the content and the educational system. Achieving this transformative experience requires unique partnerships between the private and public sector, university systems and state infrastructure focused on innovation that provides breakthrough pathways to student success and the design and deployment of disruptive educational infrastructure through technology. The result of our research is that the value of education is amplified when culturally relevant. This finding is obvious for teachers, especially those in the field. We are predicting that the same is true for universities committed to distance education, regardless of the content area.

References

2014 Alaska Offender Profile, Alaska Department of Corrections. (June, 2015). Retrieved from http://www.correct.state.ak.us/admin/docs/Final_2014_Profile.pdf

Alaska's Public Schools: 2014−2015 Report Card to the Public. (2015). State of Alaska Department of Education, Alaska Department of Education & Early Development. Retrieved from https://www.eed.state.ak.us/reportcard/2014-2015/reportcard2014-15.pdf

Ashforth, B. E., & Mael, F. (1989). Social identity theory and the organization. *The Academy of Management Review, 14*(1), 20−39. doi:10.5465/AMR.1989.4278999

Cerulo, K. A. (1997). Identity construction: New issues, new directions. *Annual Review of Sociology, 23*, 385−409. doi:10.1146/annurev.soc.23.1.385

Chande, R., Sanders, M., Borcan, O., Linos, E., Robinson, S., Luca, M., ... Kirkman, E. (2015). Curbing adult student attrition: Evidence from a field experiment. *Harvard Business School*. Working paper. Retrieved from https://papers.ssrn.com/sol3/papers.cfm?abstract_id=2563757

Demmert, W., Grissmer D., & Towner, J. (2006). A review and analysis of the research on Native American students. *Journal of American Indian Education, 45*(3), 5−23.

Demographic Profile for Alaska, 2010 Census Information. (2010). State of Alaska. Retrieved from http://live.laborstats.alaska.gov/cen/dp.cfm

Duening, T., & Metzger, M. (2015). *Identity construction in entrepreneurship education: Facilitating the process of becoming an entrepreneur.* Unpublished manuscript.

Fagioli, L. P., Rios-Aguilar, C., Deil-Amen, R. (2015). Changing the context of student engagement: Using Facebook to increase community college student persistence and success. *Teachers College Record, 117*, 1−42. Retrieved from https://

www.coe.arizona.edu/sites/coe/files/HED/Changing%20the%20Context%20of%20Engagement_0.pdf

Gay, G. (2013). Teaching to and through cultural diversity. The Ontario Institute for Studies in Education of the University of Toronto. *Curriculum Inquiry, 43*(1). doi:10.1111/curi.12002

Gee, J. P., & Hayes, E. (2009). Public pedagogy through video Games: Design, resources & affinity spaces. *Handbook of Public Pedagogy.* doi:10.4324/9780203863688.ch21

Goldsmith, S. (2008). *Understanding Alaska's remote rural economy.* UA Research Summary. Retrieved from http://www.iser.uaa.alaska.edu/Publications/researchsumm/UA_RS10.pdf

Hallett, D., Chandler, M. J., & Lalonde, C. E. (2007). Aboriginal language knowledge and youth suicide. *Cognitive Development, 22,* 392–399. doi:10.1016/j.cogdev.2007.02.001

Hattori, M. T. P. (2014). *Culturally responsive educational technology.* University of Hawai'i at Manoa. Retrieved from: https://scholarspace.manoa.hawaii.edu/bitstream/10125/100502/1/Hattori_Mary_r.pdf

Hornberger, N. (2008). *Can schools save Indigenous languages? Policy and practice on four continents.* New York, NY: Palgrave Macmillan. doi:10.1057/9780230582491

Kawagley, A. O., Tull, D., & Norris-Tull, R. A. (1998). The indigenous worldview of Yupiaq Culture: Its scientific nature and relevance to the practice and teaching of science. *Journal of Research in Science Teaching, 35*(2). doi:10.1002/(SICI)1098-2736(199802)35:2 < 133::AID-TEA4 > 3.0.CO;2-T.

Kirkness, V. J., & Barnhardt, R. (1991). First Nations and higher education: The four R's – respect, relevance, reciprocity, responsibility. *Journal of American Indian Education, 30*(3), 1–15.

Kozleski, E. B. (2010). *Culturally responsive teaching matters.* Equity Alliance at ASU. Retrieved from http://www.equityallianceatasu.org/sites/default/files/Website_files/CulturallyResponsiveTeaching-Matters.pdf

LaFromboise, T., Hardin, L., Coleman, K., & Gerton, J. (1993). Psychological impact of biculturalism: Evidence and theory. American Psychological Association, Inc. *Psychological Bulletin,* 114(3), 395–412. https://doi.org/10.1037/0033-2909.114.3.395

Leary, A., Tetpon, B., Hirshberg, D., & Hill, A. (2014). *Alaska Native-Focused teacher preparation programs. UAA Center for Alaska Education Policy Research.* University of Alaska Anchorage. Retrieved from http://www.iser.uaa.alaska.edu/Publications/2014_6-AKNative-FocusedTeacherProgs.pdf

McClure, C. L., & Monfreda, K. Crime in Alaska. (2015). Department of Public Safety. Retrieved from http://www.dps.alaska.gov/statewide/docs/UCR/UCR_2015.pdf

National Survey of Student Engagement (NSSE). (2014). *Bringing the institution into focus—Annual Results 2014.* Bloomington, IN: Indiana University Center for Postsecondary Research.

Native Youth Report. (December 2014). Executive Office of the President. Retrieved from https://www.whitehouse.gov/sites/default/files/docs/20141129nativeyouthreport_final.pdf

Ogbu, J. U., & Simons, H. D. (1998). Voluntary and involuntary minorities: A cultural-ecological theory of school performance with some implications for education. *Anthropology & Education Quarterly, 29*(2), 155–188. doi:10.1525/aeq.1998.29.2.155

Reaching the marginalised. (2010). *United Nations Educational, Scientific, & Cultural Organization.* UNESCO. Retrieved from http://www.unesco.org/en/efareport/reports/2010-marginalization/.

Reyhner, J. (1992). Plans for dropout prevention and special school support services for American Indian and Alaska Native students. *Journal of American Indian Education.* Retrieved from http://www2.nau.edu/~jar/INAR.html

Seligman, M., & Csikszentmihalyi, M. (2000). Positive psychology: An introduction. *American Psychologist, 55*(1), 5–14. doi:10.1037/0003-066X.55.1.5

Skerrett, M. (2010). A critique of the best evidence synthesis with relevance for Māori leadership in education. *Journal of Educational Leadership, Policy, and Practice, 25*(1), 42–50.

Suicide Facts at a Glance. (2015). National Center for Injury Prevention and Control, Division of Violence Prevention, Center for Disease Control. Retrieved from http://www.cdc.gov/violenceprevention/pdf/suicide-datasheet-a.PDF

Yu, A. Y., Tian, S. W., Vogel, D., & Kwok, R. C. (2010). Can learning be virtually boosted?: An investigation of online networking impacts. *Computers & Education, 55*, 1495–1503. doi:10.1016/j.compedu.2010.06.015

Chapter 9

Academic Rigour and Video Technology: A Case Study on Digital Storytelling in Graduate-level Assignments

Eva Malisius

Abstract

While some may perceive technology as disruptive in higher education, this chapter makes a case that video technology can be used to increase collaboration and engagement in learning and teaching. It is argued that digital storytelling can be integrated as part of the assessment in graduate-level courses without compromising expectations related to academic rigor. Rather, digital storytelling advances multimedia literacy for the individual and supports the generation of bounded learning communities, specifically in online and blended programmes. Covering social presence, teaching presence and cognitive presence, the chapter draws on two examples of digital storytelling used in the MA in Conflict Analysis and Management and the MA in Global Leadership at Royal Roads University, Canada. Overall, the chapter makes a contribution to the conversation of how assessment formats can be updated to match the shift from traditional, lecture formats and brick-and-mortar institutions to applied, collaborative programmes that are often delivered in blended and online formats. Thus, as the field of higher education continues to evolve and adapt alongside technological innovations, the chapter suggests that digital storytelling can be one way to complement and update assessment formats to match the evolution of the twenty-first century.

Keywords: Digital storytelling; online teaching; online learning; video assignments; academic rigor; assessment

As various formats of online and blended programme offerings become more commonplace in higher education around the globe, slowly happening alongside is a shift in the delivery of learning and teaching. This shift moves the classroom away from more traditional lectures to technologically mediated learning and teaching building on experiential learning and flipped classrooms (Keengwe, Onchwari, & Oigara, 2014; Kolb, 1984; Laster, 2012). Part of this is to make stronger efforts in accommodating different types of learners and, for example, auditory, visual and kinesthetic learning styles (Hatami, 2013; Rolfe & Cheek, 2012; Yassin & Almasri, 2015). The other part is accommodating more asynchronous and location independent learning, which allows students to study without travelling to brick-and-mortar classrooms and on their own schedule, often through video lectures formatted and posted on Learning Management Systems (LMS) such as Moodle or Blackboard. The benefits and limitations of video lectures, especially in generating diverse, interactive, collaborative, engaged and applied teaching and learning experiences that replace the traditional lectures, are widely discussed by researchers and the teaching community (Borbye, 2010; Kuosa et al., 2016; Martin & Notari, 2014; Ronchetti, 2010; Willis, 2009; Woolfit, 2015). At the same time, how do we bring traditional, written assignments into twenty-first century and online learning and teaching – without compromising expectations related to academic context and content, but rather increasing students' ability to compete in the modern job market?

The purpose of this chapter is to make a case for what some might perceive as an alternative assessment format: a case for video-based, academic assignments at the graduate-level in blended and online programmes across disciplines. While this is less commonly found in research and practice, there are efforts to include video-based assignments in higher education to complement more traditional assessment formats and academic writing (Fiorentino, 2004; Lim, Pellett, & Pellett, 2009; Malisius, 2016; Price, Strodtman, Brough, Lonn, & Luo, 2015; Willis, 2009). The chapter specifically advocates for digital storytelling as a general format for video assignment submission as it moves beyond the submission of voice-over presentations. Digital storytelling requires a more deliberate use of video technology or animation by generating a cohesive narrative in a compelling manner. Furthermore, the digital storytelling format engages students to transfer their acquired knowledge on a particular topic in an audio-visual narration, requiring critical thinking and analysis – similar to academic writing (Gregory, Steelman, & Caverly, 2009). Thereby digital storytelling as a generic format becomes comparable to academic writing, as it requires storyboarding and editing in a similar manner that essay writing requires planning and editing. Thus from both a teaching and learning approach, assignment from conception to assessment have comparability related to academic rigor and learning engagement.

Beyond that, the submission of graduate-level assignments in the format of digital storytelling has several, additional benefits (or side-effects) that contribute to the collaborative and engaged learning environment sometimes missing in blended and online programmes: the generation of a bounded learning community that brings together social presence, teaching presence and cognitive presence. Both anecdotal evidence and research suggest that the objectives of learning, engagement, retention and teacher and student satisfaction increase manifold through this approach. The format of submitting audio-visual files for assignments allows students to share their work with their peers in an easy and accessible way. By literally seeing each other and their respective approaches to content and subject matter, students in the classroom learn from each other and how they worked through the assignment, are exposed to a range of different content and views related to the same content they were exposed to. Learning overall becomes richer and more engaged through the integration of technology and related collaboration. Furthermore, students provide anecdotal evidence of how they have the ability to share their work beyond the classroom in an easy and accessible way with community members, families and friends, current or potential future employers. Learning becomes applied by both content and format through increased accessibility of materials through digital storytelling: rather than being disruptive, online learning becomes integrative and invites collaboration and dialogue beyond the classroom — similar to hallway conversations in brick-and-mortar academic institutions.

This chapter includes a case study based on the experience of integrating technology, specifically video-based assignment and digital storytelling, into blended programmes and online courses at the graduate level at a Canadian university in a social and applied sciences context. It engages with instructor and design perspectives, as well as student experiences in Conflict Analysis and Management and Global Leadership programmes at Royal Roads University, Canada. Anecdotal evidence from key stakeholders, students and instructors and interdisciplinary research on teaching and learning, the intention is to contribute to the dialogue on the improvement of student learning through technology (Dempster, Beetham, Jackson, & Richardson, 2011; Dickson & Treml, 2013; Fischer, Wild, Sutherland, & Zirn, 2013). The skills, confidence and academic learning students acquire from video assignments enables them to critically engage with audio-visual materials presented to them in professional contexts, as well as to produce succinct and relevant clips to present information at their workplace. In the digital age and at the modern workplace, audio-visual soft skills compare to enhanced report writing and research literacy stemming from academic writing and critical thinking — another marketable tool for a successful transition for students to the workforce.

While advocating for the mindful integration of video assignments at intervals throughout a programme, this chapter addresses common concerns, specifically related to video technology and academic rigor. It provides examples of how digital storytelling can be used to frame academic assignments successfully. This includes how to manage expectations of both students and instructors, how to overcome technology challenges and the wider benefits of video technology in online classrooms to generate student and instructor presence, collective learning and teaching in the online classroom community and the acquisition of technology related soft skills relevant for the workplace, and beyond the university context.

In conclusion, this chapter provides an overview of how video technology can be integrated into online learning and teaching, focusing specifically on the use of digital storytelling in graduate-level assignments. The case study is based on the experience and successful integration of video assignments blended graduate programmes at a Canadian university and argues that it is possible to maintain academic standards through video assignments while enhancing the learning and teaching experience. This includes, beyond demonstrating academic skills and knowledge in assessment, an enhanced and shared learning experience and acquisition of skills that benefit beyond the higher education classroom in preparing students for more successful engagement in their future employment.

9.1. Online Learning and Teaching: Challenges and Opportunities

The success of graduates of reputable online and blended university programmes demonstrates that the concerns related to academic rigor and quality of higher education and learning are generally unfounded. There are some caveats, of course. However, when courses and programmes adapt and integrate technology into learning and teaching in a constructive and meaningful manner, the integration of technology in the classroom is not for technology sake, but to enhance, enrich and consolidate higher education learning irrespective of the classroom format (Bates & Sangrà, 2011; Grundy et al., 2016; Issa, Isaias, & Kommers, 2014). In this regard, the rise of MOOCs and open access learning platforms such as Coursera have impacted the higher education market and provided researchers and facilitators of learning with a plethora of data and input on what interactive online learning can look like and how to decrease barriers to accessing knowledge (Koller, 2012). Furthermore, part of the success of the learning platforms has been in offering optional, by payment, micro-credits or certificates that can be transferred to credits at regular universities and/or are welcomed by employers as professional development efforts (whether or not this is disruptive to traditional universities is beyond the scope of this paper). This in turn has demonstrated a need for user related technology knowledge at the employment market. Online and blended programmes are in a unique position to advance and enhance students' abilities in this respect and thereby contribute to their employability.

9.1.1. Distance Learning and Video Technology: Managing Expectations

Expectations of what engaging use of video technology looks like to support teaching and learning vary significantly. It appears clear that the mere use of video technology as part of distance learning is insufficient to generate meaningful learning. The production process of instructional videos can be high, software and technology constantly evolving and changing: it is hard to keep up. At times, it may appear that the process is more cumbersome than meaningful, at which point it becomes counterproductive. Similarly, creating a video assignment without a distinct purpose and relevance to the context of the course and/or programme will not result in meaningful learning.

The first perceived hurdle to meaningful learning from a video assignment may be unfamiliarity of most students in producing a video clip. At the same time, the same often applies to students in relation to academic writing and all that it entails. Providing students with guidance on how to produce a clip and pointing out readily available and, often free, video editing software can be sufficient to set students off on producing meaningful video submissions with academically relevant content presented in a cohesive narrative (Willis, 2009). Resources such as a library guide and storyboarding guidance enable students to master video assignments (RRULibrary, 2015; Thorn, 2011). Depending on the framing of the assignment itself, a video assignment can be set up to ask students to address a particular question similar to an essay format, to engage with a series of questions comparable to an exam, or be used to replace an in a classroom presentation. As the latter suggests, the benefit of the video assignment format is the possibility to share with both peers and beyond.

Expectations of both faculty and students may be higher when it comes to engaging assignments, at the same time, the challenges to use technology may be perceived as an additional challenge or barrier. Anecdotal evidence from students suggests that this is often their initial reaction to facing a video assignment, for example, but that the overwhelming majority thrives in facing and overcoming the initially perceived challenge. Managing those expectations means setting the students up for success, providing guidance and creating an engaging assignment that enables students to pursue a particular learning purpose and demonstrate their academic ability and skills based on course materials and their own research in an applied and meaningful manner. Whereas traditional lecture formats may have commonly resulted in essays or short papers on particular questions pertaining to the materials covered, the creation of engaging assignments has been covered alongside the overhaul of classroom (Lim et al., 2009; Nisly, Cecire, Friesen, & Sensenig, 2015; Schultz & Quinn, 2014; Swinth & Vinton, 1994). In that respect, video assignments and digital storytelling are a logical extension of integration technology in online and blended programmes.

9.1.2. *Alternative Assessment Formats and Academic Rigor: How Different can be the Same*

As implied above, video assignments in many ways are no different than other assessment formats commonly used in higher education. Alternative assessment formats often generate concern related to academic rigor and standards, however, this can be easily addressed by setting requirements accordingly. Standard academic conventions, i.e. referencing and copyright attributions apply to video submissions in the same manner as to other academic writing. Instructors outline the scope, length, format and anticipated output for an assignment, including expectations relating the assignment to course content.

Video assignments are better suited for open-ended questions as they leave students with more space for diverse analysis and creativity in engaging with the challenge presented (Nisly et al., 2015). Similarly, the digital storytelling format enables students to determine the best-suited approach for their submission by compiling their own audio-visual materials from existing photographs, video clips, adding animation, music, interviews and their own voice to the mix (Schultz & Quinn, 2014; Truong-White & McLean, 2015). This includes students integrating their own songs and music to represent conflict; using props such as Barbie dolls or Lego to present conflict interaction or disasters; use animation software to generate images and a narrative; presenting newscast type interviews with themselves to answer the questions provided; and connecting their professional work as an air traffic controller to demonstrate conflict and competing interests. Such direct applications of the question and course materials increase engagement and retention equally, thus enhancing the impact of the assignment itself.

Some may compare video assignments to classroom presentations rather than demonstrations of critical thinking and academic writing, however, this does not have to be the case. Requiring digital storytelling as submission format sets students up to include a cohesive narrative and plan their clip in its sequences (Frazel, 2010; Page & Thomas, 2011). Rather than asking students to record their opinions or compile summaries of classroom materials, digital storytelling invites students to critically engage with the topic and materials, to apply concepts and ideas to an identified challenge and to present their reflections and application of the knowledge in a cohesive narrative. This requires students to internalise the material, to reflect on how they want to present themselves and the materials and to extend their comfort zone by giving themselves a voice. Participatory action research methods, including digital storytelling or Photovoice, are being used to engage marginalised groups and providing them with a voice (Reimers, 2016). The impact on students completing assignments in this format is arguably comparable. The goal is to allow students to stretch their comfort zone while engaging with the course materials (Borbye, 2010; Harrison, Starks, & Denhardt, 2011; Nehyba, 2011). Specifically, in online and blended formats, the ability to share assignment submission and see what others' have produced has further added value as it enables students to learn together and support their community.

9.1.3. Bounded Learning Community and the Perception of Presence: Building Relationships

One of several remarkable side-effects of video assignments is the contribution to generating a bounded learning community and perception of presence in online courses and thereby also in online or blended programmes. In online courses and programmes students often feel isolated and lacking a sense of community, even if instructors make efforts to keep engaged and interactive (Brown, Rich, & Holtham, 2014; Luppicini, 2007; Richardson et al., 2015; Tu, 2004). Students may build a relationship with the instructor but less so with their peers, specifically in comparison to more traditional in-classroom offerings where social interaction with peers organically happens. Studying online, students, who live in a range of locations across a region, country or the globe, bond in different ways. Video assignments provide an opportunity to bond in two ways: first, as students collectively face the challenge of a different format and figuring out technology; and, second, as they review each others' submissions, get a sense of the other person(s) and have a foundation for a bounded learning community. The social engagement that generates a bounded learning community encompasses social presence largely based on student-student interaction, contributes to teaching presence and the student-teacher interaction, as well and enhancing cognitive presence and student-content interaction. Thereby, student engagement can be observed to increase overall and through the bounded learning community learning appears enriched, retention increased and overall satisfaction unfolds.

Generating social presence through student–student interaction can be more difficult and less intuitive to achieve in online courses, specifically when there is little demand for students to interact directly. Some university programmes provide a framework for social presence through a cohort model in which students complete a number of courses or their entire programme largely as a group together (Hamilton, Marquez, & Agger-Gupta, 2013; Seed, 2008). This learning community is enhanced through video assignments as students have a personal frame of reference for each other, having engaged online and seen each other through their video presentation (Malisius, 2013). This can add to the safe learning environment a classroom generates and increase satisfaction with the learning experience and enabling cohorts to bond more swiftly.

The social presence extends similarly to the teaching presence and enabling enriched student-teacher interaction. Similar to students' social experience, the interaction between students and teachers in online classes can be minimal to non-existent as the barriers to move out of the LMS and the boundaries of the course can be perceived as more significant. While communication technology such as Skype can support face-to-face interactions and facilitate 'online office hours', some elements of the learning community and student – teacher conversations go missing. Video assignments, through their audio-visual and somewhat more personal approach, provide an additional dimension that facilitates teacher presence. This applies specifically when video assignments are a component in a class that is delivered through the pro-active use of video technology and enhanced coverage of course materials by the instructor (Woolfit, 2015).

Most significant, however, is the cognitive presence and student-content interaction that forms part of the bounded learning community supported by video assignments. As students share their submissions, they are individually and collectively exposed to a range of topics and materials related to course content and move being the assigned readings. Students are unlikely to read each others' written materials, but they are – as anecdotal evidence confirms – quite likely to watch at least 5–8 video submissions made by other students in their class. Often video submission range between 3 and 10 minutes depending on the assignment scope and content requirements, which is a bounded time commitment and easier access than written work. Students individually pick their take on the task and learn about other perspectives through their peers' eyes (which again, increases social presence), engage with different topics and areas of interest and expertise that may be outside their own scope. Thus video assignments can contribute to a holistic, more applied and diversified interaction of students with content.

The presence and the perception of presences have been the common thread throughout the three elements presented as part of a bounded learning community supported by video assignments. In online and blended courses presence may be a highly sought after and often underestimated contributing factor to success. While discussions around instructor presence can be found in the discussions, elements of student and content presence are less frequently at the centre of attention.

9.1.4. Video Technology and Soft Skills Acquisition: In and Beyond Classroom Learning

Despite the frequent use of video on social media and availability of recording devices through smartphones and laptops, the ability to compile and edit audio-visual materials to generate a cohesive narrative remains limited among students across disciplines. Digital storytelling is an easy access format that generates quick results, educational value and provides a structure, similar to academic writing in higher education (Chung, 2007; Price et al., 2015; Truong-White & McLean, 2015). Thus, through digital storytelling assignments, students acquire skills that enable them to succinctly present information, knowledge and content analysis in and audio-visual format.

The inherent ability to visualise, understand and critique multimedia clips is beneficial in many professions, enabling graduates to contribute and critically assess multimedia production increasingly part of modern workplaces for marketing or outreach purposes. That does not imply, however, that video assignments can replace academic writing completely. Critical thinking remains a key component of higher education; the case made her for digital storytelling simply implies to expand the portfolio of assessment to including video formats. Through academic programmes, students acquire research literacy, research and academic writing skills. Adding digital storytelling allows students to enhance their multi-media literacy, which subsequently becomes a marketable skillset at the workplace. There is an increasing demand for academic programmes to be applied and relevant to the twenty-first century workplace by enabling students to pick up soft skills alongside their academic learning journey (Kyllonen, 2013). This suggests that the output students produce in modern universities and specifically online and blended programmes, prepare graduates for their professional lives and related usage of technology.

9.2. Digital Storytelling in Graduate-level Assignments: Some Examples

In order to provide specific examples of how digital storytelling can be integrated as academic assignments in graduate-level courses, the following outlines two separate examples of online courses in blended programmes in the Faculty of Social and Applied Sciences at a Canadian university. They include an overview of the assignment itself and how it fits into the specific courses and programmes, as well as anecdotal evidence of the impact and bounded learning community generated through the assignment.

9.2.1. *MA in Conflict Analysis and Management: My Digital Conflict Story*

In the MA in Conflict Analysis and Management programme at Royal Roads University, students start their two-year blended programme with an online course running over nine weeks entitled 'CAMN 502 – Foundation: Understanding Conflict, Change, and Systems in Organisational Contexts'. Students, who are generally working professionals at a mid-career level and on average aged in their late 30s, come from diverse backgrounds that include military and police, provincial and federal ministries, human resources, healthcare professionals, as well as conflict specialists. Pre-existing knowledge and competencies related to conflict range from very little to substantial. Some students have previous online learning experience, yet many describe themselves with limited technological ability. In the first course of their programme they navigate the LMS, the content and overall technology for the first time, as well as meeting their cohort and peers within the setting of an academic course online. As their first assignment, digital storytelling is perceived by many as a deviation from their expectations and anticipation of academic writing. To many, this context appears as an outlet for anxiety and putting all students on a level playing field. The anxiety to engage in graduate studies and academic writing is quickly replaced with anxiety by using video technology, however, the barriers to overcome are met by high levels of motivation and excitement. The perceived openness of the digital storytelling format enables students to be creative and present themselves to instructor and peers.

9.2.1.1. The Assignment: My Digital Conflict Story

For the assignment itself, which is the first assignment for students within the first course of their programme, students are provided with a short introduction to digital storytelling and providing resources for storyboarding and technology advice through a library guide (RRULibrary, 2015). Students are asked to produce a video clip that is approximately 4 minutes in length and meets academic standards, i.e. is concise and analytical, makes use of references and concepts from the course materials and external research as applicable, and overall respects copyright regulations and APA standards. A dedicated Q&A forum allows students to post their questions and challenges, commiserate and share advice. More often than not, peers provide answers faster than the instructor.

As part of the assignment description students are presented with the following disclaimer:

> You may find presenting yourself and your views in a digital format challenging, and you may find yourself struggling with

technology, especially if you have never worked in this type of format before. Do not despair, reach out to your class for support, consult online tech support groups, or consider contacting computer services. Stretch your comfort zone.

Provided along with the assignment requirements is also a set of topics and questions to be addressed by the students (see Table 9.1). This provides them with further guidance for their storyboarding and planning their content; it is emphasised that they are not required to diligently answer each question, but rather to use the topics and themes as their guide.

As quickly becomes apparent from the topics and questions provided to students (see Table 9.1), the purpose and intention of the assignment combine a personal introduction with programme motivation and content knowledge, i.e. inviting students to present their take on conflict and the core theme of the programme. Students draw on a mix of personal and professional experiences, including course materials and their own research, to compile a digital conflict story.

By sharing the digital conflict stories students gain perspective of the diversity of the topic (conflict), their peers and the range of professional background and

Table 9.1. CAM 'My Digital Conflict Story' Assignment.

My personal background

- What is your name and where are you from?
- What do you do in your non-student life? What would you like to share about yourself with the class?
- What is your motivation for enroling in higher education? How did you pick your programme of study?
- What makes conflict matter to you?

How I frame conflict

- What is your experience with conflict?
- What is conflict and what does it mean to you?
- From your perspective, what makes conflict interesting and valuable or destructive and detestable? Is conflict good or bad?
- What can be done about conflict? What do you do with conflict and what do you want to do with conflict?

Beyond my digital conflict story

- What are your expectations for this course? For this programme?
- What do you expect from yourself, your classmates and your instructor?
- What is your vision for conflict?
- Any words of wisdom to share?

---

aspirations that are related to conflict analysis and management. This provides an open frame to their programme of study and enables students to experience knowledge beyond their own initial sphere of interest. The assignment itself, given its setting in reflection, further engages students in reflective practice and the application, rather than mere replication, of their conflict-related knowledge.

9.2.1.2. The Assessment: Learning Outcomes and Academic Rigor

For the assessment of the digital conflict story, the programme learning outcomes are drawn upon and adapted to the audio-visual context. The key learning domains are: critical thinking (1.3: demonstrate openness to ideas and actions), communication (2.1: articulate ideas and arguments effectively in oral and written formats) and knowledge (4.10: identify and explain the implications and impact of engaging in conflict management for self, individuals, professionals and other stakeholders. Comments are provided to students in relation to each of the learning outcome components, as well as an overall demonstration of ability, which results in a holistic assessment (see Table 9.2).

As the learning outcomes and assessment criteria show, the academic rigor and expectations related to the digital storytelling assignment are largely congruent with any other assignment in the course or programme.

Similarly, the submissions students produce display a similar range in grades and challenges with meeting the assignment criteria as would be expected with more traditional assessment formats for a first assignment. Common feedback includes length going beyond the 4 minutes' requirement (submission can vary between 3 and 8 minutes), lack of inclusion academic sources and references (pure personal narration), lack of cohesive narrative and analysis (unstructured

Table 9.2. CAM 'My Digital Conflict Story' Learning Outcomes.

- Your overall ability to present yourself, your motivations, expectations and views to the instructor and cohort in a meaningful manner that brings together theory, practice and reflection suitable to an academic context
- Your ability to demonstrate openness to ideas and action; i.e., how experiences have shaped your worldviews, how a conflict you focus on is shaped by perceptions and perspectives, how mindful (conflict) engagement informs your approach to self and others
- Your ability to articulate ideas and arguments effectively, including the clarity with which you organise your materials and thoughts, provide structure and evidence to support your analysis, and overall provide a clear flow of arguments and insights conveyed in a visually appealing and engaging format adequate for digital storytelling and
- Your ability to identify and explain the implications and impact of conflict engagement as you explore aspects of 'self' in system, distinguish between your own views and those of others, identify actors and stakeholders and engage with power as applicable

---

elements without structure and description or replication of materials). General praise includes creativity in presentation and outlook, a strong range of diverse materials and sources from course materials and beyond, focus on analysis and impact, matching content and application.

From an instructor perspective, the assessment process appears similar if not more swiftly in reviewing the submission, as the time limit for a clip is set (in this case) at 4 minutes. Generally, each submission is watched 1–3 times to complete the assessment in regards to each of the learning outcomes, and to provide feedback to the students on their performance. Again, academic standards and expectations are comparable to other assignment formats, thus making the digital storytelling an ideal starting point for students in an online and/or blended programme.

9.2.2. MA in Global Leadership: Presenting a Community in Conflict

Another example for a different use of a digital storytelling assignment comes from the course 'GBLD 522: Managing Difficult Relationships Within and Across Community Dynamics', which is delivered online over the course of 10 weeks as an optional, second-year course in the blended, two-year MA in Global Leadership at Royal Roads University. Students in this programme are encouraged throughout their course of study to engage with different assignment formats, including the production of audio-visual materials for both presentations and short, informative clips. Students compile their work in so-called e-portfolios, which enable them to share their work alongside their studies. Overall, students are generally familiar with audio-visual formats and have been encouraged to engage in digital storytelling prior to taking this course and assignment. This shifts the purpose of the assignment beyond the building of a bounded learning community into the sustaining of community that has already been established: the student-student presence is further deepened, the student – teacher presence set anew with a new instructor and the student-content presence is expanded to the materials covered in this particular course.

Given the different starting point, the assignment, in this case, serves an additional purpose: students research and submit 'community in conflict' cases from which the class then chooses several which provide the basis for a following, team assignment which takes on the design of a change process for the community, leading through conflict. What the digital storytelling format in this assignment facilitates is both the reflection of the individual student on the case of their choosing, which requires internalisation of materials, analysis and presentation and enables the class to review cases and make informed decisions as to which cases to pursue further. Different from a written format, the audio-visual format makes this a quick turnaround and easy to follow step for students. The content transfer for students to learn from all cases submitted by their peers is immense and informs learning beyond the course itself.

9.2.2.1. The Assignment: Presenting a Community in Conflict

Within the topic of the course, the purpose of the assignment is to enable the student to analyse a particular community in depth, increasing their awareness of dynamics and tensions between and across stakeholders. Students are invited to pick a community that they are familiar with and where they have access to public information or research that enables them to analyse the challenges facing the community. It could be a community covered in a different course, a community they have worked with in the past or would like to work with or a community they live in. Reminding students to avoid duplication of previous work, including self-plagiarism, they are advised to generate new perspectives if they choose a case they previously worked on in the academic context and to comply with academic integrity regulations. Furthermore, students are reminded of potential challenges of working too close to a case, i.e. ensuring their ability to take a balanced stance to analyse and present the dynamics of their chosen community without bias or passion for a particular group or cause. Students identify their audience for the assignment, i.e. the community leadership, a potential donor organisation or a more general audience to be alerted to the conflict. Generally, students choose to present a community they work with or live in, and present to the wider public appealing to a need for action (see Table 9.3).

Table 9.3. MAGL 'Presenting a Community in Conflict' Assignment.

The purpose of this assignment is to enhance your awareness of the dynamics and tensions between and across stakeholders in an existing community. Identify a community that you are familiar with and/or one where you have access to public information about conflicts, tension and challenges in that community.

You may choose:

(1) a community that you have covered or heard about in a different course;

(2) a community that you have worked with or would like to work in, or

(3) the community you live in.

The key guiding questions for your assignment are:

- What defines this community?
- Who are the key actors?
- What are the dynamics, key challenges, and conflicts that face the community?

Describe your community in all its richness, highlighting its assets, analysing its dynamics and acknowledging its challenges and complexities. Provide a brief background and basic statistical data for your community (geographical location, demographics and some historical facts). Limit this section to what is essential for understanding the wider context

Focus your assignment on the key dynamics of the community: what are key values shared by the community? What are some underlying conflicts and how do they affect the relationships between the community groups? How has the community dealt with conflict in the past? How does the community make

Table 9.3. (*Continued*)

decisions? How does the community interact with the national/regional level? How does it interact with other communities? What are the key challenges for community development?

At the end of your assignment indicate your recommendations for the future of the community and what could be done to address difficult relationships within and with other communities

---

To provide students with a basic structure and focus for their assignment, they are provided with key guiding questions and a suggested focus for the information they present. While this guidance may be perceived as extensive, it enables students to focus on the content of their case and provides them with sufficient flexibility to focus the assignment on the parameters most relevant to the conflict they focus on. This enables them to go into analytical depth within the confines of their submission format.

9.2.2.2. The Assessment: Learning Outcomes and Academic Rigor

While digital storytelling is encouraged, students have the options to submit in form of a written assignment as well. Students are required to submit either a 3- to 5-minute audio-visual clip or a 2000-word essay. The assessment criteria for the assignment are the same, irrespective of submission format, which reiterates the equivalency regarding expectations of academic standards and rigor.

Aligned with the assessment process within the MA in Global Leadership, the submissions are assessed based on learning outcomes that focus on competencies and skills acquisition (see Table 9.4).

Table 9.4. MAGL 'Presenting a Community in Conflict' Learning Outcomes.

A2.1. Demonstrates the ability to adapt, learn and change through self-awareness and self-management, and development of supportive and productive relationships.

- Identifies a relevant conflict and presents how it impacts a community and relevant stakeholders.
- Analyses a community and its culture, including values, (inter)relationships and history as relevant to the conflict.
- Engages in reflective practice so that it becomes an integral part of the analysis and identifies recommendations for future action that are feasible and based on relevant research and/or practice.
- Is able to assess existing skills and strengths, as well as limitations for dealing with conflict and tension within a community.

Table 9.4. (*Continued*)

- Reflects on different roles in a system to ensure the successful engagement with a conflict.

B2.2. Applies culturally appropriate approaches to communicate and interact with diverse audiences.

- Uses culturally appropriate communication methods, protocols, language and norms, taking into consideration cultural differences relevant to the identified target audience and community context.

B3.1. Demonstrates the ability to facilitate culturally diverse groups and teams.

- Recognises one's own biases, assumptions and understandings, and seeks to understand others' biases, assumptions and understandings in a culturally appropriate and sensitive manner.
- Offers readings, ideas and alternatives willingly and appropriately in a culturally sensitive manner.

Given the placement of the course within the programme of study, expectations for quality of the submission, analytical depth and scope are higher in comparison to the previously presented case of a first assignment. The acquisition of skills in generating video assignments has been acquired and strengthened by students throughout their programme. Nevertheless, common struggles remain to maintain the focus on analysis and within the scope of the assignment requirements. Successes include presentations that inspire further action, including sharing of their work with stakeholder communities and action groups that work in the context in real life. The applied nature of the assignment (and programme) empowers students to take their classroom learning beyond their academic journey.

9.3. Conclusions

In pursuit of the question how to bring traditional, written assignments into twenty-first century and online learning and teaching, this chapter has made a contribution to the conversation by advocating for digital storytelling as a form of academic assessment in graduate-level courses. Drawing on relevant research and examples of digital storytelling assignments from two different programmes at a Canadian university, the above has shown that video assignments can be created compromising expectations related to academic rigor, context and content. Rather, students' ability to critically engage with multimedia technology has been shown as an additional soft skill desirable in the job market. Digital storytelling has also been compared to academic writing and the ability to generate bounded learning communities that are specifically relevant in online and blended programmes to generate presence. Social presence, teaching presence and cognitive presence all contribute to engagement, learning, retention and overall satisfaction of students and instructors. Thereby, mindful integration of video assignments has been shown to advance online classrooms into the twenty-first century through relevant acquisition and application of academic and professional skills and knowledge.

Acknowledgement

The author would like to thank the students at RRU who provided the inspiration to engage in research on transformative teaching and learning and who have completed assignments that are described here. The goal was always to extend comfort zones and explore creativity!

References

Bates, T., & Sangrà, A. (2011). *Managing technology in higher education: Strategies for transforming teaching and learning*. San Francisco, CA: Jossey-Bass.

Borbye, L. (2010). *Out of the comfort zone: new ways to teach, learn, and assess essential professional skills: An advancement in educational innovation* (Vol. 2; 2). San Rafael, CA: Morgan & Claypool Publishers.

Brown, A., Rich, M., & Holtham, C. (2014). Student engagement and learning. *Journal of Management Development*, *33*(6), 603–619. doi:10.1108/JMD-04-2014-0038

Chung, S. K. (2007). Art education technology: digital storytelling. *Art Education*, *60*(2), 17.

Dempster, J. A., Beetham, H., Jackson, P., & Richardson, S. (2011). Creating virtual communities of practice for learning technology in higher education: Issues, challenges and experiences. *Research in Learning Technology*, *11*(3). doi:10.3402/rlt.v11i3.11288

Dickson, K. L., & Treml, M. M. (2013). Using assessment and SoTL to enhance student learning. *New Directions for Teaching and Learning*, *2013*(136), 7–16. doi:10.1002/tl.20072

Fiorentino, L. H. (2004). Digital video assignments: focusing a new lens on teacher preparation programs. *JOPERD – The Journal of Physical Education, Recreation & Dance*, *75*(5), 47. doi:10.1080/07303084.2004.10607240

Fischer, F., Wild, F., Sutherland, R., & Zirn, L. (2013). Grand challenges in technology enhanced learning. *Outcomes of the 3rd Alpine Rendez-Vous* (Vol. 1; 2014). Dordrecht: Springer International Publishing.

Frazel, M. (2010). *Digital storytelling guide for educators*. Eugene, OR.: International Society for Technology in Education.

Gregory, K., Steelman, J., & Caverly, D. C. (2009). Techtalk: Digital storytelling and developmental education. *Journal of Developmental Education*, *33*(2), 42–43.

Grundy, S., Hamilton, D., Veletsianos, G., Agger-Gupta, N., Marquez, P., Forssman, V., & Legault, M. (Eds.). (2016). *Engaging students in life-changing learning. Royal Roads University's Learning and Teaching Model in Practice*. Victoria: PressBook.

Hamilton, D., Marquez, P., & Agger-Gupta, N. (2013). Royal Roads University's Learning and Teaching Model. Retrieved from http://media.royalroads.ca/media/marketing/viewbooks/2013/learning-model/index.html

Harrison, L., Starks, B., & Denhardt, K. (2011). Outside the comfort zone of the classroom. *Journal of Criminal Justice Education, 22*(2), 203–225. doi:10.1080/10511253.2010.517773

Hatami, S. (2013). Learning styles. *ELT Journal, 67*(4), 488. doi:10.1093/elt/ccs083

Issa, T., Isaias, P., & Kommers, P. A. M. (2014). *Multicultural awareness and technology in higher education: Global perspectives.* Hershey, Pennsylvania (701 E. Chocolate Avenue, Hershey, Pa., 17033, USA): IGI Global.

Keengwe, J., Onchwari, G., & Oigara, J. N. (2014). *Promoting active learning through the flipped classroom model.* Hershey, PA: Information Science Reference.

Kolb, D. A. (1984). *Experiential learning: experience as the source of learning and development.* Canada: Prentice Hall.

Koller, D. (2012). What we're learning from online education. Retrieved from https://www.youtube.com/watch?v=U6FvJ6jMGHU: TEDTalks.

Kuosa, K., Distante, D., Tervakari, A., Cerulo, L., Fernandez, A., Koro, J., & Kailanto, M. (2016). Interactive visualization tools to improve learning and teaching in online learning environments. *International Journal of Distance Education Technologies (IJDET), 14*(1), 1–21.

Kyllonen, P. C. (2013). Soft skills for the workplace. *Change: The magazine of higher learning, 45*(6), 16–23. doi:10.1080/00091383.2013.841516

Laster, S. J. (2012). Rethinking higher education technology. *EDUCAUSE Review, 47*(3), 62.

Lim, J., Pellett, H. H., & Pellett, T. (2009). Integrating digital video technology in the classroom: digital-video assignments enhance experiential learning. *JOPERD – The Journal of Physical Education, Recreation & Dance, 80*(6), 40. doi:10.1080/07303084.2009.10598339

Luppicini, R. (2007). *Online learning communities.* Charlotte, NC: IAP.

Malisius, E. (2013). *Learning communities: Explanation of the popcorn maker assignment. Learning and Teaching Model Series.* Victoria: Royal Roads University.

Malisius, E. (2016). Creativity takes courage. Integrating video assignments into academic courses and blended programs. In R. R. University (Ed.), *Engaging students in life-changing learning: Royal Roads University's Learning and Teaching Model in Practice* (pp. 175–192). Victoria: PressBooks.

Martin, S., & Notari, M. (2014). Affordances, approaches, and challenges for blended, technology-enhanced learning: Present and future development. *Educational Research and Evaluation, 20*(7), 513–515. doi:10.1080/13803611.2014.997466

Nehyba, J. (2011). Experiential reflective learning and comfort zone. *Pedagogicka Orientace, 21*(3), 305–321.

Nisly, L. L., Cecire, S., Friesen, M., & Sensenig, A. (2015). Creating engaging assignments. *The National Teaching & Learning Forum, 24*(3), 9–11. doi:10.1002/ntlf.30025

Page, R. E., & Thomas, B. (2011). New narratives. *stories and storytelling in the digital age.* Lincoln, TX: University of Nebraska Press.

Price, D. M., Strodtman, L., Brough, E., Lonn, S., & Luo, A. (2015). Digital Storytelling: An innovative technological approach to nursing education. *Nurse educator, 40*(2), 66–70. doi:10.1097/NNE.0000000000000094

Reimers, B. C. (2016). Building a bridge across the conflict theory-practice gap: Comprehensive conflict engagement in community contexts. *Conflict Resolution Quarterly, 33*(4).

Richardson, J. C., Koehler, A. A., Besser, E. D., Caskurlu, S., Lim, J., & Mueller, C. M. (2015). Conceptualizing and investigating instructor presence in online learning environments. *International Review of Research in Open and Distance Learning, 16*(3).

Rolfe, A., & Cheek, B. (2012). Learning styles. *InnovAiT, 5*(3), 176–181. doi:10.1093/innovait/inr239

Ronchetti, M. (2010). A different perspective on lecture video-streaming: How to use technology to help change the traditional lecture model. *International Journal of Knowledge Society Research, 1*(2), 50–60.

RRULibrary. (2015). Video essays and digital storytelling: Video essays. LibGuides. Retrieved from http://libguides.royalroads.ca/videoessayhowto

Schultz, P. L., & Quinn, A. S. (2014). Lights, camera, action! learning about management with student-produced video assignments. *Journal of Management Education, 38*(2), 234–258. doi:10.1177/1052562913488371

Seed, A. H. (2008). Cohort building through experiential learning. *Journal of Experiential Education, 31*(2), 209–224. doi:10.5193/JEE.31.2.209

Swinth, R. L., & Vinton, K. L. (1994). The video case assignment. *Journal of Management Education, 18*(3), 359–363. doi:10.1177/105256299401800309

Thorn, K. (2011). The art of storyboarding. *eLearn, 2011*(8). doi:10.1145/2016016.2024072

Truong-White, H., & McLean, L. (2015). Digital storytelling for transformative global citizenship education. *Canadian Journal of Education, 38*(2), 1.

Tu, C.-H. (2004). *Online collaborative learning communities: Twenty-one designs to building an online collaborative learning community.* Westport, CT: Libraries Unlimited.

Willis, H. (2009). Video: The good, the bad, and the ugly. *EDUCAUSE Review, 44*(6), 106.

Woolfit, Z. (2015). The effective use of video in higher education. Retrieved from https://www.inholland.nl/media/10230/the-effective-use-of-video-in-higher-education-woolfitt-october-2015.pdf

Yassin, B. M., & Almasri, M. A. (2015). How to accommodate different learning styles in the same classroom: Analysis of theories and methods of learning styles. *Canadian Social Science, 11*(3), 26.

Chapter 10

Game-based Learning as Education Method in the Digital Age: Experiences at the Highest Military Education Institution in Germany with Online and Offline Game Formats Related to Developing Competencies [☆]

Ronald Deckert, Felix Heymann and Maren Metz

Abstract

Game-based learning or simulation-based learning — especially Serious Games — are notions of the contemporary discourse on digitalisation in the higher education sector in Germany. These methods offer a more vivid and motivating learning context and they help to improve important competencies for reaching work-related higher education goals. This explorative study focuses on experts' experiences with digital and non-digital serious games and their contribution towards developing self, social and management competencies, in the Bundeswehr Command and Staff College in Hamburg (Germany). Whilst there are numerous opportunities for using serious games in higher education, their use creates barriers for addressing social, as well as leadership/management competencies. In the future, game-based learning — and more specifically, digital game-based learning — could challenge the relation between learning as hard work and

---

[☆]The Military Education Institution of the study is Führungsakademie der Bundeswehr, Hamburg.

learn for fun, and between explicit and goal-oriented learning and implicit, incidental and explorative learning.

Keywords: Serious Games; gamification; edutainment; digital game-based learning; simulation-based learning; digital competency development

10.1. Introduction

Game-based learning or simulation-based learning – particularly Serious Games – are concepts across the methodological spectrum of learning approaches, which are currently in the focus of discussion in higher education circles (Schmid, Thom, & Görtz, 2016; Wannemacher, 2016; Willcox, Sarma, & Lippel, 2016). Simulation-based learning is associated with a kind of digitalised reality Wannemacher, 2016) and game-based learning is considered to enable contextual learning (Willcox et al., 2016). Thinking about and bringing forward advances in technology and learning methods is one side of the coin, but ultimately, the purpose of education is not to use technology or methods, but rather, to enable learners to construct, apply and develop their knowledge and competencies (Willcox et al., 2016). Competency-based approaches allow the learner to focus on the context, intentions and sources of learning, as it will be discussed in the following section.

This study focused on experts' experiences in the Bundeswehr Command and Staff College with the effective use of simulation-based methods. Specifically, the purpose of the present study was to explore participants' experiences with: (1) simulations – mainly combat simulations – being a well-known military training method, (2) military education and training, which help learners to 'be able to act' in diverse situations, ranging from the battle field to diplomacy matters and (3) developing competencies – a strong focus of the present study – which is well-known and frequently practiced in military training. This study was guided by the following research questions:

- What are the participants' experiences with simulation-based learning?
- What are the participants' experiences with military education and training?
- What are theparticipants' experiences with competency-based learning in the context of military training?

10.2. The Competency-based View

Higher education in Germany along with many other countries passed through the Bologna Reform Process (European Commission, 2017) at the end of the twentieth century with the Declarations of Sorbonne and Bologna in 1998 and 1999 (EHEA Secretariat, 2017). Competence orientation is a core aspect related to this process. Competency-based learning is particularly relevant for game-based learning, such as Serious Games, which could support skill and competencies' development in an individualised and flexible way.

However, the implementation of competency-based learning approaches has been questioned (Tenberg, 2014) and extensive research is on its way in Germany (Wilhelm et al., 2014; Zlatkin-Troitschanskaia, Pant, Lautenbach, & Toepper, 2016). Competency-based learning offerings in Germany focus on developing the following competencies:

- Self-competencies – What is someone able to do on his own? (e.g. problem-solving competence for special kinds of problems).
- Social competencies – What is someone able to do related to others? (e.g. communication competence).
- Leadership/management competencies – How is someone able to lead and/or manage? (e.g. team leader competence) (HRK, KMK, & BMBF, 2005).

Competencies like the ones mentioned earlier, can be used to provide structure (Neuberger, 2002), particularly within a higher education context (Schlüter & Winde, 2009) and they create a vision for education, as they may also promote social and emotional learning through technology (World Economic Forum, 2015, 2016). Table 10.1 provides a short description of each of those competencies:

10.3. Digital Learning

This section discusses the use of serious games as a learning method, placing it in the context of digital learning concepts and more specifically, game-based learning. We begin with a discussion of various digital learning concepts, where we reflect on the commonalities and differences between them. Subsequently, we turn our focus to game-based learning and its key characteristics and we then go on to examine the concept of Serious Games and their uses in higher and further education.

10.3.1. Digital Learning Concepts

In our attempt to understand game-based learning and more specifically, Serious Games, in this section, we analyse the landscape of digital learning concepts. With regard to digital learning concepts, digitalisation may have far-reaching consequences for how people learn in the future. In line with the connectivistic view (Siemens, 2005), the question arises, whether learning in the future might be more implicit, incidental and explorative, occurring through the information, events, problems or challenges of our social networks. This could imply that learning will bear a greater resemblance to children's learning. Children gain maturity and they learn from their surroundings through social learning and understanding, and more specifically, they learn through imitation, shared attention, empathy and social emotions (Meltzoff, Kuhl, Movellan, & Sejnowski, 2009).

Table 10.1. Description of the Competencies Based on HRK, KMK and BMBF (2005); World Economic Forum (2015, 2016); Tenberg (2014).

Competencies	Description
Self-competencies	
Critical thinking/ problem-solving	Identifying, analysing and evaluating complex problems (situations, ideas, information) and identifying and formulating appropriate solutions; primarily in new and unfamiliar situations and also in broad and multidisciplinary contexts
Creativity	Imagining and crafting new, innovative ways of addressing problems, answering questions or expressing meaning through the application, synthesis or re-purposing of knowledge
Curiosity	Asking questions and demonstrating open-mindedness and inquisitiveness
Initiative	Undertaking self-paced new tasks or goals and acquiring new knowledge and abilities independently
Persistence/grit	Sustaining interest and effort and persevering in tasks or goals
Adaptability	Changing plans, methods or goals in light of new information
Social Competencies	
Communication	Listening carefully, understanding correctly, conveying information clearly and reasonably and placing this information in context through verbal, non-verbal, visual and written means
Collaboration	Working in a team towards a common goal and ability to prevent and manage conflicts successfully
Social and cultural awareness	Interacting with other people in a socially, culturally and ethically appropriate way
Leadership/Management Competencies	
Leadership/ Management	Directing, guiding and inspiring others to accomplish a common goal, particularly in complex situations, without complete information and related to ethical aspects
Cognitive Dispositions	
Knowledge and understanding	Verifiable availability of fundamental understanding and expertise, including application and transfer of knowledge and methodological competence

E-learning, edutainment, gamification and (digital) game-based learning are different approaches, formats and concepts using the entertainment potential of computer games to deliver educational content (Vollbrecht, 2008). Although these concepts differ in terms of their educational intention and setting, the boundaries between them are sometimes blurred. Transitions between intentional, purposeful learning and non-systematic implicit learning constantly occur and are nowadays virtually unavoidable in many modern media (Kübler, 1997). Aside from purposeful learning, taking place for instance, as part of a formal education programme or training, opportunities for non-systematic, implicit learning are ubiquitous for instance, through social media, online networks, but also within the game-based learning method, which combines explicit with implicit learning. Correspondingly, overlaps become evident at various points and clear boundaries cannot be drawn.

The most general category among the digital learning concepts mentioned earlier – e-learning, edutainment, gamification and game-based learning – is e-learning, which according to Hodson, Connolly and Saunders (2001) refers mainly to aspects of computer-based learning, to interactive technologies and, more widely, to distance learning. Edutainment is a concept that emerged in the 1990s and is a cross between education and entertainment. It refers to educational activities or multi-media learning environments that are entertaining or to entertainment activities that are at the same time educational (Aufenanger, 2005). Essentially, the aim of edutainment is to impart content in a school-based context, for instance when teaching languages, mathematics, physics or chemistry. It focuses on the training of skills and basic competencies (Egenfeldt-Nielsen, 2006). In the edutainment format, the game element generally rewards the learner for his or her efforts and is therefore subsidiary to, and typically not an integral part of what is being learned. Gamification is still a new concept used to describe the additional application of elements that are typical of games in a non-game context. The focus is therefore not on playing a game but on adding playful elements to different areas of application in order to motivate users and award them with a feeling of success as well as pride and joy (Deterding, Khaled, Nacke, & Dixon, 2011; Groh, 2012). In particular, this includes elements such as ranking lists, progress bars, high scores experience points or awards. In a learning context, these elements are intended to motivate the user, to encourage him or her to keep on learning, to promote a feeling of learning success and also to help the learner identify with the learning concept.

10.3.2. Game-based Learning

Game-based learning and digital game-based learning are further concepts using games for educational purposes for learners of any age.

A classical game-based learning format is the simulation game. This method simulates complex real (socio-technical) systems in a stimulating learning context. Digital game-based learning is restricted to digital formats using a playful approach on a computer or online (Prensky, 2007). In digital game-based learning settings, a product must have distinct features (Lampert, Schwinge, &

Tolks, 2009). For instance, (1) the context and content must be related in such a manner that the user of the game actually feels like a player rather than a learner. (2) Moreover, digital game-based learning only works if the same (high) value is placed both on the game's ability to engage and reward the user and on the learning component. If this is not the case, the game becomes either a learning programmeme or a regular computer game mainly for entertainment. In addition, (3) these two dimensions must be kept on an equally high level during the entire course of the game.

The learning tasks are embedded in the game world. The learner must collect objects, answer questions or pass tricky tests that are linked to content-related information and questions. Digital game-based learning works primarily because of the motivation generated by playing the game, which makes the player learn automatically. Rieber, Smith and Noah (1998) describe this as 'stealth learning'. This refers to a setting in which, either the setting itself or the teacher conceals the relevant content by applying clever and stimulating non-traditional tools (e.g. games). The idea is to encourage students to have fun while learning. For the player, it is motivating and rewarding not only to solve the tasks by acquiring relevant knowledge and putting it in an appropriate context but also to remain in the game and finish or win it. The learning activity is embedded in a gaming act so that learning takes place incidentally in the game setting. This is based on the idea that the (learning) game itself, and therefore the element of play, is not a method restricted to a former, infantile or purpose-free way of learning, but it is a purpose-guided learning method to be used freely across all development phases and ages.

Game-based learning incorporates an educational intention and it is designed around didactic principles, whilst it also maintains the features of a game (Meier & Seufert, 2003). It allows learning through trial and error and the mastering of tasks, to alternate between implicit and explicit learning, and to follow personal interest and motivation.

The counterpart to educationally motivated games is entertainment games, i.e. commercial computer games. These games sometimes contain elements that draw the player into the game world, thus leading to an immersive experience. As a rule, entertainment games are played primarily for the purpose of entertainment, which does not preclude learning processes, though these tend to occur, if at all, at an informal level.

10.3.3. The Serious Games Concept

Digital learning games are also called 'serious games'. They represent a format that primarily belongs to the category of digital game-based learning formats and to e-simulations. As with gamification, serious games are not a stand-alone learning format, but an additional element in a learning process. Serious games go far beyond the aspect of pure knowledge transfer and are intended for training (Michael & Chen, 2006). In contrast to educationally oriented TV programmemes, computer games have the advantage of requiring a high level of activity and providing opportunities for interaction. In addition, the involvement of other players in multiplayer games creates the thrill of unpredictability, but also provides opportunities to work together. The target group (individuals or groups) includes all age groups but particularly addresses digital natives (Prensky, 2001). Due to their online format, serious games can usually be played independently of time and place. There is still no standard definition of the concept of 'serious games' and its categorisation as a learning format. There is a multitude of definitions, but none of them has so far become a standard definition. Consequently, the terms serious games, educational games, edutainment, digital game-based learning, social impact games, persuasive games and games for change are sometimes used synonymously (Sawyer & Smith, 2008; Susi, Johannesson, & Backlund, 2007). In Germany, the term 'serious games' is currently used for all computer games that serve the purpose of simulation, training and education in different fields (e.g. educational sector, medicine, military). This makes a clear delineation of the term difficult. Wannemacher (2016) has developed a structural representation of digitalised learning elements and formats used in higher education in Germany. In this diagram, serious games are of relevance in the categories 'Game-Based Learning' and – depending on the kind of game – 'Computer-Mediated Reality' and 'Simulation-Aided Learning' (Wannemacher, 2016, p. 13).

Whether digital or not, simulations are models representing real systems in which players assume a task or role and apply skills or act in certain ways that require them to make decisions in a vivid and social learning context in order to acquire knowledge for use in the real system (Kriz, 2001). Virtual reality situations in the form of serious games are useful, not only in cases where the situation rarely occurs in real life or would be too expensive or dangerous to be practiced, but also because they allow content to be presented in an attractive and motivating form.

Serious games developed from military board games and simulation games and from flight simulators developed by the aviation industry. Military simulation games date back to a modified version of the board game chess that was used to try out different military strategies in the seventeenth century. The chess pieces were altered to represent military units of the time and the board was modified to reflect the actual terrain of the area in question. Between 1812 and 1824, Prussian Baron von Reisswitz developed his 'tactical war game apparatus' (Marr, 2010). This resembled a cabinet that contained various utensils including the pieces, military equipment and realistic terrain features. In the following centuries, the complexity of war simulators steadily increased, as wars were fought not only on land but also in the air and at sea. Moreover, military equipment was constantly being enhanced. Abt (1971) also had a strong influence on the concept of serious games with his 1968 book of the same name. With the development of personal computers in the 1980s and the rapid growth of their popularity in the 1990s, Germany saw further technological advancements in game visualisation. Nevertheless, Germany was behind the developments and experiences in the field of serious games, in particular, the US. Since 2007, different institutions have been established and various research projects carried out in this field. For the first time, the Serious Games Conference was held within the framework of the CeBIT Exhibition, and the Serious Games Award was sponsored by the Ministry of Economic Affairs of the German state of Hesse. Experts in the field of serious games have no doubts that this field will continue to evolve (Sawyer, 2005, 2007; Susi et al., 2007; van Eck, 2006).

Like all formats combining entertainment and education, serious games must also be considered in terms of the relationship between education and entertainment (see also Lampert, 2007; Singhal, Cody, Rogers, & Sabido, 2004; Singhal & Rogers, 1999). Some authors believe that the main feature of serious games is that the entertainment aspect is subordinate to the educational aspect (Michael & Chen, 2006). According to Abt (1971), these games must have a clear and well-thought-out educational purpose rather than offering mainly entertainment. Other experts argue that the educational element should be subordinate to the entertainment element (Zyda, 2005). The only consensus that has been reached so far is that serious games are computer games that are not designed solely for entertainment. However, opinions still differ with regard to the other purposes of such games. The context of the game and its adequate employment are the key to its effectiveness. Contextual factors refer to the place in which the game is employed, technological support and the learning environment. For serious games to be successful, they must have the best possible quality and functionality, as well as an appealing design and a high visual and acoustic quality. Tempo and immediate reward are further factors determining the success of a game. However, content is also essential, as players are tested by having to accomplish tasks and reach goals. The players are awarded points for their actions and these points allow them to compare their performance to that of other players. There is another type of serious game that is not oriented towards competition but focuses on learning by doing, which means that the player can try out a particular process or action in a virtual environment to see whether it produces the desired results. In terms of content, the tasks to be performed can be dependent on, or independent of, the game story. An immersive game ensures success and motivation. The game should be neither too easy nor too difficult to play. It should never be boring and it should not constantly overtax the player. The level of difficulty is gradually increased and the player continuously experiences progress. Serious games adapt to the player's level of proficiency and thus lead to a feeling of success on the part of the player (Fritz, 2003; Vollbrecht, 2008). Moreover, serious games combine the features characteristic of commercial computer games, such as a high level of motivation (Egenfeldt-Nielsen, 2006). Other essential factors that must be sufficiently taken into account when designing the game's content are social complexity, problem management and problem-solving, as well as self-regulation. Consequently, an educational goal, an attractive learning structure and the game's skilful technological realisation are of utmost importance for the success of this method.

It makes sense to embed serious games in a set of activities and processes that follow an educational approach in encouraging players to experiment and seek solutions to problems (Boud & Feletti, 1991). Action, thought and communication patterns can then be observed. A subsequent analysis and reflection phase provides the players with the opportunity not only to become aware of experiences, mental models, values, goals or behavioural rules associated with the game but also to discuss and understand them and perhaps even change them. This transfer from the game situation to the learning and working context depends not so much on factual knowledge as on other aspects such as personal learning competencies, procedures for acquiring knowledge and assistance with retrieving knowledge (Wesener, 2004). Therefore, follow-up activities are essential, whether as a subsequent discussion or a period of reflection together with other learners or a coach (Peters & Vissers, 2004). Coaching-based reflection is a very helpful means to accompany the learning process over a period of time (Theis & Helm, 2009). The conscious development and practice of action strategies enable the learner to develop new action patterns (Kris, 2001). Learning in a secure and manageable environment that simulates reality is an essential requirement for the sustainability of this learning method. Different learning aids can be included in this process to support learning (Bopp, 2005). These may be tutorials, forums or introductory missions in a simplified and reduced gaming environment can help to explain the rules of the game. Serious games are based on traditional computer games and combine two aspects, namely a medium that is already familiar to the player and a guided digital learning space. Other types of media may also be integrated into serious games such as e-mails, text messaging or supporting (educational) messages.

Serious games are employed in the fields of personnel recruitment, training, personnel and organisational development, health management and leadership development. In a business context, for example, the target groups are (potential) apprentices, employees and leadership personnel or, in the health sector, specific groups such as patients. Serious games can be used to address a variety of specific topics ranging from product and communication training to complex decision-making processes. Serious games are used in higher education to support classroom teaching. In Anglo-American countries, game-based concepts have already been employed many times with success (Antunes, Pacheco, & Giovanela, 2012; Stringfield & Kramer, 2014). In Germany, higher education institutions such as the RWTH Aachen University and Düsseldorf University have used game-based scenarios, such as 'Die Rettung der Zink & Co.' (Liauw, 2012) and 'Die Legende von Zyren' (Knautz, Soubusta, & Orszullok, 2013), respectively.

Moreover, Serious Games have long been used to train top-level military personnel at the Bundeswehr Command and Staff College. They can be subdivided into the categories of staff exercises, simulation exercises and (computer-aided/non-computer-aided) simulations/simulation games. Whereas staff exercises focus on the basic, advanced and follow-on training of military leaders and staffs in the command and control of armed forces, simulation exercises are especially suitable for training and for exercising predefined military decision-making processes. Simulation exercises are usually conducted with one or two parties. These exercises are supported by various simulation models such as SIRA (simulation system in support of command post exercises) and KORA/OA (corps-level framework model for officer training). When it comes to non-computer-aided simulations/simulation games, commercially available conflict simulation games such as Commands & Colors by GMT Games are used. Similar to specifically developed simulation games, these games are aimed not so much at training the implementation of processes as at enhancing individual leadership skills based on reflection on one's own actions.

10.3.3.1. Learning with Serious Games

Playing games is a voluntary and intrinsically motivated activity that is pursued its own sake and not with the intention of achieving specific teaching/learning objectives (Huizinga, 2006; Oerter, 1999). Moreover, some people still have certain associations when it comes to learning, for example that learning always requires a disagreeable amount of additional work. In a culture of learning, many assume that learning is a serious business involving hard work and little fun (Meier & Seufert, 2003). They believe that discovering their environment in a playful manner is only possible during their leisure time and with considerable freedom to do so. Natural, fun-based learning has largely been excluded from the adult world. This apparent contradiction – that game-playing and 'more serious' activities, such as learning, are mutually exclusive – is refuted by serious games. There is empirical evidence that educational video games are indeed effective and those game elements can successfully support learning processes (Consider this abbreviation (among others) instead of for example Egenfeldt-Nielsen, 2006; Einsiedler, 1991).

Serious games are based on the concept of knowledge acquisition, as well as on interaction (learning by doing/by pursuing an activity), as well as on testing one's own limits and trying out different roles (Theis & Helm, 2009). Playing and learning take place simultaneously in serious games. Explicit learning is accomplished by acquiring knowledge within the framework of intentional and targeted learning activities, and the learners are aware that they are learning. With implicit learning, knowledge acquisition occurs incidentally. Incidental learning is generally understood as a process that takes place without the students being aware that they are learning. Both explicit and implicit learning are stimulated as students' game-playing competence increases and by a didactic-immersive game design (Lampert et al., 2009). In addition, serious games impart declarative and procedural knowledge that relates to the world outside the game. Declarative knowledge refers to the knowledge of facts and concepts and it is gained through the transfer of knowledge. Procedural knowledge builds upon the already acquired declarative knowledge and it is manifest in subconscious routines and learning processes. Whilst declarative knowledge is explicit, consciously accessible and it can be expressed verbally, procedural knowledge is typically acquired through skills and it is difficult to articulate.

According to Klimmt (2008), both problem-solving and explorative actions must be part of serious games. As long as the player is subjectively 'within' the game world, implicit/incidental learning will take place throughout the game cycle. If the player is unable to proceed, he or she will shift to a script of explicit learning, but only as long as it takes to become re-immersed in the game world and to apply the newly gained knowledge to the problem at hand. Therefore, game worlds should alternate between these two phases, while keeping the explicit learning phases short and succinct. These explicit learning phases should not require the user to abandon the game but should be part of the course of the game (Bopp, 2005). In serious games, learning happens incidentally. At least, this is the players' impression. In fact, players go through a process of acquiring knowledge both explicitly and implicitly.

The combination of knowledge transfer and the game's setting has a positive effect on motivation. Players, therefore, engage with a game and consequently with a specific topic for a longer period. A high level of motivation and engagement also ensures that players remember in-game experiences longer and retain what they have learned more effectively than with other forms of learning (Egenfeldt-Nielsen, 2006). Serious games can generate high levels of intrinsic motivation while they are being played and this motivation can be transferred to the learning process (Marr, 2010). Another special characteristic is immersion, which has addictive potential. Serious games are fun to play and generate a flow effect. The term 'flow' refers to a state of complete concentration as the player is absorbed in the activity he or she is performing and forgets the world outside the game (Csikszentmihalyi, 2000). In a state of flow, learning happens almost incidentally. The same applies to the process of acquiring and making use of skills. Once a challenge is overcome, the player feels good and receives approval. This leads to a feeling not only of competence but also success and elation. The player is encouraged to repeat previous actions. His or her responses can be tried and tested a number of times and practiced or adapted as long as necessary. Moreover, a high level of motivation on the part of the learner is a basic requirement for initiating and maintaining learning processes. Eckert (2009) and also Theis and Helm (2009) regard this emotional involvement as the advantage of serious games compared to other learning formats.

An important element in this context, and one that is also fun, is being able to try things out. In the digital game world, the player does not have to know everything. He or she has the opportunity to try out certain moves and receives feedback from the system. Completing more game rounds, the player increasingly expands his or her knowledge. Recurring patterns are memorised implicitly and ensure that the player improves his or her performance and is able to master the task more quickly and therefore control the game. The knowledge gained in such game worlds can be thought of as a collection of 'scripts'. A script contains the knowledge required to deal with a certain type of situation, what things need to be borne in mind when such a situation occurs, and which sequence of actions would be appropriate in such a case. This knowledge is routinised by applying it a number of times and is implemented automatically as soon as a situation occurs that can be associated with a certain script. Expertise is characterised by the fact that a person has a whole range of elaborate scripts at his or her disposal and can apply them in a highly routine manner. This growing game-playing competence leads to a feeling of joy and of being able to take appropriate action. Feeling elated about one's growing skills is an essential source of motivation, as described by Behr, Klimmt and Vorderer (2008). In complex game worlds, players not only have to apply previously established rules, i.e.

transform declarative knowledge into procedural knowledge, they also have to generate procedural knowledge by interacting with the system. Players often have difficulty explicating the knowledge they acquired implicitly while playing. They know how to deal with certain situations, but in many cases, they are hardly able to express this knowledge in words. The learning effect is strengthened by the didactic structuring of self-observation and self-reflection (Theis & Helm, 2009).

10.4. Digital and Non-digital Game-based Learning

10.4.1. Digital Game-based Learning Settings at the Bundeswehr Command and Staff College

Within the framework of education and training at the Bundeswehr Command and Staff College, online and offline simulations are a good opportunity to quickly introduce new topics. Both forms are used effectively in contexts where there is limited scope for action and players are guided towards a previously determined set of goals.

The digital game-based learning settings are uploaded from a DVD to a computer and can be used without accessing the internet. SIRA (a simulation system in support of command post exercises) is a constructive simulation system developed by CAE. The initiative for employing this simulation system was launched in 1988 in order to ensure that training of Bundeswehr command personnel at battalion and brigade level takes place in a cost-effective and environmentally-friendly manner. KORA/OA, designed for one or multiple parties, focuses on the realistic depiction of the deployment of land forces and the support rendered to them by air and naval forces. Ecopolicy®, on the other hand, which is advertised as a simulation and strategy game, recreates social, economic and political interdependencies to generate a highly dynamic and complex game scenario. In this setting, different scenarios can be played out, different roles assumed and alternative solutions tried out. Decisions can be reconstructed and reflected on, just as in a simulator. The reactions and reflections following a decision lead to a change of perspective and the development of new patterns of action. Interaction within such formats conveys first and foremost a feeling of self-efficacy. Finally, the latest innovation in the digitalisation of education is the implementation of a digital map table. This device allows to reach training objectives regarding to operational planning processes in a far higher quality. As it is possible to implement a time dimension within the process, this raises the spectre of application also for war gaming. As there will be a further development towards the additional dimension of simulation, the digital map table will provide an enormous potential for the future development of digital game-based learning.

Digital learning at the Bundeswehr Command and Staff College generally focuses on developing management skills aimed at improving and expanding the systematic application of previously learned military decision-making processes. Special emphasis is placed on practicing the processes of situation assessment, decision-making and operations planning. Critical thinking, collaboration and other soft skills are key elements of training conducted at the Bundeswehr Command and Staff College. They are a by-product of the simulations. When it comes to learning soft skills, non-computer-aided simulations and/or simulation games are used. Similar to specifically developed simulation games, these games are aimed not so much at training the implementation of processes as at enhancing individual leadership skills, for example with regard to creativity or intercultural competence based on the reflection of one's own actions. This format ensures that players quickly receive feedback.

10.5. Discussion Digital and Non-digital Game-based Learning Formats at the Bundeswehr Command and Staff College

First of all, digital and non-digital game-based learning formats have certain things in common. Both formats place the learning process in the hands of the learner while being thoroughly structured and guiding the player towards certain knowledge domains. Both formats are vehicles in the sense that they are part of a methodology within a learning setting. They simulate and construct content in such a way that experience leads to reflection. Common to both learning methods is supporting a high level of intrinsic motivation to learn, leading to the development of a motivating learning scenario (Behr et al., 2008).

There are differences between the two methods in terms of observable competencies and knowledge acquisition. Whereas digital serious games generally use a playful approach to imparting knowledge, non-digital game-based learning formats, such as strategy games, focus especially on testing or ascertaining what the player has already learned or knows and on encouraging the player to reflect on his or her abilities and skills. Non-digital formats also focus on the player's ability to handle complex and stressful situations. Training conducted in a classroom setting without digital support offers far greater scope for personality development. Group dynamics become apparent particularly in situations where there is direct contact and where players have to perform a task together. Players take action, make decisions and communicate instinctively, which can be observed and analysed. Transfer of knowledge and feedback can take place immediately. By contrast, digital serious games lack the haptic effect and cannot activate the full range of sensory channels. They mainly require and stimulate mental flexibility and imagination, whereas unconscious thoughts or actions are not revealed or analysed to the same extent that they would be when playing non-digital games. Digital serious games, however, generate a slightly higher level of learner autonomy, because learning rate, place and time can be adapted to individual needs. Moreover, knowledge and action processes can be repeated (i.e. simulated) under the same framework conditions. There are also better possibilities for documenting on-going processes because the course of the game can be digitally recorded.

If one compares the competencies essential to higher education (see Chapter 2) with the content and skills addressed by the two formats, one arrives at the comparison shown in Table 10.2.

Neither format places much emphasis on developing creativity, because routines and fixed structures are required to complete them and because practising these routine actions is, in fact, the object of these formats. Depending on the

Table 10.2. Comparing Digital and Non-digital Game Settings with Regard to Competencies.

Competencies	Digital Game-based Learning (Serious Games)	Non-digital Game-based Learning (Simulation Games)
Personal Competencies		
Critical thinking/ problem-solving	Can be addressed	Can be addressed and formally reflected in a social context
Creativity	Can be addressed within the limits of pre-specified, digitally realised problem structures and solution pathways	The focus lies on the handling of routines; time and space for creativity have to be included
Curiosity	Can be addressed	Can be addressed and formally reflected in a social context
Initiative	If this is part of the specific aspect of the game is addressing	Can be addressed and formally reflected in a social context
Persistence/grit	If this is part of the specific aspect of the game is addressing	Can be addressed and formally reflected in a social context
Adaptability	Can be addressed	Can be addressed and formally reflected in a social context
Social Competencies		
Communication	If this is part of the specific aspect the game is addressing, to a limited extent due to the spatial distance between the players	Can be addressed and formally reflected in a social context
Collaboration	If this is part of the specific aspect the game is addressing, to a limited extent due to spatial distance between the players	Can be addressed and formally reflected in a social context

Table 10.2. (*Continued*)

Competencies	Digital Game-based Learning (Serious Games)	Non-digital Game-based Learning (Simulation Games)
Social and cultural awareness	If the serious game includes a group scenario and on the basis of digital realisation	Can be addressed and formally reflected in a social context
Leadership/Management Competencies		
Leadership/ management	If it is part of the serious game and on the basis of digital realisation	Can be addressed and formally reflected in a social context

game's topic and parameters, all competencies described earlier can be covered by both methods, although social competencies, in particular, can develop in very different ways. Compared to simulations, and depending on the type of serious game, the possibilities for creating relationships may vary considerably.

One advantage of digital game formats is that a large number of people can be trained simultaneously. A lot of information can be passed on. This approach is very efficient in terms of the resources needed. Content must be prepared in different ways, however, depending on whether digital or non-digital formats are used. A webinar, for example, requires a different kind of preparation than classroom training and synchronous and asynchronous web-based communication entails other challenges than face-to-face communication, but digital formats still allow interaction within the learning environment and among the students. For some, there may be too little interpersonal contact in digital educational formats. In such cases, the wider learning framework should include the establishment of contacts, for example by setting up learning groups and discussion forums or involving a learning consultant. Group processes can be observed in serious games when players communicate or interact directly.

The use of digital game formats thus provides numerous possibilities for supporting and enriching university studies in general and the treatment of specific topics in particular.

10.6. Summary and Future Perspectives

Digital learning has become a firmly established form of learning and it is showing positive developments. Greater emphasis is now being placed on adaptive learning. Moreover, there will be a close connection between modern technologies and the education sector in the future according to expert interviews conducted by the MMB-Institute for Media and Competence Research (mmb Learning Delphi, 2015/2016).

Despite limited amount of empirical data on the subject, the lack of evaluation studies and the resulting necessity to conduct further evaluations and impact studies for the purpose of analysing the effectiveness of games in individual cases, current findings indicate that digital game-based learning formats are especially in areas with limited scope for action. In this manageable area, learning goals and action processes can be identified and trained. The more accurate objectives are formulated and the game is tailored to its target group, the more effective the game will be and the more successful the learning experience. Games, whether digital or not, have great potential and are much more than fun and entertainment. Education through play remains an effective way to support learning efforts.

Digital game-based learning formats, in particular, make it possible to impart knowledge and generate interest and motivation for a given topic. Digital game-based learning formats are a very new medium in the field of education and still require further development. Universities and their departments should actively contribute to shaping this modern format and should adapt it to the transfer of knowledge and pursuit of learning objectives. This means that digital game-based learning formats should be technically improved, but also that the content should be tailored to the learning goal. The learning objective must be clearly defined and the game-based learning format adapted to this goal. Game didactics, game methodology and system requirements might need to be adjusted to promote user group motivation.

In addition, questions remain as to whether and how group processes can be digitalised or how relationships can be integrated and built into the digital process. Another question that arises is how students could be supported through digital learning. Developing a solid student identity will present a general challenge to digitalised education. Like in other topics, an important step forward would be to learn from other universities around the world that have already introduced Serious Games and also in a wider context, other digital forms of education, and to join other platforms in order to gain some initial experience. This will mean to continue to involve all higher education stakeholders in the experiment of new digital game-based learning formats to create digital structures as a basis for further learning.

References

Abt, C. (1971). *Ernste Spiele: Lernen durch gespielte Wirklichkeit*. Köln: Kiepenheuer & Witsch.

Antunes, M., Pacheco, M., & Giovanela, M. (2012). Design and implementation of an educational game for teaching chemistry in Higher Education. *Journal of Chemical Education, 89*, 517–521.

Aufenanger, S. (2005). *Edutainment. Grundbegriffe Medienpädagogik* (pp. 60–73.). J. von Hüther & B. Schorb (Eds.), Munich: Kopaed.

Behr, K.-M., Klimmt, C., & Vorderer, P. (2008). Leistungshandeln und Unterhaltungserleben im Computerspiel. In T. Quandt, J. Wimmer, & J. Wolling (Eds.), *Die Computerspieler. Studien zur Nutzung von Computergames.* (pp. 225–240). Wiesbaden: VS Verlag für Sozialwissenschaften.

Bopp, M. (2005). Immersive Didaktik: Verdeckte Lernhilfen und Framingprozesse in Computerspielen. *Kommunikation@gesellschaft: Journal für alte und neue Medien aus soziologischer, kulturanthropologischer, und kommunikationswissenschaftlicher Perspektive*, 6, article 2. Retrieved from http://www.kommunikation-gesellschaft.de/B2_2005_Bopp.pdf

Boud, D., & Feletti, G. (Eds.). (1991). *The challenge of problem-based learning*. London: Kogan Page.

Csikszentmihalyi, M. (2000). *Das Flow-Erlebnis. Jenseits von Angst und Langeweile im Tun aufgehen* (8th ed.). (Unpublished text), Stuttgart: Klett.

Deterding, S., Khaled, R., Nacke, L. E., & Dixon, D. (2011). Gamification: Toward a definition. *CHI 2011 Gamification Workshop Proceedings* (pp. 1–4). Vancouver: ACM.

Eck, v. R. (2006). Digital game-based learning: It's not just the digital natives who are restless. *EDUCAUSE Review*, *41*(2), 16–18.

Eckert, A. (2009). Serious Games: Einführung und Best-Practice-Beispiel: Der Vodafone Code. Sonderdruck. Auszug aus: Eckert, Angelika: MarktCHECK: *Serious Games im Unternehmensumfeld*.

Egenfeldt-Nielsen, S. (2006). Overview of research on the educational use of video games. *Digital Kompetanse*, *1*(3), 184–213.

EHEA Secretariat. (2017). *History*. Retrieved from http://www.ehea.info/article-details.aspx?ArticleId=3

Einsiedler, W. (1991). Das Spiel der Kinder. *Zur Pädagogik und Psychologie des Kinderspiels*. Klinkhardt: Bad Heilbrunn.

European Commission. (2017). *The Bologna Process and the European Higher Education Area*. Retrieved from http://ec.europa.eu/education/policy/higher-education/bologna-process_en.htm

Fritz, J. (2003). Zwischen Frust und Flow. *Computerspiele*. Bonn: Bundeszentrale für politische Bildung. Retrieved from http://www.bpb.de/themen/8GADVU,0,0,Zwischen_Frust_und_Flow.html

Groh, F. (2012). Gamification: State of the Art Definition and Utilization. In B. Asaj, Könings, M. Poguntke, F. Schaub, & B. W. Weber (Eds.), *Proceedings of 4the seminar on Research Trends in Media Informatics* (pp. 39–46). Ulm: Eigenverlag.

Hodson, P., Connolly, M., & Saunders, D. (2001). Can computer-based learning support adult learners? *Journal of Further and Higher Education*, *25*(3), 325–335.

HRK, KMK, BMBF. (2005). *Qualifikationsrahmen für Deutsche Hochschulabschlüsse*. Retrieved from: http://www.kmk.org/fileadmin/Dateien/veroeffentlichungen_beschluesse/2005/2005_04_21-Qualifikationsrahmen-HS-Abschluesse.pdf

Huisinga, J. (2006). *Homo Ludens: Vom Ursprung der Kultur im Spiel*. Hamburg: Rowohlt Verlag.

Klimmt, C. (2008). Unterhaltungserleben bei Computerspielen. In K. Mitgutsch & H. Rosenstingl (Eds.), *Faszination Computerspielen. Theorie – Kultur – Erleben*. (pp. 7–17). Wien: Braumüller.

Knautz, K., Soubusta, S., & Orszullok, L. (2013). Game-based learning for digital natives: Knowledge is just a click away. In D. Tan (Eds.), *International Conference on Advanced Information and Communication Technology for Education* (ICAICTE 2013) (pp. 74–78). Hainan, China: Atlantis Press.

Kris, W.-C. (2001). Die Planspielmethode als Lernumgebung. In H. Loebe & E. Severing (Eds.), *Planspiele im Internet: Konzepte und Praxisbeispiele für den Einsatz in Aus- und Weiterbildung* (pp. 41–64). Bielefeld: Bertelsmann.

Kübler, H. D. (1997). Bildungsmedien. In J. Hüther & B. Schorb (Eds.), *Grundbegriffe Medien Pädagogik* (pp. 40–47). Munich: KoPäd.

Lampert, C. (2007). *Gesundheitsförderung im Unterhaltungsformat: Wie Jugendliche gesundheitsbezogene Botschaften in fiktionalen Fernsehangeboten wahrnehmen und bewerten*. Baden Baden: Nomos Verlag.

Lampert, C., Schwinge, C., & Tolks, D. (2009). Der gespielte Ernst des Lebens: Bestandsaufnahme und Potenziale von Serious Games (for Health). *Zeitschrift für Theorie und Praxis der Medienbildung*, Special Issue 15/16. Retrieved from http://www.medienpaed.com/15/#lampert0903Zeitschrift

Liauw, M. (2012). *WBV-Fachtagung, 24. Oktober 2012*. Retrieved from http://www.wbv_fachtagung.de/fileadmin/user_upload/2012/Unterlagen/aktuell_Forum%203_Liauw_Game%20Based%20Learning.pdf

Marr, A. C. (2010). Serious Games für die Informations- und Wissensvermittlung. In: R. Fuhlrott, U. Krauß-Leichert, & C. H. Schütte (Eds.), *B.I.T. online – Innovativ, 28*. Wiesbaden: Dinges & Frick GmbH.

Meier, C., & Seufert, S. (2003). Game-based learning: Erfahrungen mit und Perspektiven für digitale Lernspiele in der beruflichen Bildung. In A. Hohenstein & K. Wilbers (Eds.), *Handbuch E-Learning* (pp. 1–17). Köln: Fachverlag Deutscher Wirtschaftsdienst.

Meltzoff, A. N., Kuhl, P. K., Movellan, J., & Sejnowski, T. J. (2009). Foundations for a new science of learning. *Science, 325*(5938), 284–288.

Michael, D., & Chen, S. (2006). *Serious games: Games that educate, train, and inform*. Boston: Thomson CourseTechnology.

mmb Learning Delphi. (2015/2016). *Mobiles Lernen wird der Umsatzbringer No. 1*. Retrieved from https://mmb-institut.de/mmb-trendmonitor/

Neuberger, O. (2002). *Führen und führen lassen: Ansätze, Ergebnisse und Kritik der Führungsforschung*. 6th completely revised and expanded edition. Stuttgart: Lucius & Lucius.

Oerter, R. (1999). *Psychologie des Spiels*. Weinheim: Beltz.

Peters, V. A., & Vissers, G. A. (2004). A simple classification model for debriefing simulation games. *Simulation & Gaming, 35*(1), 70–84.

Prensky, M. (2001). Digital natives, digital immigrants. *On the Horizon, 9*(5), 1–6.

Prensky, M. (2007). *Digital game-based learning*. St. Paul, Minnesota, USA: Paragon House.

Rieber, L. P., Smith, L., & Noah, D. (1998). The value of serious play. *Educational Technology, 38*(6), 29–37.

Sawyer, B. (2005). *The state of serious games*. Retrieved from http://www.gamasutra.com/features/20051024/sawyer_01.shtml

Sawyer, B. (2007). *10 Myths about Serious Games*. Retrieved from http://www.escapistmagazine.com/articles/view/issues/issue_121/2575-Ten-Myths-About-Serious-Games

Sawyer, B., & Smith, P. (2008). *Serious Games Taxonomy*. Presentation given at the Game Developers Conference. Retrieved from http://www.seriousgames.org/presentations/serious-gamestaxonomy-2008_web.pdf

Schlüter, A., & Winde, M. (Eds.) (2009). *Akademische Personalentwicklung. Eine strategische Perspektive*. Essen: Edition Stifterverband.

Schmid, U., Thom, S., & Görtz, L. (2016). *Ein Lebenlang Digital Lernen*. Working Paper No. 20 of HFD, MMB-Institute. Retrieved from: https://hochschulforumdigitalisierung.de/sites/default/files/dateien/HFD_AP_Nr20_Lebenslanges_Lernen.pdf

Siemens, G. (2005). Connectivism: A learning theory for the digital age. *International Journal of Instructional Technology and Distance Learning, 2*(1). Retrieved from http://www.itdl.org/journal/jan_05/article01.htm

Singhal, A., Cody, M. J., Rogers, E. M., & Sabido, M. (Eds.). (2004). *Entertainment-education and social change: History, research, and practice*. Mahwah: Lawrence Erlbaum.

Singhal, A., & Rogers, E. (1999). *Entertainment-education: A communication strategy for social change*. Mahwah, NJ: Lawrence Erlbaum Associates.

Stringfield, T., & Kramer, E. (2014). Benefits of a game-based review module in chemistry courses for non-majors. *Journal of Chemical Education, 91*, 56−58.

Susi, T., Johannesson, M., & Backlund, P. (2007). *Serious games: An overview*. Technical Reports, HS-IKI-TR-07-001. Retrieved from https:// www.his.se/upload/19354/HS-%20IKI%20-TR-07-001.pdf

Tenberg, R. (2014). Competence-oriented study: Didactic reform of higher education or Bologna-rhetoric? *Journal of Technical Education, 2*(1), 1−15. Retrieved from http://www.journal-of-technical-education.de/index.php/joted/article/view/32

Theis, F., & Helm, M. (2009). Serious Games als Instrument in der Führungskräfteentwicklung. In S. Laske, A. Orthey, & M. J. Schmidt (Eds.), *Personal Entwickeln: Das aktuelle Nachschlagewerk für Praktiker*. 127(7.40), 1−14.

Vollbrecht, R. (2008). Computerspiele als medienpädagogische Herausforderung. In J. Fritz (Ed.), *Computerspiele(r) verstehen: Zugänge zu virtuellen Spielwelten für Eltern und Pädagogen* (pp. 236−262). Bonn: Bundeszentrale für politische Bildung.

Wannemacher, K. (2016). *Digitale Lernszenarien im Hochschulbereich. Im Auftrag der Themengruppe Innovationen in Lern- und Prüfszenarien koordiniert vom CHE im Hochschulforum Digitalisierung. Submitted by the HIS Institute for Development in Higher Education (HIS-HE)*. Essen: Edition Stifterverband. Retrieved from https://hochschulforumdigitalisierung.de/sites/default/files/dateien/HFD%20AP%20Nr%2015_Digitale%20Lernszenarien.pdf

Wesener, S. (2004). *Spielen in virtuellen Welten: Eine Untersuchung von Transferprozessen in Bildschirmspielen*. Wiesbaden: VS Verlag.

Wilhelm, O., Baumert, J., von Davier, M., Jeschke, S., Seeber, S., Stemmler, G., & Sumfleth, E. (2014). *Audit-Bericht zur Förderbekanntmachung „Kompetenzmodellierung und Kompetenzerfassung im Hochschulsektor*. Retrieved from http://www.kompetenzen-im-hochschulsektor.de/Dateien/Auditbericht_08_09_2014.pdf

Willcox, K. E., Sarma, S., & Lippel, P. H. (2016). *Online education: A catalyst for Higher Education reforms: Online Education Policy Initiative*. Cambridge: Massachusetts Institute of Technology. Retrieved from: https://oepi.mit.edu/sites/default/files/MIT%20Online%20Education%20Policy%20Initiative%20April%202016_0.pdf

World Economic Forum / The Boston Consulting Group. (2015). *New vision for education: Unlocking the potential of technology*. Retrieved from http://www3.weforum.org/docs/WEFUSA_NewVisionforEducation_Report2015.pdf

World Economic Forum/ The Boston Consulting Group. (2016). *New Vision for Education: Fostering Social and Emotional Learning through Technology*. Retrieved from http://www3.weforum.org/docs/WEF_New_Vision_for_Education.pdf

Zlatkin-Troitschanskaia, O., Pant, H. A., Lautenbach, C., & Toepper, M. (Eds.). (2016). *Kompetenzmodelle und Instrumente der Kompetenzerfassung im Hochschulsektor – Validierungen und methodische Innovationen (KoKoHs): Übersicht der Forschungsprojekte (KoKoHs Working Papers, 10)*. Berlin & Mainz: Humboldt University & Johannes Gutenberg University. Retrieved from http://www.kompetenzen-im-hochschulsektor.de/Dateien/WP10_final_032016.pdf

Zyda, M. (2005). From visual simulation to virtual reality to games. *Computer, 38*(9), 25–32.

Index

Academic lead, 49, 50
Academic resistance, 60
Academic rigor/rigour, 171–172, 177–178, 179–180
  digital storytelling in graduate-level assignments, 174–180
  online learning and teaching, 170–174
Acculturation, 153
Acknowledgement, 36
Adaptability, 188
Administrative processes, 20–21
Administrators, key issues by, 32
  competition, 34–35
  guiding principles, 33
  implications on our brand name, 33
  measuring instructional effectiveness, 34
  MOOCs representing legitimate way of delivering education, 32
Adult learning principles, 91–92
Alaska, disrupting higher education in
  Alaska Natives immigrants, 151–152
  Alaska's educational model, 153–154
  Alaska's for disruption in teacher education, 148–150
  barriers to success of programme offerings, 154–155
  crisis in Alaska Native education, 150–151
  education's role in identity formation, 152–153
  NTCP, 156–163
Alaska Department of Education & Early Development (DEED), 150
Alaska education system, 150
Alternation models, 153
Alternative assessment format, 168, 171–172
American Psychological Association (APA), 87
American University, 30
American University of Beirut (AUB), 29–30, 33
Ancestral homelands, 152–153
Andragogy, 57
Appreciation, 36, 103
Arab world, 28, 38, 40, 41
Assessment
  MA in conflict analysis and management, 177–178
  MA in global leadership, 179–180
Assignment
  MA in conflict analysis and management, 175–177
  MA in global leadership, 179
Assimilation, 153

Belonging in community, 87–90
Biculturalism, 153–154
Bilingual, bicultural teacher certification pipeline, 160
Bilingualism, 153–154
Blended double degree model, 75

Blended dual degree programme partnership, 71
Blended learning, 15, 130
  course, 159
Blended MBA-MGM double degree programme, 72
Bounded learning community, 172–174
Building community, 92–93
Building relationships, 172–174
Bundeswehr Command and Staff College
  digital and non-digital game-based learning formats at, 197–199
  digital game-based learning settings at, 196–197
Business model, 59
  academic resistance, 60
  cost, 60
  cross-functional teams, 59

CAM 'Digital Conflict Story'
  assignment, 176
  learning outcomes, 177
Classical game-based learning format, 189–190
Classroom
  delivery, 56
  dynamics in digital teaching space, 3–4
  learning, 174
Client lead, 149
Co-constructed knowledge, 112
Co-constructed summaries, 110
Co-constructive process, 105–106
Co-creation of course design, 49–50
Coaching-based reflection, 193
Cognitive dispositions, 188
Cognitive load, 111
Cohort model, 159, 173

Cohort-based approach, 131–132, 137
Collaboration, 112–113, 188
  behaviours, 105
Collaborative learning, 55–56, 103–104, 127–130, 131
  approaches, 3, 142
  core affordances of SCPs for, 104–106
  enabling through SCPs, 103–106
  monitoring and regulation, 106
Collaborative tasks, 104–105, 110, 112, 114–115
Commissioning client, 45–46, 52
Communication, 105, 188
Communities of Learning (CoL), 92
Communities of Practice (CoP), 92
Community in conflict, 178, 179
Competencies based on HRK, KMK and BMBF, 188
Competency-based view, 186–187
Competition, 34–35
Computer-mediated communication systems (CMC systems), 129
Computer-supported collaborative learning (CSCL), 104, 113
Computer-supported social collaborative learning environment, 108–111
Conflict analysis and management, MA in, 175
  assessment, 177–178
  assignment, 175–177
Constructivist elements, 106
Contextual factors, 192
Corporate executive education, 55
Corps-level framework model for officer training (KORA/OA), 193, 196

Course
    activities, 91
    description, 107
    instructors, 38
    reconceptualisation, 108–111
Course commissioning and design, technology role in, 48
    co-creation of course design, 49–50
    course design, 53–54
    roles in executive education course design, 51–53
Course delivery, technology role in, 54
    collaborative learning, 55–56
    participants' experience with teaching and learning, 55
    participation and engagement, 57–58
    peer-to-peer learning, 56–57
    tailoring to learning styles, 55
Creativity, 84, 188
Critical thinking/problem-solving, 188
Cross-border collaborations, 67–68
Cross-border internationalization, 65
Cross-border online education, benefits and barriers to, 68–70
Cross-functional teams, 59
Cultural programmes, 158
Culturally responsive curriculum and technology, positive power of, 157–159
Culturally responsive project-based learning, 159
Culturally responsive teaching, 158
Curiosity, 188
Customised executive education, 45–47
    business model and inhibitors, 59–60
    evaluation and outcomes, 58–59
    technology role in course commissioning and design, 48–54
    technology role in course delivery, 54–58
Customised executive education, 45–47
    differences with MOOCs, 47
    field, 51

Declarative knowledge, 194
Differentiated instruction, 101, 102
Digital and non-digital game settings comparison, 198
Digital conflict, 175–178
Digital game-based learning, 189–190, 196
    formats, 197–199
    settings at Bundeswehr Command and Staff College, 196–197
Digital learning, 187
    game-based learning, 189
    serious games concept, 190–196
Digital storytelling, 168, 169, 172, 174
    in graduate-level assignments, 174–180
Digital teaching space, changing classroom dynamics in, 3–4
Discipline, MOOCs work in, 36–37
Disruptive power of online education, 1

changing classroom dynamics in digital teaching space, 3–4
online programmes and programme design, 2
Disruptive technology discourse, 29
Distance
  degrees, 84
  learning, 170–171
  in online education, 126–127
Double degree model, 75
Double degree partnership, 74
Double degree programmes, internationalisation and, 65
  benefits and barriers to cross-border online education, 68–70
  expanding access to international education, 66–68

e-Learning, 8–9, 189
  at Austrian Universities, 11–12
  environment, 131
  implementation at programme level, 16
  institutional change, administrative processes and policy development, 20–21
  learning resources, 20
  quality and quality assurance, 21–22
  strong leadership and institutional commitment, 16–17
  supporting and developing teaching staff in transition, 17–18
  supporting students in adapting to new way of learning, 18–19
  systemic innovation and sustainability, 22
  technology use at programme level, 19–20
  See also Online learning; Scaling online learning
e-portfolios, 178
Edraak, 30, 34–35
Education(al), 91, 149–150
  role in identity formation, 152–153
  setting, 127
  technology, 9–10
  theory, 55
Edutainment, 189
Engagement, strategies for, 92
  assignments, 95
  learning community forum, 94
  Q&A forum, 94
  behind scenes outreach, 94
  synchronous meetings, 95
  weekly forum, 93–94
Engagement in online learning
  engagement script, 85
  online teaching principles, 90–96
  welcome/orientation, 85–90
Erasmus Mundi, 66
EU-US Atlantis Program, 66
European standards in on-campus programmes, 137
Evaluation and outcomes, 58–59
Executive courses, 46–47
Executive Development Directors (EDD), 45
Executive education
  context, 46
  course design, 51–53
  environment, 59
Expectation management, 170–171
Explicit learning, 194

Face-to-face classroom teaching, 55
Faculty, 65
  appreciation and acknowledgement, 36
  benefits to, 73–74
  effort, 36
  key issues raised by, 35
  making sense, 37
  MOOCs representing legitimate way of delivering education, 35–36
  MOOCs work in discipline, 36–37
  See also Teaching staff
Financial aid systems, 69
Fusion model, 154

Game-based learning, 189
  competency-based view, 186–187
  digital and non-digital game-based learning, 196–199
  digital learning, 187–196
Gamification, 55, 189
Global leadership, MA in, 178
  assessment, 179–180
  assignment, 179
Government funded programmes, 66
Graduate-level assignments, digital storytelling in, 174
  MA in conflict analysis and management, 175–178
  MA in global leadership, 178–180
Guiding principles, 33

Higher Education Institutions (HEIs), 44–45
  academic delivery team, 51
Human Resources (HR), 45

IBM, 116
Implicit learning, 194
Incidental learning, 194
Individual attention from instructor, 38
Information technology, 11
Inhibitors, 59–60
Initiative, 188
Institution(al), 65
  benefits to, 73–74
  change, 20–21
  commitment, 16–17
  programme-level approach for, 14–15
Instructional designs, 115
Instructional effectiveness, measuring, 34
Instructor, individual attention from, 38
International double degree, 74
International education, 68
  expanding access to, 66–68
International models, 162–163
  of success, 162–163
International online collaborations, 68–69
Internationalisation of online learning
  internationalisation and double degree programmes, 65–70
  RRU-MCI double degree, 70–76

Knowledge and understanding, 188

Leadership, 16–17, 107
  leadership/management competencies, 187, 188
  skills training in small-group learning settings, 110, 112

210   Index

Learning
  collaborative learning enabling through SCPs, 103–106
  communities, 92–93
  in community, 87–90
  community forum, 86–87, 94
  community room, 86
  concepts, 100
  differentiated instruction and personalised learning, 102
  enhancement using TEL, 56
  outcomes, 177–178, 179–180
  participants' experience with, 55
  process, 115, 128, 136
  resources, 20
  with serious games, 194–196
  solutions team, 17–18
  beyond standardised lecture-based instruction, 101
  supporting students in adapting to new way of, 18–19
  tailoring to learning styles, 55
  See also Social collaborative learning environments
Learning management system (LMS), 19, 55, 133, 136, 168
Learning paths, 102
  personalised learning through, 111–112, 114
  personalised learning through provision, 109–110
Lebanon, AUB in, 30
Lecture-based learning setting, 101
Legitimate way of delivering education, MOOCs representing, 32, 35–38
LOGIC LEADS LEARNing, 32
  methodology, 31
  MOOC, 31–39

Lone Ranger approach, 13–15
Longer-term engagement, 67

MAGL 'presenting community in conflict'
  assignment, 180
  learning outcomes, 181
Management Centre Innsbruck (MCI), 15–16, 19–20, 64, 71
Management education, 126
Massive Open Online Courses (MOOCs), 2, 9, 28–29, 31, 44, 45, 48, 68
  administrators, key issues raised by, 32–35
  faculty, key issues raised by, 35–37
  students, key issues raised by, 37–39
Master of Global Management (MGM), 70
MBA, 64, 70
MCI MBA-RRU MGM partnership, 65
MGM-MBA double degree programme, 72, 73
Military simulation games, 191
Multi-media literacy, 174
Multicultural models, 153
Mutual high tech, 49, 50
Mutual low tech, 49

National Survey of Student Engagement (NSSE), 159–160
Native Teacher Certification Pathway (NTCP), 156
  international models of success, 162–163
Net outcome for enrolment in MOOC, 39

Network technology, 104
Networked learning, 129
Non-digital game-based learning, 196–197
   formats, 197–199
Non-traditional students, 67

Ogbu, John, 151–152
Omnidirectional mentorship, 92–93
Online
   double degree partnership, 75
   environment, 142
   executive education, 54
Online education, 67, 69, 126, 136–137, 142–143
   case, 131–134
   collaborative learning and, 127–130
   distance in, 126–127
   method, 131
   strengths, 134–137, 139
   weaknesses, 137–141
Online learning, 11–13, 64, 66–68, 84
   alternative assessment formats and academic rigor, 171–172
   bounded learning community and perception of presence, 172–174
   distance learning and video technology, 170–171
   programme-level approach to, 13–14
   and teaching, 170
   video technology and soft skills acquisition, 174
   See also Scaling online learning
Online programmes, 64
   implementation, 17
   online MBA programmes, 68
   and programme design, 2
Online teaching principles, 90
   applying adult learning principles, 91–92
   building community, 92–93
   strategies for engagement, 92
Open Educational Resources (OER), 9, 20
Open Space dialogue, 95
Organisational impact, 59
'Our brand name', implications on, 33

Participants' experience with teaching and learning, 55
Participation and engagement, 57–58
Participatory action research methods, 172
Peer-to-peer learning, 56–57
Perception of presence, 172–174
Persistence/grit, 188
Personalised learning, 102
   through learning paths, 111–112, 114
   through provision of learning paths, 109–110
Photovoice, 172
Playing games, 194
Policy development, 20–21
Positive psychology, 157
Preliminary evaluation findings, 111–112
Primary learning environment, SCPs as, 103
   collaborative learning, 103–104
   core affordances of SCPs for collaborative learning, 104–106
Programme offerings, barriers to success of, 154–155

Programme-level development and implementation, 13
   advantages of programme-level approach, 14–15
   eLearning implementation at programme level, 16–22
   for institution, 14–15
   programme-level approach to online learning, 13–14
   for students, 14
   for teaching staff, 14
Public subsidies, 138

Quality and quality assurance, 21–22

Recognition, 38–39
Reflection
   blog post, 110
   co-construction, 110
Royal Roads University (RRU), 64, 70, 90
RRU-MCI double degree, 70
   benefits to students, faculty and institutions, 73–74
   lessons learned from RRU-MCI online double degree partnership, 74–76
   program development and design, 71–73
   RRU and MCI profile, 70–71

Scalability, 15
Scaling online learning
   eLearning implementation at programme level, 16–22
   beyond Lone Ranger approach, 13–15
   setting scene, 8–9
   short profile of MCI, 15–16
   strategic imperative, 9–11
   strategic scope, 11–13

   See also Online learning
Self-competencies, 187, 188
Serious Games, 187, 190
   learning with, 194–196
Serious Games Conference, 191–192
Settler society, 151
Short-term online collaborations, 76
Simulation system in support of command post exercises (SIRA), 193, 196
Simulation-based learning, 186
Skype, 173
Small Private Online Course (SPOC), 44
Social and cultural awareness, 188
Social collaboration platforms (SCPs), 3, 100, 104, 113
   collaborative learning, 103–104
   core affordances for collaborative learning, 104–106
   social enterprise network as, 109, 111
Social collaborative learning environments
   case, 107
   course description, 107
   encountered challenges of traditional learning setting, 107–108
   learning beyond standardised lecture-based instruction, 101–106
   limitations, 117
   potential for educating tomorrow's leaders, 113–115
   potential for tomorrow's universities, 116–117

preliminary evaluation findings, 111–112
reconceptualisation of course, 108–111
Social competencies, 187, 188
Social enterprise network as social collaboration platform, 109, 111
Social identity theory, 137
Social interaction, 103
Social isolation, 126
Socio-cultural learning setting, 111
SOCRATES programme, 66
Soft skills acquisition, 174
Standardised lecture-based instruction, learning beyond, 101–106
Students, 68–69, 75–76, 91
  in adapting to new way of learning, supporting, 18–19
  benefits to, 73–74
  effort, 38
  individual attention from instructor, 38
  key issues raised by, 37
  MOOCs representing legitimate way of delivering education, 37–38
  net outcome for enrolment in MOOC, 39
  programme-level approach for, 14
  recognition, 38–39
Sustainability, 22
Symbolism, 91
Synchronous meetings, 95
Systemic approach, 9
Systemic innovation, 22

Teaching, participants' experience with, 55

Teaching staff
  programme-level approach for, 14
  in transition, 17–18
  See also Faculty
Technology-enhanced learning (TEL), 44, 52–54
  learning enhancement using, 56
Traditional learning setting challenges, 107–108
Transactional distance, 126–127
Twelve Skills of Master Teachers, 159

United Nations Educational, Scientific and Cultural Organisation (UNESCO), 163
University learning settings, 115

Video assignments, 171–173
  format, 171
Video lectures, 168
Video technology, 170–171, 174
Virtual Classroom Access, 133–134
Virtual community, 159
Virtual learning course, 159

Web 2.0 platforms, 104
Western Association of Management (WAM), 84, 90
Wordl^{TM}, 93
World Indigenous Nations Higher Education Consortium (WINHEC), 150

Yukon-Kuskokwim Delta, 151
Yupiit School District, 151
Yupik teaching, 157

www.ingramcontent.com/pod-product-compliance
Lightning Source LLC
Chambersburg PA
CBHW071204240426
43668CB00032B/2071